The Leader's SMARTbook

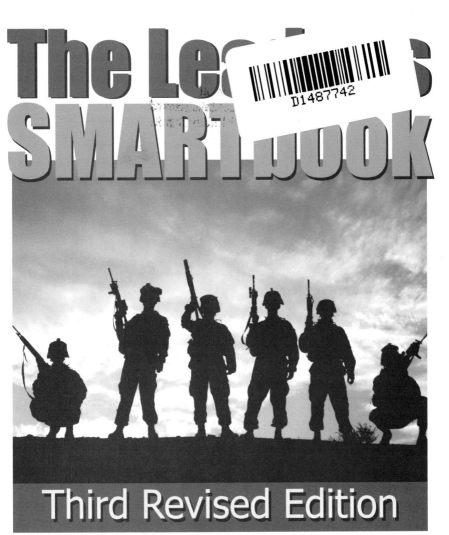

Third Revised Edition

With CHANGE 1
(FM 7-0 SMARTupdate)

Change 1 (FM 7-0 SMARTupdate) updates/replaces material in the
first printing of the third edition Leader's SMARTbook (ISBN 0-9675748-5-3)
from the 2002-version of "FM 7-0, Training the Force" to new material from the
Dec 2008-version of "FM 7-0, Training for Full Spectrum Operations."

Readers of the first printing TLS3 (ISBN 0-9675748-5-3) can obtain
Change 1 (FM 7-0 SMARTupdate) online at: www.TheLightningPress.com

The Lightning Press
Norman M. Wade

The Lightning Press

2227 Arrowhead Blvd
Lakeland, FL 33813
24-hour Voicemail/Fax/Order: 1-800-997-8827
E-mail: SMARTbooks@TheLightningPress.com
www.TheLightningPress.com

The Leader's SMARTbook (3rd Revised Edition) with Change 1 (FM 7-0 SMARTupdate)

Doctrinal Guide to Military Leadership & Training for Full Spectrum Operations

This is the second printing of The Leader's SMARTbook, 3rd Rev. Ed., incorporating Change 1 (FM 7-0 SMARTupdate). Change 1 updates/replaces material in the first printing of the third edition Leader's SMARTbook (ISBN 0-9675748-5-3) from the 2002-version of "FM 7-0, Training the Force" to new material from the Dec 2008-version of "FM 7-0, Training for Full Spectrum Operations."
Pages marked with asterisks denote updated pages.

Compiled, Edited, and Illustrated by Norman M. Wade

Copyright © 2009 Norman M. Wade

ISBN: 978-0-9824859-0-3

About our cover photo: Bravo Battery, 3rd Battalion, 320th Field Artillery, 101st Airborne Division at Forward Operating Base O'Ryan (near Balad) taken on or about Dec 2005. Battery Commander: CPT John J "Monty" Montgomery. Battalion Commander: LTC Richard Root. Soldiers in photo, from left to right: SPC Leroy Minion, SGT Christopher McCallum, SGT Harrington, SPC Thomason, SGT Hamby and SGT Robert Gordon. Photo by Department of the Army.

Printed and bound in the United States of America.

The Leader's SMARTbook (3rd Rev. Ed.)
CHANGE 1 to TLS3

CHANGE 1 (FM 7-0 SMARTupdate) to
The Leader's SMARTbook, 3rd Revised Edition

Change 1 (FM 7-0 SMARTupdate) updates/replaces material in the first printing of the third edition Leader's SMARTbook (ISBN 0-9675748-5-3) from the 2002-version of "FM 7-0, Training the Force" to new material from the Dec 2008-version of "FM 7-0, Training for Full Spectrum Operations." *Pages marked with asterisks denote updated pages.*

Readers of the first printing TLS3 (ISBN 0-9675748-5-3) can obtain Change 1 (FM 7-0 SMARTupdate) online at www.TheLightningPress.com

FM 6-22, Army Leadership, is the Army's keystone field manual on leadership. It establishes leadership doctrine and fundamental principles for all officers, noncommissioned officers, and Army civilians across all components.

FM 7-0, Training for Full Spectrum Operations (Dec '08), establishes the Army's keystone doctrine for training. FM 7-0 is the guide for Army training and training management. It addresses the fundamental principles and tenets of training. FM 7-0 addresses the fundamentals of training modular, expeditionary Army forces to conduct full spectrum operations—simultaneous offensive, defensive, and stability or civil support operations—in an era of persistent conflict.

FM 7-1, Battle Focused Training, is the Army's doctrinal foundation for how to train, and it is applicable to all units and organizations of the Army. FM 7-1 builds on task, condition, and standards-based training. Warfighting readiness is about developing confidence through trust—soldier-to-soldier, leader-to-led, and unit-to-unit—and the will to succeed. It is about leadership.

SMARTbooks - The Essentials of Warfighting!
Recognized as a doctrinal reference standard by military professionals around the world, SMARTbooks are designed with all levels of Soldiers, Sailors, Airmen, Marines and Civilians in mind.

SMARTbooks can be used as quick reference guides during actual tactical combat operations, as study guides at military education and professional development courses, and as lesson plans and checklists in support of training. Serving a generation of warfighters, military reference SMARTbooks have become "mission-essential" around the world. *Visit www.TheLightningPress.com for complete details!*

SMARTregister for Updates
Keep your SMARTbooks up-to-date! The Lightning Press will provide e-mail notification of updates, revisions and changes to our SMARTbooks. Users can register their SMARTbooks online at **www.TheLightningPress.com**. Updates and their prices will be announced by e-mail as significant changes or revised editions are published.

The Leader's SMARTbook (3rd Rev. Ed.)

References

The following references were used in part to compile The Leader's SMARTbook. Additionally listed are related resources useful to the reader. All references are available to the general public and designated as "approved for public release; distribution is unlimited." The Leader's SMARTbook does not contain classified or sensitive information restricted from public release.

Field Manuals

FM 3-0	TBP (2008)	Operations
FM 5-19	Aug 2006	Composite Risk Management
FM 6-22	Oct 2006	Army Leadership
*FM 7-0	***Dec 2008**	***Training for Full Spectrum Operations**
~~FM 7-0~~	~~Oct 2002~~	~~Training the Force~~ (SUPERSEDED)
FM 7-1	Sept 2003	Battle Focused Training
FM 7-2	TBP	How to Conduct Training Exercises
FM 7-22.7	Dec 2002	The Army Noncommissioned Officer Guide
FM 7-3	TBP	Training for Mobilization and War

Training Circulars

TC 25-8	Apr 2004	Training Ranges
TC 25-10	Aug 1996	A Leader's Guide to Lane Training
TC 25-30	Apr 1994	A Leader's Guide to Company Training Meetings

Additional Resources and Publications

APS	2007	Army Posture Statement 2007
AMP	2007	Army Modernization Plan 2007
FM 22-100	Aug 1999	Army Leadership (superceded by FM 6-22)
FM 25-101	Sept 1990	Battle Focused Training (superceded by FM 6-22)

The Leader's SMARTbook (3rd Rev. Ed.)
Table of Contents

Chap 1
The Basis of Leadership

Leading, Developing, Achieving

IV. Influences on Leadership

Chap 4
Counseling, Coaching, Mentoring

Chap 5

FM 7-0 (Dec '08): Training for Full Spectrum Opns

Chap 6

Training Plans, Meetings & Schedules

Chap 7
Training Execution & Training Exercises

Chap 8

Training Assessments & After Action Reviews

Index

Index

Order

The Essentials of Warfighting!

Military SMARTbooks

Army Leaders for the 21st Century (AL21)

Ref: 2007 Army Posture Statement, addendum B (Train and Equip Soldiers to Serve as Warriors and Grow Adaptive Leaders).

More than a half-million Soldiers now are serving in over 80 countries worldwide. Virtually all the Army's operational brigades are either conducting combat operations, preparing to do so, or are positioned forward to deter confl ict in critical regions. Some brigades are on their third and even fourth combat tour. To date, over 700,000 Active and Reserve Soldiers have answered the "call to duty," supporting the Global War on Terror.

Even as the Army continues to fight the current battle, it must transform and modernize the force, creating the strategic depth and breadth for readiness, both now and in the future. Iraq has proven to be a non-linear battlefield, where distinctions between combatant and noncombatant have blurred as have those between combat and stability operations. Simultaneous operations across the range of military operations, rather than sequential operations, will likely be the rule. Being ready to succeed in this environment requires Soldiers and leaders who are capable of using all the resources at their disposal. They must be able to use the best and latest equipment available; employing all capabilities available in a Joint and combined environment.

In the years since 9-11, the international security environment has become increasingly dangerous. Military commitments – requiring ground and Special Operations Forces – have increased on a global scale. Sustained levels of force deployment have stressed our Soldiers, their equipment, and the institutions that generate them. The likelihood of sustained strategic demand for Army forces underscores the need to improve our readiness for both current and future challenges. Soldiers are serving today in one of the most dangerous periods in our history. They are making enormous contributions and sacrifices at the forefront of the Global War on Terror. Their "boots on the ground" have enabled historic elections in Afghanistan and Iraq and will be required for democratic institutions to take hold. Operating as part of the Joint Team, our Soldiers are preventing attacks on the Nation, responding to natural disasters at home and abroad, helping to secure our borders, and underwriting our nation's commitment to defend its interests.

The goal of Army Leaders for the 21st Century (AL21) is to prepare Soldiers for the rigors of war and developing our leaders to serve as multi-skilled pentathletes able to thrive amidst complexity and uncertainty. Recognizing that intellectual change precedes physical change, the AL21 is designed to:

- Produce Soldiers armed with the mindset, values, and combat skills to serve as competent, resilient warriors.
- Reinforce a commitment to the Warrior Ethos among all Soldiers and Army Civilians.
- Enhance education and training programs throughout the Army: at home stations, at Combat Training Centers, within schools, by leveraging distance learning methods – and by increasing opportunities for graduate level education.
- Grow innovative, adaptive leaders through training and education programs that quickly apply lessons learned during combat, stability operations, reconstruction, and in providing support to civil authorities.

- Enhance capabilities by providing the best possible training, weapons, sensors, protection, and equipment to our Soldiers.
- Expand emphasis on language training and enhancing cultural awareness in our military education programs.
- Improve Soldiers' abilities to operate in complex environments overseas and with other governments and militaries to strengthen the capacity of partner nations.

I. Training Soldiers

To accomplish the mission, the Army is preparing Soldiers from all components to conduct the full spectrum of operations as part of joint, interagency, and coalition teams. This spectrum ranges from engaging with friends, allies, and partners to strengthen their capacity to conducting major combat operations.

The Army is transforming how it trains and educates Soldiers to better prepare them to deal with the challenges they will face today and tomorrow. The Army is envisions a "lifelong approach" to enhancing knowledge and skills, begining upon entry into service and by furnishing opportunities for professional growth and learning throughout their careers.

A. Warrior Tasks and Battle Drills

To better prepare Soldiers for combat, we have enhanced the rigor and relevance of training for newly enlisted Soldiers and recently commissioned officers. Today, every Soldier and officer, regardless of specialty, becomes a warrior first. A grouping of carefully selected Warrior Tasks and Battle Drills, developed from lessons learned on the battlefield, builds proficiency and confidence to function in today's operational environment. We conduct a biannual review of these tasks and drills to ensure continued relevance.

Through a program we call Operation Warrior Trainer, we are using the recent combat experiences of junior leaders from the Army National Guard and the Army Reserve to better prepare leaders for the challenges they will encounter. This program relies upon officers and noncommissioned officers who volunteer to serve in our Training Support Brigades. They teach, coach, and mentor their fellow Soldiers in the tactics, techniques, and procedures that were successful during their recent combat tours.

Note: See p. 1-12 to 1-13 for additional discussion.

B. Cultural Awareness and Foreign Language Training

We are increasing our investment in our Soldiers to develop foreign language capability and to increase their appreciation, understanding, and respect for other cultures. These two areas establish the foundation for improving our Soldiers' abilities to operate in complex environments overseas and to work closely with other governments and militaries to strengthen the capacity of partner nations.

Our operations in recent years have underscored the important role that language proficiency plays in the execution of successful operations. It accelerates the process of building rapport with the local populace, partner nations, and other organizations. In addition to language training in our schoolhouses, we also provide training on 30 languages to all Soldiers and Army Civilians through modern distance learning methods. Language proficiency, coupled with focused instruction, is helping to improve cultural awareness and enhance leader development. In addition, we are expanding opportunities for graduate level studies in all aspects of foreign cultures, which has the additional benefit of helping to retain our junior officers.

Note: See p. 1-9 for additional discussion.

The Army Vision

Ref: 2007 Army Posture Statement.

The Army Vision: Relevant and Ready Landpower In Service To The Nation

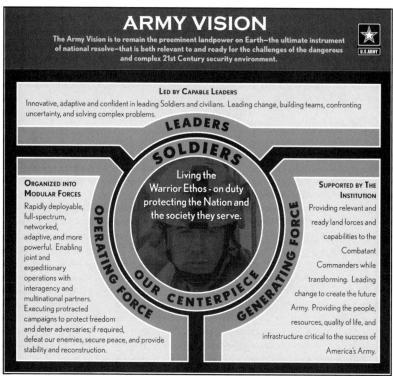

ARMY VISION

The Army Vision is to remain the preeminent landpower on Earth—the ultimate instrument of national resolve—that is both relevant to and ready for the challenges of the dangerous and complex 21st Century security environment.

U.S.ARMY

LED BY CAPABLE LEADERS

Innovative, adaptive and confident in leading Soldiers and civilians. Leading change, building teams, confronting uncertainty, and solving complex problems.

LEADERS

SOLDIERS

Living the Warrior Ethos - on duty protecting the Nation and the society they serve.

OUR CENTERPIECE

OPERATING FORCE

GENERATING FORCE

ORGANIZED INTO MODULAR FORCES

Rapidly deployable, full-spectrum, networked, adaptive, and more powerful. Enabling joint and expeditionary operations with interagency and multinational partners. Executing protracted campaigns to protect freedom and deter adversaries; if required, defeat our enemies, secure peace, and provide stability and reconstruction.

SUPPORTED BY THE INSTITUTION

Providing relevant and ready land forces and capabilities to the Combatant Commanders while transforming. Leading change to create the future Army. Providing the people, resources, quality of life, and infrastructure critical to the success of America's Army.

The challenges posed by the 21st Century security environment drive our vision of the force we must become to continue to accomplish our mission, to preserve peace and freedom for the Nation. Maintaining our focus on Soldiers – who are well led and organized into flexible, adaptive formations in our Operating Force, and properly supported by our Generating Force – we will ensure that our Army continues to be relevant, in terms of its design, and ready, in terms of its capabilities, for whatever the Nation demands. America has entrusted us to preserve peace, maintain freedom, and defend democracy – a role we have performed for over 230 years. Today, because of our Soldiers and our record of accomplishment, the American people regard the Army as one of the Nation's most respected institutions. We will maintain this trust.

C. Army Force Generation (ARFORGEN)

In addition to these enhancements in training Soldiers and leaders, we are improving how we develop the readiness of our units. Our Combined Arms Training Strategy is designed to provide trained and ready forces to meet the Combatant Commanders' operational requirements. This strategy features specific activities throughout what we refer to as multiple training domains: institutional, unit, and self-development. The cycles of Army Force Generation (ARFORGEN) – RESET and TRAIN ,READY, and AVAILABLE– allow commanders to optimize available training time in each of these domains, in a progressive manner, from individual training and education to more complex tasks in which whole units are involved. We carefully manage the flow of equipment throughout the cycles of ARFORGEN to ensure units have the tools they need to conduct demanding, realistic unit training. Applying the latest technology to use simulated training experiences and other tools is helping us to remain ahead of our adversaries and to quickly adapt our doctrine and training methods to prepare for a complex, dynamic environment.

We are also expanding our distributed learning program to enhance opportunities to develop our Soldiers and Army Civilians. On an average day over 22,000 Soldiers participate in one or more of the over 2,600 available online courses, including foreign language and cultural awareness training, to improve job proficiency and to work toward civilian degrees. Army Knowledge Online, the largest and most mature of all Department of Defense (DoD) portals, is the model for development of Defense Knowledge Online (DKO). DKO will be established as the DoD portal for personnel from all services, and will be the interface for providing DoD users with the services needed to accomplish their mission.

Note: See facing page (p. 1-5) for additional discussion.

II. Growing Adaptive Leaders

Today's security environment requires more of Army leaders at all levels. The evolving Transition Team mission that our officers and noncommissioned officers are performing – to train foreign nation's security forces – is but one example of the challenges our leaders are dealing with. As we have seen in Iraq, Afghanistan, Korea, Europe, across the Americas, in peace enforcement operations around the world, and while providing civil support, the actions of individual Soldiers and leaders are vital to success and can have strategic consequences.

A. Review Education, Training and Assignments for Leaders (RETAL)

To better prepare our leaders to develop creative solutions to the complex, ambiguous problems they will face, we formed a special task force to Review Education, Training and Assignments for Leaders. We drew upon the ideas and experiences of the finest leaders inside and outside of the Army.

Note: See p. 1-16 for additional discussion.

B. Army Leaders for the 21st Century (AL21)

The results of the RETAL task force's work is now being incorporated into Army Leaders for the 21st Century (AL21) – a comprehensive initiative designed to build leaders akin to pentathletes, skilled in many disciplines and able to rapidly transition between complex tasks with relative ease.

Note: See p 1-7 for additional discussion.

Army Force Generation [ARFORGEN]

Ref: 2007 Army Posture Statement, addendum B and 2007 Army Modernization Plan, pp. 4 to 5.

Army Force Generation (ARFORGEN) is the structured progression of increased unit readiness over time resulting in recurring periods of availability of trained, ready, and cohesive units. These units are prepared for operational deployment in support of Combatant Commanders' or civil authorities' requirements. Units are task organized in modular expeditionary forces, tailored for mission requirements. They are sustainable and have the capabilities and depth required to conduct the full range of operations in a persistent conflict. Operational requirements drive the ARFORGEN training and readiness process.

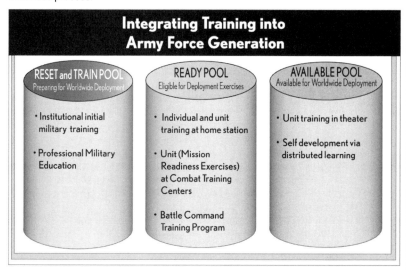

Army units will proceed through the Reset and Train, Ready and Available force pools to meet operational requirements with increased predictability. Units in the Reset and Train force pool redeploy from operations, receive and stabilize personnel, reset equipment, and conduct individual and collective training. Unit collective training is focused on core Mission Essential Task List (METL) tasks, such as offensive and defensive operations.

Reset and Train Pool
The Reset and Train phase culminates in a brigade-level collective training event. Units in the Reset and Train force pool are not ready or available for major combat operations. However, they should be ready to respond to homeland defense requirements and provide defense support to civil authorities at all times.

Ready Force Pool
Units in the Ready force pool continue mission-specific collective training and are eligible for sourcing if necessary to meet joint requirements. Their collective training is designed to focus on its directed METL, such as stability operations.

Available Force Pool
Units in the Available force pool are in their planned deployment windows and are fully trained, equipped, and resourced to meet operational requirements. In this way, ARFORGEN enables units to be fully-trained to conduct full-spectrum operations.

C. Pentathlete Leaders

We are evolving our training and education programs for our officers, noncommissioned officers, and civilians to grow military and civilian pentathletes. We are teaching our leaders critical thinking skills – emphasizing how to think, not what to think. Our focus is to develop highly adaptive leaders who have the intellectual agility needed to thrive in adverse, dynamic situations.

Note: See facing page (p. 1-7) for additional discussion.

D. Basic Officer Leader Course (BOLC)

For our newly commissioned officers we implemented the Basic Officer Leader Course (BOLC). Consistent with our warrior first approach, this tough, standardized, small-unit leadership experience ensures that all junior officers, in all of our branches, master the skills they will need to lead in combat. Our warrant officer and noncommissioned officer programs are experiencing similar improvements in the rigor and relevance of training and education.

Basic Officer Leader Course (BOLC) is a three phase training program to provide initial military training for officers in both active and reserve components.

- **BOLC Phase I** is the pre-commissioning phase. It includes all required preparatory training at the U.S. Military Academy, Reserve Officer Training Corps, Officer Candidate Schools and Direct Commissioned Officers (DCO). In February 2007, the Army implemented a four week DCO course to adequately prepare "off the street" direct commissioned officers for the rigors of BOLC II.

- **BOLC Phase II** is a new initial-entry, common core, field-leadership experience after Lieutenants are commissioned. BOLC II is a rigorous six-week, branch-immaterial course focused on small-unit leadership and tactics designed to challenge officers physically and mentally. Fort Benning, GA and Fort Sill, OK host this phase.

- **BOLC Phase III** is the branch technical phase where Lieutenants will learn the specialized skills, doctrine, tactics and techniques of their assigned branch. Since BOLC III is branch-specific, these courses are taught at the appropriate TRADOC schoolhouse or training center and range from 6 to 15 weeks.

The Army created a common core, tactical leadership phase of training - BOLC II. The old style of training at the schools/centers has been revamped to make greater use of experiential training to enhance the quality and effectiveness of the branch-specific course. All is part of the transformation of the Officer Education System so it better supports the goals of increased readiness, greater relevance of the force and a more Joint and expeditionary Army.

The Army will continue to identify training shortfalls from the Contemporary Operating Environment (COE) using a Gap Analysis process to improve training for BOLC I, II and III. Those gaps will be identified, prioritized and integrated into training as the COE changes. Beginning in FY 09, newly appointed warrant officers will be integrated into BOLC II. This will give the tactical leadership training to better prepare them to lead Soldiers in combat.

BOLC is developing leaders with a common warrior experience - more competent, confident and adaptable - effective at solving problems, making rapid decisions and leading Soldiers in any Contemporary Operating Environment. Each leader will be ready to train and lead small units in combat immediately upon arrival at his or her first unit of assignment.

Army Leaders in the 21st Century (AL21) - The Pentahlete

Ref: 2007 Army Posture Statement, addendum B and 2007 Army Modernization Plan, p. 38. Note: See also p. 1-4.

Army Leaders for the 21st Century (AL21) is an initiative to improve the Army leader development process. It responds to the Secretary of the Army (SA) and Chief of Staff of the Army (CSA) directive to review education, training and assignments for leaders (RETAL) and determine how to best develop leaders to serve in operational and institutional capacities, into the "pentathletes" needed to operate and win in the contemporary operating environment. Approved in June 2006, AL21 supersedes the Army Training and Leader Development program, implemented in November 2003.

Army Leaders in the 21st Century "The Pentathlete"

Multi-skilled Leader

- Strategic and creative thinker
- Builder of leaders and teams
- Competent full spectrum warfighter or accomplished professional who supports the Soldier
- Effective in managing, leading, and changing large organizations
- Skilled in governance, statesmanship, and diplomacy
- Understands cultural context, and works effectively across it

U.S.ARMY

Personifies the Warrior Ethos in all aspects, from war fighting to statesmanship to enterprise management ... It's a way of life.

Leader Attributes

- Sets the standard for integrity and character
- Confident and competent decision-maker in uncertain situations:
  - Prudent risk taker
  - Innovative
  - Adaptive
  - Accountable
- Empathetic and always positive
- Professionally educated and dedicated to life-long learning
- Effective communicator

Army Leaders for the 21st Century will produce multi-skilled, professionally educated warriors. "The Pentathlete" will be the confident, competent decision-maker who can overcome the challenges the Army will face in the future defense of the Nation. Through the proper balance of unit experiences, self-development, training, and education at all levels, the Army will grow leaders who are decisive, innovative, adaptive, culturally astute, and effective communicators. This balance is dynamic and continually adjusted based on future force needs. In addition to being experts in the art and science of the profession of arms and demonstrating character and integrity in everything they do, Army leaders must be astute at building teams, boldly confronting uncertainty, and solving complex problems. Above all, future senior leaders must be strategic and creative thinkers dedicated to lifelong learning. The goal is to develop leaders who as skilled in leadership as they are in governance, statesmanship, and diplomacy.

E. Warrant Officer Education System (WOES)

The goal of Warrant Officer Education is to produce highly specialized experts, trainers, and leaders who are fully competent in technical, tactical, and leadership skills. Warrant Officers must be creative problem solvers able to function in highly complex and dynamic environments. They must also be proficient operators, maintainers, administrators, and managers of Army equipment, support activities, and technical systems. WO leader development is a continuous process that begins with pre-appointment training and education.

The Warrant Officer Education System (WOES) is being redesigned and has begun integration into the Officer Education System (OES). This integration will allow development and implementation of shared leadership education and training opportunities among officer and warrant officer cohorts. The Army has also begun a WO technical/functional training and education needs analysis for CW3-CW5 to determine what training is required for senior warrant officers to maintain their technical expertise while performing in non-traditional leadership/staff positions. Full implementation of an integrated OES and technical training for senior WOs will meet the requirements of Army Force Generation.

As the Army transforms, there is an expanded role for WOs. Senior leaders in the field agree that the role of WOs in the planning, preparation, execution and assessment of training should be expanded. By taking advantage of their technical and operational experience, their contributions to the combat readiness of their units can be realized. Ensuring WOs receive progressive, relevant and timely technical/functional training ensures WOs can provide specialized technical mentorship and training to soldiers, especially non-commissioned officers, and provide valuable insights to commanders for collective training. WOs spend 80 percent of their careers in direct or organizational leadership positions leading Soldiers. The changes to the WO education system will help ensure they are fully prepared to execute these responsibilities.

Warrant Officers are the technical leaders in the Army that must develop and maintain technical skills regardless of rank or position. However, as WOs progress in their respective careers, leadership development is as important as technical training. This base knowledge is complemented through life long learning in institutional training, operational assignments, and self development.

F. Civilian Education System (CES)

The Civilian Education System (CES) is a progressive and sequential leader development program that provides enhanced educational opportunities for Army civilians throughout their careers comparable to that provided to officers, warrant officers, and noncommissioned officers. CES is comprised of four courses delivered via distributed learning and resident instruction, and is based on leadership competencies from the Office of Personnel Management and FM 6-22, Army Leadership.

The Command and General Staff College and the Army Management Staff College have directed the development of four courses that are being piloted during FY07—Foundation Course (FC), Basic Course (BC), Intermediate Course (IC), and Advanced Course (AC). While the FC is for all new Army civilians, the BC is for team leaders or first-line supervisors, the IC for both direct and indirect supervisors, and the AC for more senior level managers or supervisors of programs. Initial CES policy has been published to provide guidance for this new Army civilian leader development program, and a new on-line course management system, CES Civilian Human Resources Training Application System (CHRTAS), was fielded in June 2007. CES CHRTAS will manage the training and education application process for potential students and provide notification of application status to applicants and

Cultural Awareness and Foreign Language Capabilities

Ref: 2007 Army Posture Statement, addendum B.

Cultural awareness capability is the ability to understand the "how and why" of foreign cultures and the roles that culture, religion, and geography have in military operations. Foreign language capability extends beyond linguists, intelligence analysts, and interrogators to every Soldier and leader; ranging from the ability to communicate with the aid of language survival tools to high levels of proficiency in skilled linguists.

What has the Army done?

The Army is pursuing a variety of initiatives to enhance its capability in cultural awareness and foreign language. In accordance with the Defense Language Transformation Roadmap, the Army is incorporating cultural awareness training into all levels of professional military education. The US Army Training and Doctrine Command Culture Center at Fort Huachuca, Arizona developed an 80-hour modular cultural awareness training program for deploying units and branch schools. This center also provides mobile training teams (MTT) which bring cultural awareness training to units in their pre-deployment training. The Defense Language Institute Foreign Language Center (DLIFLC) at the Presidio of Monterey in Monterey, California incorporates cultural awareness in its language familiarization training for deploying units. DLIFLC also provides CD-ROM language survival kits to deploying Soldiers. Combat Training Centers (CTC) have completely transformed, using native-speaking role players, to replicate the sights and culture of the contemporary operational environment. In pre-commissioning, US Military Academy and ROTC have incorporated cultural awareness lessons into their curriculums.

The Army offers Soldiers a variety of ways to obtain foreign language skills and actively recruits native speakers from heritage communities. Language specialists primarily attend DLIFLC which offers online sustainment training through its Global Language Network (http://www.lingnet.org) and its Global Language Online Support System (http://gloss.lingnet.org). The Army provides online basic language training with "Rosetta Stone®." This is a state-of-the-art commercial software product intended for use by all Soldiers and Army civilians. MTTs and Language Training Detachments from DLIFLC bring language training at various skill levels to home station, CTCs, and mobilization training sites.

What continued efforts does the Army have planned?

The Army continues to develop, update, and expand its offering of cultural awareness training and foreign language materials at all levels. The Army plans to expand exchange and cultural immersion programs at the US Military Academy and increase advanced civil schooling opportunities.

Why is this important to the Army?

The human dimension is such a critical factor in today's complex environments demanding that Soldiers at all levels possess some cultural awareness and foreign language capability. It is no longer sufficient for limited numbers of Soldiers in specialized skill sets and units to possess these capabilities.

supervisors. In addition, three civilian leader development on-line courses—Action Officer Development Course (AODC), Supervisor Development Course (SDC) and Manager Development Course (MDC) have been revised and updated for civilian use as mandatory or self-development courses.

In order to ensure maximum participation in the appropriate CES courses for civilian leaders, the Army will continue to address policy issues as the new CES evolves and will publish periodic updates. The latest policy will also be published in the next revision of Army Regulation 350-1, Army Training and Leader Development. As additional resources are provided, the CES infrastructure to support the system will be ramped up and increased training opportunities provided to our civilian leaders.

Although Army civilians have historically made significant contributions in the execution of the Army's mission, our reliance on civilians today is even more pronounced. The Global War on Terrorism has diverted uniformed leaders increasingly from Generating Force roles to warfighting missions. As the Army transforms, Army civilians will assume a greater number of leadership roles and responsibilities to support Army operations at war. Freeing-up military manpower to perform more military-specific tasks required in the contemporary operating environment is critical. A fully implemented CES will help meet the Secretary of the Army's vision to develop leaders who are multi-skilled and possess the attributes of the 21str Century Army Pentathlete.

G. Army Career Intern/Fellows Program

The Army Career Intern/Fellows Program serves as the bench for the officer component of the civilian workforce. Like second lieutenants, Army's interns/fellows form an elite pool of trainees who represent the feeder group for future senior level professional, managerial, and executive civilian positions. These employees are provided progressive and sequential formal classroom and on-the-job developmental assignments that prepare them for placement in one or more of Army's 23 civilian professional programs.   The end result of these highly structured programs are Army Civilian Corps members with the requisite skills, abilities and leadership competencies required to immediately fill critical voids in the Civilian Corps upon graduation. All interns/fellows sign a mobility agreement and their final placements are based on the priority needs of the Army.

Army has extensively analyzed workforce trends and has clearly defined replenishment requirements, the Army adjusted the program to increase work year which resulted in an execution from 846 in Fiscal Year (FY) 2003 to an average of 1430 in FY 2004 through 2006.

Forecasts have identified the need to replace approximately 4,000 skilled professional employees on an annual basis. The Intern/Fellows Program is by far the best vehicle we have for replacing these losses. It produces employees who are ready to step in and support our warfighters as they defend our national security interests. Army is now focused on gradually increasing the program to bring it closer to required levels. This approach will allow us to stabilize the program while slowly increasing the number of interns and fellows we place into key positions each year. Army remains strongly committed to the Intern/Fellows Program. It supports the Global War on Terror and produces civilian pentatheletes while serving as a building block for transformation.

The Army Civilian Corps is a critical part of the institution. Its members ensure that we have the best equipped, trained and ready warfighters in the world. Civilians are deploying alongside our warfighters in greater numbers every year and will continue to do so in the future. In addition to accompanying our warfighters to the field Army civilians support them and their families in all aspects of their life. They gather

Battle Command

Ref: FM 3-0 Operations. See: www.battle-command.army.mil for additional information.

In battle, commanders face a thinking and adaptive enemy. Commanders estimate, but cannot predict, the enemy's actions and the course of future events. Two key concepts for exercising command and control in operations are battle command and mission command. Battle command describes the commander's role in the operations process. Mission command is the Army's preferred means of battle command.

Battle command is the art and science of understanding, visualizing, describing, directing, leading, and assessing forces in operations against a hostile, thinking, and adaptive enemy. Battle command applies leadership to translate decisions into actions—by synchronizing forces and warfighting functions in time, space, and purpose—to accomplish missions. Battle command is guided by professional judgment gained from experience, knowledge, education, intelligence, and intuition.

Successful battle command demands timely and effective decisions based on applying judgment to available information. It requires knowing both when and what to decide. It also requires commanders to evaluate the quality of information and knowledge. Commanders identify important information requirements and focus subordinates and the staff on answering them. Commanders are aware that, once executed, the effects of their decisions are frequently irreversible. Therefore, they anticipate the actions that follow their decisions.

Analytic and Intuitive Approaches to Decisionmaking

Commanders combine analytic and intuitive approaches to decisionmaking to exercise battle command. Analytic decisionmaking approaches a problem systematically. The analytic approach aims to produce the optimal solution to a problem from among the solutions identified. The Army's analytic approach is the military decisionmaking process (MDMP). In contrast, intuitive decisionmaking is the act of reaching a conclusion that emphasizes pattern recognition based on knowledge, judgment, experience, education, intelligence, boldness, perception, and character. This approach focuses on assessment of the situation vice comparison of multiple options (FM 6-0). It relies on the experienced commander's and staff member's intuitive ability to recognize the key elements and implications of a particular problem or situation, reject the impractical, and select an adequate solution.

Note: FM 5-0 discusses the MDMP. FM 6-0 discusses analytic and intuitive decisionmaking.

The two approaches are not mutually exclusive. Commanders may make an intuitive decision based on situational understanding gained during the MDMP. If time permits, the staff may use a specific MDMP step, such as wargaming, to validate or refine the commander's intuitive decision. When conducting the MDMP in a time-constrained environment, many techniques—such as selecting a single course of action—rely heavily on intuitive decisions. Even in the most rigorous analytic decisionmaking processes, intuition sets boundaries for analysis.

Understand, Visualize, Describe, Direct, Lead and Assess

Commanders understand, visualize, describe, direct, lead, and assess throughout the operations process. First, they develop an understanding of the operational environment. Then they visualize the desired end state and a broad concept of how to transform the current conditions into it. Commanders describe their visualization through the commander's intent, planning guidance, and concept of operations. They also express gaps in relevant information as commander's critical information requirements (CCIRs). Direction is implicit in command; commanders direct actions to achieve results and lead forces to mission accomplishment.

Warrior Tasks and Battle Drills

Ref: 2007 Army Posture Statement, addendum B.

Warrior Tasks and Battle Drills (WTBD) are defined as a skills taught in Basic Combat Training (BCT) or One Station Unit Training (OSUT) to train Soldiers how to survive in the combat environment.

- Warrior Tasks are a collection of individual Soldier skills deemed critical to Soldier survival. Examples include weapons training, tactical communications, urban operations, and first aid.
- Battle Drills are group skills designed to teach a unit to react and survive in common combat situations. Examples include react to ambush, react to chemical attack, and evacuate injured personnel from a vehicle.

What has the Army done?

- WTBD increase the relevance of training to current combat requirements and enhance the rigor in training. The driving force behind the change was lessons learned from Operation Iraqi Freedom (OIF), Operation Enduring Freedom (OEF), and comments from OIF/OEF veterans. The WTBD continue to evolve to meet the needs of the operational Army. For example as resources become available, Combat Life Saver certification will be conducted in BCT and OSUT.
- In Advanced Individual Training (AIT), selected WTBD (urban operations, combatives, convoy operations (convoy live-fire for OD, TC, QM, MI, SC), advanced rifle marksmanship, and rifle qualification if the AIT is longer than 23 weeks) are reinforced. Additionally, AIT school commandants may retrain any of the WTBD they deem critical to specific specialties.
- Currently there are 40 Warrior Tasks and 11 Battle Tasks being taught.

An annual review of the WTBD is conducted to maintain relevance to current operations. Army Warrior Training the new program that replaced common task testing focuses on WTBD training for all military personnel throughout the Army.

Shoot

- Qualify with assigned weapon
- Correct malfunctions with assigned weapon
- Engage targets with M-240B machine gun
- Engage targets with M-249 machine gun
- Engage targets with M-2 .50-caliber machine gun
- Engage targets with MK-19 machine gun
- Correct malfunctions with M-2
- Correct malfunctions with M-240B
- Correct malfunctions with M-249
- Correct malfunctions with MK-19
- Engage targets with weapon using night-vision sight
- Engage targets using aiming light
- Employ mines (manned) and hand grenades

Communicate

- Use visual-signaling techniques
- Perform voice communications: situation report/spot report
- Perform voice communications: MEDEVAC

Joint urban operations

- Perform movements techniques during an urban operation
- Engage targets during an urban operation
- Enter a building during an urban operation

Move

- Determine location on the ground (terrain association, map and Global   Positioning System)
- Navigate from one point to another (dismounted)
- Move over, through or around obstacles (except minefields)

Fight

- Move under direct fire
- React to indirect fire (dismounted and mounted)
- React to direct fire (dismounted and mounted)
- React to unexploded ordnance hazard
- React to man-to-man contact (combatives)
- React to chemical or biological attack/hazard
- Decontaminate yourself and individual equipment using chemical decontaminating kits
- Maintain equipment
- Evaluate a casualty
- Perform Combat Lifesaving for open wound (abdominal, chest, head)
- Perform Combat Lifesaving for bleeding of extremity
- Perform Tactical Combat Casualty Care
- Perform Field Sanitation and Preventative Medicine Fieldcraft
- Select a temporary fighting position
- Soldier as a Sensor
- Escalation of Force
- Personnel Recovery
- Improvised Explosive Device (IED) Detect & Defeat

Battle Drills

- React to contact: (visual, improvised explosive device, direct fire [includes rocket-propelled grenade])
- React to ambush (near)
- React to ambush (far)
- React to indirect fire
- React to chemical attack
- Break contact
- Dismount a vehicle
- Evacuate a casualty (dismounted & mounted)
- Establish security at a halt
- Checkpoint entry operations
- Vehicle Roll-Over Drill

intelligence; design, purchase, maintain and transport weapons and supplies; and provide housing, jobs, and recreational activities for soldiers and their families worldwide. Interns and Fellows provide the contemporary skills and practical experience needed to infuse the Civilian Corps with the agility required to meet the challenges of a rapidly changing environment. They are a key to assuring that the mission and our warfighters receive the highest level of support possible.

III. Enhancing the Combat Training Centers

To better prepare forces for the rigors of an increasingly uncertain, complex, and dangerous environment, the Army is continuing to enhance our Combat Training Center Program. The Army maintains three Combat Training Centers (CTC) which support large scale training operations. A fourth center supports the execution of the Battle Command Training Program, which facilitates training through advanced simulation based exercises. The Army is adapting the settings, conditions, and scenarios used at all of its centers based on operational experience. To better prepare Soldiers, leaders, and units, the Army's goal is to accurately reproduce the complex environments—terrain, culture, language, and information—in which they will operate.

At the CTCs, Brigade Combat Teams and other units conduct pre-deployment training on their core mission skills. As units practice their missions at the CTCs, they will encounter nongovernmental organizations, media, coalition forces, hundreds of civilians, interagency organizations and often, special operations forces. This training is crucial to developing readiness for combat. It enables our units to hone their skills and to develop into effective, cohesive teams before they deploy to our theaters of operation.

As the Army transforms to a larger, more capable operational force, we require additional training capacity. In addition, training centers are exceeding their capacity because of sustained high levels of strategic demand for Army forces. To meet the increasing need for world-class training to certify our units before they deploy, we are developing an exportable training capability. This capability is providing an experience that is close to what is provided at our actual centers at units' home stations. This initiative provides greater flexibility to meet the schedules established by the Combatant Commanders. It can also serve to reduce the time that our Soldiers are away from their home stations.

The rigor and relevance of the CTC Program is enhancing Army capabilities across the full spectrum of operations. By improving pre-deployment preparation, it is also reducing risk to Soldiers.

Note: See facing page (p. 1-15) for additional information.

Battle Command Training Program (BCTP)

The Battle Command Training Program provides realistic, stressful training, and leader development for corps, division, and brigade commanders and their staffs. We use the latest simulation technology and developments in operational scenarios to create the challenging, dynamic conditions these headquarters will encounter when deployed. This program prepares them to serve as joint and coalition task force operational headquarters in combat.

Note: See facing page (p. 1-15) for additional information.

Combat Training Center Program
Ref: 2007 Army Posture Statement, addendum B.

The mission of the Combat Training Center Program (CTC) is to provide highly realistic and stressful joint, combined arms training for Soldiers, leaders, and units according to Army and joint doctrine.

The Battle Command Training Program (BCTP)
Based at Fort Leavenworth, Kansas, BCTP supports realistic, stressful training and leader development for corps, division, and brigade commanders and their staffs.

The Joint Readiness Training Center (JRTC)
Located at Fort Polk, Louisiana primarily trains light infantry brigade combat teams against a "live" replicated opposing force. Though JRTC primarily trains light forces, it can and has trained heavy (mechanized) forces and Stryker brigade combat teams.

The National Training Center (NTC)
Located at Fort Irwin, California primarily trains heavy brigade combat teams against a "live" replicated opposing force. Though NTC primarily trains heavy forces, it can and has trained light infantry forces and Stryker brigade combat teams.

The Joint Multi-National Training Center (JMRC)
Formerly known as the Combat Maneuver Training Center (CMTC) - at Hohenfels, Germany primarily trains brigade combat teams assigned to the United States Army in Europe against a "live" replicated opposing force.

What has the Army done?
Since 2003, the CTCs have primarily been planning, coordinating, and conducting Mission Rehearsal Exercises (MREs) for maneuver BCTs and Mission Readiness Exercises (MRXs) for commanders and staff to prepare units to operate in the Contemporary Operational Environment (COE) within a joint or multi-national force during stability and support operations or contingency operations. Training innovations at the CTCs are continually incorporated to replicate the current COE in Iraq and Afghanistan. The MREs are specifically tailored to prepare units for the conditions in the combat zone, either Iraq or Afghanistan, to which they will deploy.

The CTCs have reconfigured the training areas that replicate threat environments to include Improvised Explosive Device (IED) lanes, tunnel and cave complexes and walled compounds. Additional buildings and shantytowns, populated with Iraqi or Afghani natives, throughout the training area were added with regional names to better replicate the urban environment the Soldiers will see in theater. Forward Operating Bases (FOBs) were added to replicate and stress the force protection requirements and measures that units will have to develop in theater. While the CTCs retain the capability to train to major combat operations unit training needed for other potential theaters of war and the new modular brigades, the current focus has shifted to counter-insurgency operations and lessons from combat in Iraq and Afghanistan.

Why is this important to the Army?
Overall, the training environment at our CTCs must be rapidly adaptable to the COE as our enemies change tactics and our operations shift. Additionally, the CTCs must assist in anticipating the future needs for units in theater. The complex, event-driven scenarios use cause and effect interactions and challenges the brigade combat team to execute multiple, simultaneous missions. This dynamic and demanding training prepares units for their next stop – combat operations in Iraq or Afghanistan.

Review of Education, Training and Assignments for Leaders (RETAL)

Ref: 2007 Army Posture Statement, addendum B.

The review of education, training and assignments for leaders (RETAL) is a Secretary of the Army (SA) and Chief of Staff of the Army (CSA) initiative to determine how the Army should develop its military and civilian leaders. These personnel will serve in both operational and institutional capacities to become the "pentathlete" leaders needed to operate and win in the contemporary operating environment. To accomplish this, the Director of the Army Staff established the RETAL Task Force to examine the policies and programs that govern educating, training, and assigning Army leaders.

The RETAL Task Force, staffed with co-chairs (ASA(M&RA) and G-3/5/7), a senior mentor (retired general officer consultant), a chief of staff, three teams, and a consulting body, conducted the review from October 2005 to June 2006. The review focused on developing "pentathlete" civilian, officer, and noncommissioned officer leaders.

What has the Army done?

The Army's effort to train, educate and provide relevant experiences develops leaders of character who are innovative and adaptive on today's battlefield. Modern warfare will continue to present increasingly more demanding challenges - beyond those traditionally thought to be of a military nature. Soldiers and civilians are capable of exercising leadership, provided they are competent to perform in their assigned roles and their organizations properly institute leadership practices.

The SA and CSA approved the Task Force's recommendations to improve the Army's ability to train, develop, and assign military and civilian leaders, capable of accomplish-ing the missions required among the complexities and challenges of the 21st Century national security environment. Based on the SA-CSA vision for a 21st Century "Pentathlete" leader, the Task Force identified: resource requirements; voids, gaps, and redundancies in Army policies and programs; successful elements of current policies and programs to sustain; additions and modifications to achieve an optimal develop-mental continuum; and culminated with integrating the approved resource requirements into the Planning, Programming, and Budgeting System guidance.

What continued efforts does the Army have planned?

In October 2006, the Army published the Army Leaders for the 21st Century (AL21) Implementation Guidance – the plan to implement the RETAL recommendations. This document directs merging the open tasks from the Army Training and Leader Development (ATLD) Implementation Plan with the RETAL recommended tasks; thus, creating an integrated and synchronized plan for improving the leader development process.

Why is this important to the Army?

Implementing these recommendations will allow the Army to achieve its goal of "building" military and civilian leaders, who master their military or core career field tasks and develop skills in the broader, more complex, politico-military arena. These "pentathlete" leaders will be better prepared to operate amongst the increasing complexity of the 21st Century security environment.

I. Leadership Defined

Ref: FM 6-22 Army Leadership, part 1, chap 1.

All Army team members, Soldiers and civilians alike, must have a basis of understanding for what leadership is and does. The definitions of leadership and leaders address their sources of strength in deep-rooted values, the Warrior Ethos, and professional competence. National and Army values influence the leader's character and professional development, instilling a desire to acquire the essential knowledge to lead. Leaders apply this knowledge within a spectrum of established competencies to achieve successful mission accomplishment. The roles and functions of Army leaders apply to the three interconnected levels of leadership: direct, organizational, and strategic. Within these levels of leadership, cohesive teams can achieve collective excellence when leadership levels interact effectively.

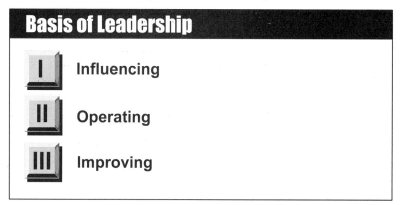

Basis of Leadership

I   Influencing

II Operating

III Improving

Ref: FM 6-22, chap. 1.

Leadership is the process of **influencing** people by providing purpose, direction, and motivation while **operating** to accomplish the mission and **improving** the organization.

I. Influencing

Influencing is getting people—Soldiers, Army civilians, and multinational partners—to do what is necessary. Influencing entails more than simply passing along orders. Personal examples are as important as spoken words. Leaders set that example, good or bad, with every action taken and word spoken, on or off duty. Through words and personal example, leaders communicate purpose, direction, and motivation.

A. Purpose and Vision

1. Purpose
Purpose gives subordinates the reason to act in order to achieve a desired outcome.
Leaders should provide clear purpose for their followers and do that in a variety
of ways. Leaders can use direct means of conveying purpose through requests or
orders for what to do.

2. Vision
Vision is another way that leaders can provide purpose. Vision refers to an organizational purpose that may be broader or have less immediate consequences than
other purpose statements. Higher-level leaders carefully consider how to communicate their vision.

B. Direction

Providing clear direction involves communicating how to accomplish a mission:
prioritizing tasks, assigning responsibility for completion, and ensuring subordinates
understand the standard. Although subordinates want and need direction, they
expect challenging tasks, quality training, and adequate resources. They should be
given appropriate freedom of action. Providing clear direction allows followers the
freedom to modify plans and orders to adapt to changing circumstances. Directing
while adapting to change is a continuous process.

For example, a battalion motor sergeant always takes the time and has the patience
to explain to the mechanics what is required of them. The sergeant does it by calling
them together for a few minutes to talk about the workload and the time constraints.
Although many Soldiers tire of hearing from the sergeant about how well they are
doing and that they are essential to mission accomplishment, they know it is true and
appreciate the comments. Every time the motor sergeant passes information during
a meeting, he sends a clear signal: people are cared for and valued. The payoff
ultimately comes when the unit is alerted for a combat deployment. As events unfold
at breakneck speed, the motor sergeant will not have time to explain, acknowledge
performance, or motivate them. Soldiers will do their jobs because their leader has
earned their trust.

C. Motivation

Motivation supplies the will to do what is necessary to accomplish a mission. Motivation comes from within, but is affected by others' actions and words. A leader's role
in motivation is to understand the needs and desires of others, to align and elevate
individual drives into team goals, and to influence others and accomplish those
larger aims. Some people have high levels of internal motivation to get a job done,
while others need more reassurance and feedback. Motivation spurs initiative when
something needs to be accomplished.

Soldiers and Army civilians become members of the Army team for the challenge.
That is why it is important to keep them motivated with demanding assignments and
missions. As a leader, learn as much as possible about others' capabilities and limitations, then give over as much responsibility as can be handled. When subordinates
succeed, praise them. When they fall short, give them credit for what they have done
right, but advise them on how to do better. When motivating with words, leaders
should use more than just empty phrases; they should personalize the message.

BE-KNOW-DO
Ref: FM 6-22, pp. 1-1 to 1-2.

Leadership is the process of **influencing** people by providing purpose, direction, and motivation while **operating** to accomplish the mission and **improving** the organization.

An enduring expression for Army leadership has been **BE-KNOW-DO**.

BE
Army leadership begins with what the leader must **BE**—the values and attributes that shape character. It may be helpful to think of these as internal and defining qualities possessed all the time. As defining qualities, they make up the identity of the leader.

An Army leader is anyone who by virtue of assumed role or assigned responsibility inspires and influences people to accomplish organizational goals. Army leaders motivate people both inside and outside the chain of command to pursue actions, focus thinking, and shape decisions for the greater good of the organization.

Values and attributes are the same for all leaders, regardless of position, although refined through experience and assumption of positions of greater responsibility. For example, a sergeant major with combat experience may have a deeper understanding of selfless service and personal courage than a new Soldier.

KNOW
The knowledge that leaders should use in leadership is what Soldiers and Army civilians **KNOW**. Leadership requires knowing about tactics, technical systems, organizations, management of resources, and the tendencies and needs of people. Knowledge shapes a leader's identity and is reinforced by a leader's actions.

DO
While character and knowledge are necessary, by themselves they are not enough. Leaders cannot be effective until they apply what they know. What leaders **DO**, or leader actions, is directly related to the influence they have on others and what is done. As with knowledge, leaders will learn more about leadership as they serve in different positions.

New challenges facing leaders, the Army, and the Nation mandate adjustments in how the Army educates, trains, and develops its military and civilian leadership. The Army's mission is to fight and win the Nation's wars by providing prompt, sustained land dominance across the spectrum of conflicts in support of combatant commanders. In a sense, all Army leaders must be warriors, regardless of service, branch, gender, status, or component. All serve for the common purpose of protecting the Nation and accomplishing their organization's mission to that end. They do this through influencing people and providing purpose, direction, and motivation.

Indirect approaches can be as successful as what is said. Setting a personal example can sustain the drive in others. This becomes apparent when leaders share the hardships. When a unit prepares for an emergency deployment, all key leaders should be involved to share in the hard work to get the equipment ready to ship. This includes leadership presence at night, weekends, and in all locations and conditions where the troops are toiling.

II. Operating

Operating encompasses the actions taken to influence others to accomplish missions and to set the stage for future operations. One example is the motor sergeant who ensures that vehicles roll out on time and that they are combat ready. The sergeant does it through planning and preparing (laying out the work and making necessary arrangements), executing (doing the job), and assessing (learning how to work smarter next time). The motor sergeant leads by personal example to achieve mission accomplishment. The civilian supervisor of training developers follows the same sort of operating actions. All leaders execute these types of actions which become more complex as they assume positions of increasing responsibility.

III. Improving

Improving for the future means capturing and acting on important lessons of ongoing and completed projects and missions. After checking to ensure that all tools are repaired, cleaned, accounted for, and properly stowed away, our motor sergeant conducts an after-action review (AAR). An AAR is a professional discussion of an event, focused on performance standards. It allows participants to discover for themselves what happened, why it happened, how to sustain strengths, and how to improve on weaknesses. Capitalizing on honest feedback, the motor sergeant identifies strong areas to sustain and weak areas to improve. If the AAR identifies that team members spent too much time on certain tasks while neglecting others, the leader might improve the section standing operating procedures or counsel specific people on how to do better.

Developmental counseling is crucial for helping subordinates improve performance and prepare for future responsibilities. The counseling should address strong areas as well as weak ones. If the motor sergeant discovers recurring deficiencies in individual or collective skills, remedial training is planned and conducted to improve these specific performance areas.

By stressing the team effort and focused learning, the motor sergeant gradually and continuously improves the unit. The sergeant's personal example sends an important message to the entire team: Improving the organization is everyone's responsibility. The team effort to do something about its shortcomings is more powerful than any lecture.

II. The Foundations of Leadership

Ref: FM 6-22 Army Leadership, part 1, chap 2.

The foundations of Army leadership are firmly grounded in history, loyalty to our country's laws, accountability to authority, and evolving Army doctrine. By applying this knowledge with confidence and dedication, leaders develop into mature, competent, and multiskilled members of the Nation's Army. While Army leaders are responsible for being personally and professionally competent, they are also charged with the responsibility of developing their subordinates.

To assist leaders to become competent at all levels, the Army identifies three categories of core leader competencies: lead, develop, and achieve. These competencies and their subsets represent the roles and functions of leaders.

I. Army Leadership Requirements Model

FM 1, one of the Army's two capstone manuals, states that the Army exists to serve the American people, protect enduring national interests, and fulfill the Nation's military responsibilities. To accomplish this requires values-based leadership, impeccable character, and professional competence. The Army leadership requirements model provides a common basis for thinking and learning about leadership and associated doctrine. All of the model's components are interrelated.

Leadership Requirements Model

Attributes	Core Leader Competencies
What an Army Leader is	*What an Army Leader Does*
A Leader of Character	**A. Leads**
■ Army Values	■ Leads others
■ Empathy	■ Extends influence beyond the chain of command
■ Warrior Ethos	■ Leads by example
	■ Communicates
A Leader with Presence	
■ Military bearing	**B. Develops**
■ Physically fit	■ Creates a postive environment
■ Composed, confident	■ Prepares self
■ Resilient	■ Develops others
A Leader with Intellectual Capacity	**C. Achieves**
■ Mental agility	■ Gets results
■ Sound judgement	
■ Innovation	
■ Interpersonal tact	
■ Domain knowledge	

Ref: FM 6-22, fig. 2-2, p. 2-4.

The model's basic components center on what a leader is and what a leader does. The leader's character, presence, and intellect enable the leader to master the core leader competencies through dedicated lifelong learning. The balanced application of the critical leadership requirements empowers the Army leader to build high-performing and cohesive organizations able to effectively project and support landpower. It also creates positive organizational climates, allowing for individual and team learning, and empathy for all team members, Soldiers, civilians, and their families.

II. The Founding Documents of Our Nation

The Army and its leadership requirements are based on the Nation's democratic foundations, defined values, and standards of excellence. The Army recognizes the importance of preserving the time-proven standards of competence that have distinguished leaders throughout history. Leadership doctrine acknowledges that societal change, evolving security threats, and technological advances require an ever-increasing degree of adaptability.

Although America's history and cultural traditions derive from many parts of the civilized world, common values, goals, and beliefs are solidly established in the Declaration of Independence and the Constitution. These documents explain the purpose of our nationhood and detail our specific freedoms and responsibilities.

Declaration of Independence and the Constitution

On 4 July 1776, the Declaration of Independence formally sealed America's separation from British rule and asserted her right as an equal participant in dealings with other sovereign nations. Adopted by Congress in March of 1787, the U.S. Constitution formally established the basic functions of our democratic government. It clearly explains the functions, as well as the checks and balances between the three branches of government: the executive, the legislative, and the judicial. The Constitution sets the parameters for the creation of our national defense establishment, including the legal basis for our Army. Amended to the Constitution in December 1791, the Federal Bill of Rights officially recognized specific rights for every American citizen, including freedom of religion, of speech, and of the press.

III. Leadership And Command Authority

Command is a specific and legal leadership responsibility unique to the military.

Command is the authority that a commander in the military service lawfully exercises over subordinates by virtue of rank or assignment. Command includes the leadership, authority, responsibility, and accountability for effectively using available resources and planning the employment of, organizing, directing, coordinating, and controlling military forces to accomplish assigned missions. It includes responsibility for unit readiness, health, welfare, morale, and discipline of assigned personnel.

Command is about sacred trust. Nowhere else do superiors have to answer for how their subordinates live and act beyond duty hours. Society and the Army look to commanders to ensure that Soldiers and Army civilians receive the proper training and care, uphold expected values, and accomplish assigned missions.

In Army organizations, commanders set the standards and policies for achieving and rewarding superior performance, as well as for punishing misconduct. In fact, military commanders can enforce their orders by force of criminal law. Consequently, it should not come as a surprise that organizations often take on the personality of their commanders. Army leaders selected to command are expected to lead beyond merely exercising formal authority. They should lead by example and serve as role models, since their personal example and public actions carry tremendous moral force. For that reason, people inside and outside the Army recognize commanders as the human faces of the system, the ones who embody the Army's commitment to readiness and care of people.

IV. The Civilian-Military Linkage
Ref: FM 6-22 Army Leadership, pp. 2-1 to 2-2.

The U.S. Constitution grants Congress the ability to raise and support armies. Subsequently, the armed forces are given the task of defending the United States of America and her territories. Membership in the Army and its other Services is marked by a special status in law. That status is reflected in distinctive uniforms and insignia of service and authority. To be able to function effectively on the battlefield, the Army and other Services are organized into hierarchies of authority. The Army's hierarchy begins with the individual Soldier and extends through the ranks to the civilian leadership including the Secretary of the Army, Secretary of Defense, and the President of the United States.

To formalize our ties to the Nation and to affirm subordination to its laws, members of the Army—Soldiers and Army civilians—swear a solemn oath to support and defend the Constitution of the United States against all enemies, foreign and domestic. Soldiers simultaneously acknowledge the authority of the President as Commander in Chief and officers as his agents. The purpose of the oath is to affirm military subordination to civilian authority.

Oath of Enlistment

I do solemnly swear (or affirm) that I will support and defend the Constitution of the United States against all enemies, foreign and domestic; that I will bear true faith and allegiance to the same; and that I will obey the orders of the President of the United States and the orders of the officers appointed over me, according to regulations and the Uniform Code of Military Justice. So help me God.

Oath of Office (taken by commissioned officers and Army civilians)

I do solemnly swear (or affirm) that I will support and defend the Constitution of the United States against all enemies, foreign and domestic; that I will bear true faith and allegiance to the same; that I take this obligation freely, without any mental reservation or purpose of evasion; and that I will well and faithfully discharge the duties of the office on which I am about to enter. So help me God.

Army Values

The oath and values emphasize that the Army's military and civilian leaders are instruments of the people of the United States. The elected government commits forces only after due consideration and in compliance with our national laws and values. Understanding this process gives our Army moral strength and unwavering confidence when committed to war.

Note: See p. 2-16 to 2-17 for a list of Army Values.

As General George Washington expressed more than 200 years ago, serving as a Soldier of the United States does not mean giving up being an American citizen with its inherent rights and responsibilities. Soldiers are citizens and should recognize that when in uniform, they represent their units, their Army, and their country. Every Soldier must balance the functions of being a dedicated warrior with obedience to the laws of the Nation. They must function as ambassadors for the country in peace and war. Similarly, self-disciplined behavior is expected of Army civilians.

V. Core Leader Competencies

Ref: FM 6-22 Army Leadership, pp. 2-7 to 2-8.

Leader competence develops from a balanced combination of institutional schooling, self-development, realistic training, and professional experience. Building competence follows a systematic and gradual approach, from mastering individual competencies, to applying them in concert and tailoring them to the situation at hand. Leading people by giving them a complex task helps them develop the confidence and will to take on progressively more difficult challenges.

Core Leader Competencies & Supporting Behaviors

	Leads Others	Extends Influence	Leads by Example	Communicates
Leads	■ Provide purpose, motivation, inspiration ■ Enforces standards ■ Balances mission and welfare of Soldiers	■ Build trust to outside lines of authority ■ Understand sphere, means and limits of influence ■ Negotiate, build consensus, resolve conflict	■ Display character ■ Lead with confidence in adverse conditions ■ Demonstrate competence	■ Listen actively ■ State goals for action ■ Ensure shared understanding

	Creates Positive Environment	Prepares Self	Develops Leaders	
Develops	■ Set the conditions for positive climate ■ Build teamwork and cohesion ■ Encourage initiative ■ Demonstrate care for people	■ Be prepared for expected and unexpected challenges ■ Expand knowledge ■ Maintain self-awareness	■ Assess developmental needs, develop on the job ■ Support professional and personal growth ■ Help people learn ■ Counsel, coach, mentor ■ Build team skills and processes	

	Gets Results			
Achieves	■ Provide direction, guidance and priorities ■ Develop and execute plans ■ Accomplish tasks consistently			

Ref: FM 6-22, fig. 2-3, p. 2-7.

Competencies provide a clear and consistent way of conveying expectations for Army leaders. Current and future leaders want to know what to do to succeed in their leadership responsibilities. The core leader competencies apply across all levels of the organization, across leader positions, and throughout careers. Competencies are demonstrated through behaviors that can be readily observed and assessed by a spectrum of leaders and followers: superiors, subordinates, peers, and mentors.

Leader competencies improve over extended periods. Leaders acquire the basic competencies at the direct leadership level. As the leader moves to organizational and strategic level positions, the competencies provide the basis for leading through change. Leaders continuously refine and extend the ability to perform these competencies proficiently and learn to apply them to increasingly complex situations.

These competencies are developed, sustained, and improved by performing one's assigned tasks and missions. Leaders do not wait until combat deployments to develop their leader competencies. They use every peacetime training opportunity to assess and improve their ability to lead Soldiers. Civilian leaders also use every opportunity to improve.

III. Leadership Levels, Roles and Teams

Ref: FM 6-22 Army Leadership, part 1, chap 3.

I. Levels of Leadership

There are three levels of Army leadership: direct, organizational, and strategic. Factors determining a position's leadership level can include the position's span of control, its headquarters level, and the extent of influence the leader holding the position exerts. Other factors include the size of the unit or organization, the type of operations it conducts, the number of people assigned, and its planning horizon.

Army Leadership Levels

Global/Regional/National Perspective

Strategic

Organizational/Systems and Processes Perspective

Organizational

Team/Unit/Task Force Perspective

Direct

Ref: FM 6-22, fig. 3-3, p. 3-6.

Army leaders of character lead by personal example and consistently act as good role models through a dedicated lifelong effort to learn and develop. They achieve excellence for their organizations when followers are disciplined to do their duty, committed to the Army Values, and feel empowered to accomplish any mission, while simultaneously improving their organizations with focus towards the future.

The Army cannot accomplish its mission unless all Army leaders, Soldiers, and civilians accomplish theirs—whether that means filling out a status report, repairing a vehicle, planning a budget, packing a parachute, maintaining pay records, or walking guard duty. The Army consists of more than a single outstanding general or a handful of combat heroes. It relies on hundreds of thousands of dedicated Soldiers and civilians—workers and leaders—to accomplish missions worldwide.

Each of their roles and responsibilities is unique, yet there are common ways in which the roles of various types of leaders interact. Every leader in the Army is a member of a team, a subordinate, and at some point, a leader of leaders.

Levels of Leadership

Ref: FM 6-22 Army Leadership, pp. 3-6 to 3-8.

There are three levels of Army leadership: direct, organizational, and strategic. Factors determining a position's leadership level can include the position's span of control, its headquarters level, and the extent of influence the leader holding the position exerts. Other factors include the size of the unit or organization, the type of operations it conducts, the number of people assigned, and its planning horizon.

Most NCOs, company and field grade officers, and Army civilian leaders serve at the direct leadership level. Some senior NCOs, field grade officers, and higher-grade Army civilians serve at the organizational leadership level. Primarily general officers and equivalent senior executive service Army civilians serve at the organizational or strategic leadership levels.

Often, the rank or grade of the leader holding a position does not indicate the position's leadership level. A sergeant first class serving as a platoon sergeant works at the direct leadership level. If the same NCO holds a headquarters job dealing with issues and policy affecting a brigade-sized or larger organization, that NCO works at the organizational leadership level. However, if the sergeant's primary duty is running a staff section that supports the leaders who run the organization, the NCO is a direct leader.

It is important to realize that the headquarters echelon alone does not determine a position's leadership level. Leaders of all ranks and grades serve in strategic-level headquarters, but they are not all strategic-level leaders. The responsibilities of a duty position together with the various factors usually determine its leadership level. For example, an Army civilian at a post range control facility with a dozen subordinates works at the direct leadership level. An Army civilian deputy garrison commander with a span of influence over several thousand people is an organizational-level leader.

A. Direct Leadership

Direct leadership is face-to-face or first-line leadership. It generally occurs in organizations where subordinates are accustomed to seeing their leaders all the time: teams and squads; sections and platoons; companies, batteries, troops, battalions, and squadrons. The direct leader's span of influence may range from a handful to several hundred people. NCOs are in direct leadership positions more often than their officer and civilian counterparts.

Direct leaders develop their subordinates one-on-one and influence the organization indirectly through their subordinates. For instance, a squadron commander is close enough to the Soldiers to exert direct influence when he visits training or interacts with subordinates during other scheduled functions.

Direct leaders generally experience more certainty and less complexity than organizational and strategic leaders. Mainly, they are close enough to the action to determine or address problems. Examples of direct leadership tasks are monitoring and coordinating team efforts, providing clear and concise mission intent, and setting expectations for performance.

B. Organizational Leadership

Organizational leaders influence several hundred to several thousand people. They do this indirectly, generally through more levels of subordinates than do direct leaders. The additional levels of subordinates can make it more difficult for them to see and judge immediate results. Organizational leaders have staffs to help them lead their people and manage their organizations' resources. They establish policies and the organizational climate that support their subordinate leaders.

Organizational leaders generally include military leaders at the brigade through corps levels, military and civilian leaders at directorate through installation levels, and civilians at the assistant through undersecretary of the Army levels. Their planning and mission focus generally ranges from two to ten years. Some examples of organizational leadership are setting policy, managing multiple priorities and resources, or establishing a long-term vision and empowering others to perform the mission.

While the same core leader competencies apply to all levels of leadership, organizational leaders usually deal with more complexity, more people, greater uncertainty, and a greater number of unintended consequences. Organizational leaders influence people through policymaking and systems integration rather than through face-to-face contact.

Getting out of the office and visiting remote parts of their organizations is important for organizational leaders. They make time to get to the field and to the depot warehouses to verify if their staff's reports, e-mails, and briefings match the actual production, the conditions their people face, and their own perceptions of the organization's progress toward mission accomplishment. Organizational leaders use personal observation and visits by designated staff members to assess how well subordinates understand the commander's intent and to determine if there is a need to reinforce or reassess the organization's priorities.

C. Strategic Leadership

Strategic leaders include military and Army civilian leaders at the major command through Department of Defense (DOD) levels. The Army has roughly 600 authorized military and civilian positions classified as senior strategic leaders. Strategic leaders are responsible for large organizations and influence several thousand to hundreds of thousands of people. They establish force structure, allocate resources, communicate strategic vision, and prepare their commands and the Army as a whole for their future roles.

Strategic leaders work in uncertain environments that present highly complex problems affecting or affected by events and organizations outside the Army. The actions of a geographic combatant commander often have critical impacts on global politics.

Strategic leaders apply all core leader competencies they acquired as direct and organizational leaders, while further adapting them to the more complex realities of their strategic environment. Since that environment includes the functions of all Army components, strategic leader decisions must also take into account such things as congressional hearings, Army budgetary constraints, new systems acquisition, civilian programs, research, development, and inter-service cooperation.

Strategic leaders are important catalysts for change and transformation. Because these leaders generally follow a long-term approach to planning, preparing, and executing, they often do not see their ideas come to fruition during their limited tenure in position. The Army's transformation to more flexible, more rapidly deployable, and more lethal unit configurations, such as brigade combat teams, is a good example of long-range strategic planning. It is a complex undertaking that will require continuous adjustments to shifting political, budgetary, and technical realities. While the Army relies on many leadership teams, it depends predominantly on organizational leaders to endorse the long-term strategic vision actively to reach all of the Army's organizations.

Comparatively speaking, strategic leaders have very few opportunities to visit the lowest-level organizations of their commands. That is why they need a good sense of when and where to visit. Because they exert influence primarily through staffs and trusted subordinates, strategic leaders must develop strong skills in selecting and developing talented and capable leaders for critical duty positions.

II. Roles and Responsibilities

When the Army speaks of Soldiers, it refers to commissioned officers, warrant officers, noncommissioned officers (NCOs), and enlisted Soldiers. The term commissioned officer refers to officers serving under a presidential commission in the rank of chief warrant officer 2 through general. An exception is those in the rank of warrant officer 1 (WO1) who serve under a warrant issued by the Secretary of the Army. Army civilians are employees of the Department of the Army and, like all Soldiers, are members of the executive branch of the federal government. All Army leaders, Soldiers, and Army civilians share the same goals: to support and defend the Constitution against all enemies, foreign and domestic, by providing effective Army landpower to combatant commanders and to accomplish their organization's mission in peace and war.

Although the Army consists of different categories of personnel serving and empowered by different laws and regulations, the roles and responsibilities of Army leaders from all organizations overlap and complement each other. Formal Army leaders come from three different categories: commissioned and warrant officers, noncommissioned officers, and Army civilians.

Members of all these categories of service have distinct roles in the Army, although duties may sometimes overlap. Collectively, these groups work toward a common goal and should follow a shared institutional value system. Army leaders often find themselves in charge of units or organizations populated with members of all these groups.

A. Commissioned And Warrant Officers

1. Commissioned Officers

Commissioned Army officers hold their grade and office under a commission issued under the authority of the President of the United States. The commission is granted on the basis of special trust and confidence placed in the officer's patriotism, valor, fidelity, and abilities. The officer's commission is the grant of presidential authority to direct subordinates and subsequently, an obligation to obey superiors. In the Army, commissioned officers are those who have been appointed to the rank of second lieutenant or higher or promoted to the rank of chief warrant officer two or higher.

Commissioned officers are essential to the Army's organization to command units, establish policy, and manage resources while balancing risks and caring for their people. They integrate collective, leader and Soldier training to accomplish the Army's missions. They serve at all levels, focusing on unit operations and outcomes, to leading change at the strategic levels. Commissioned officers fill command positions. Command makes officers responsible and accountable for everything their command does or fails to do. Command, a legal status held by appointment and grade, extends through a hierarchical rank structure with sufficient authority assigned or delegated at each level to accomplish the required duties.

Serving as a commissioned officer differs from other forms of Army leadership by the quality and breadth of expert knowledge required, in the measure of responsibility attached, and in the magnitude of the consequences of inaction or ineffectiveness. An enlisted leader swears an oath of obedience to lawful orders, while the commissioned officer promises to, "well and faithfully discharge the duties of the office." This distinction establishes a different expectation for discretionary initiative. Officers should be driven to maintain the momentum of operations,

B. Noncommissioned Officers

Ref: FM 6-22 Army Leadership, pp. 3-3 to 3-4.

NCOs conduct the daily operations of the Army. The NCO corps has adopted a vision that defines their role within the Army organization.

The NCO Vision

An NCO corps, grounded in heritage, values, and tradition, that embodies the Warrior Ethos; values perpetual learning; and is capable of leading, training, and motivating Soldiers.

We must always be an NCO corps that --
Leads by example.
Trains from experience.
Maintains and enforces standards.
Takes care of Soldiers.
Adapts to a changing world.

Ref: FM 6-22, fig. 3-1, p. 3-3.

The Army relies on NCOs who are capable of executing complex tactical operations, making intent-driven decisions, and who can operate in joint, interagency, and multinational scenarios. They must take the information provided by their leaders and pass it on to their subordinates. Soldiers look to their NCOs for solutions, guidance, and inspiration. Soldiers can relate to NCOs since NCOs are promoted from the junior enlisted ranks. They expect them to be the buffer, filtering information from the commissioned officers and providing them with the day-to-day guidance to get the job done. To answer the challenges of the contemporary operating environment, NCOs must train their Soldiers to cope, prepare, and perform no matter what the situation. In short, the Army NCO of today is a warrior-leader of strong character, comfortable in every role outlined in the NCO Corps' vision.

NCO leaders are responsible for setting and maintaining high-quality standards and discipline. They are the standard-bearers. Throughout history, flags have served as rallying points for Soldiers, and because of their symbolic importance, NCOs are entrusted with maintaining them. In a similar sense, NCOs are also accountable for caring for Soldiers and setting the example for them.

NCOs live and work every day with Soldiers. The first people that new recruits encounter when joining the Army are NCOs. NCOs process Soldiers for enlistment, teach basic Soldier skills, and demonstrate how to respect superior officers. Even after transition from civilian to Soldier is complete, the NCO is the key direct leader and trainer for individual, team, and crew skills at the unit level.

possess courage to deviate from standing orders within the commander's intent when required, and be willing to accept the responsibility and accountability for doing so. While officers depend on the counsel, technical skill, maturity, and experience of subordinates to translate their orders into action, the ultimate responsibility for mission success or failure resides with the commissioned officer in charge.

The cohorts differ in the magnitude of responsibility vested in them. The life and death decisions conveyed by noncommissioned officers and executed by Soldiers begin with officers. There are different legal penalties assigned for offenses against the authority of commissioned and noncommissioned officers, and there are specific offenses that only an officer can commit. Officers are strictly accountable for their actions. Senior officers bear a particular responsibility for the consequences of their decisions and for the quality of advice given—or not given—to their civilian superiors.

As they do with all Army leaders, the Army Values guide officers in their daily actions. These values manifest themselves as principles of action. Another essential part of officership is a shared professional identity. This self-concept, consisting of four interrelated identities, inspires and shapes the officer's behavior. These identities are warrior, servant of the Nation, member of a profession, and leader of character. As a warrior and leader of warriors, the officer adheres to the Soldier's Creed and the Warrior Ethos. An officer's responsibility as a public servant is first to the Nation, then to the Army, and then to his unit and his Soldiers. As a professional, the officer is obligated to be competent and stay abreast of changing requirements. As a leader of character, officers are expected to live up to institutional and National ethical values.

2. Warrant Officers

Warrant officers possess a high degree of specialization in a particular field in contrast to the more general assignment pattern of other commissioned officers. Warrant officers command aircraft, maritime vessels, special units, and task organized operational elements. In a wide variety of units and headquarters specialties, warrants provide quality advice, counsel, and solutions to support their unit or organization. They operate, maintain, administer, and manage the Army's equipment, support activities, and technical systems. Warrant officers are competent and confident warriors, innovative integrators of emerging technologies, dynamic teachers, and developers of specialized teams of Soldiers. Their extensive professional experience and technical knowledge qualifies warrant officers as invaluable role models and mentors for junior officers and NCOs.

Warrant officers fill various positions at company and higher levels. Junior warrants, like junior officers, work with Soldiers and NCOs. While warrant positions are usually functionally oriented, the leadership roles of warrants are the same as other leaders and staff officers. They lead and direct Soldiers and make the organization, analysis, and presentation of information manageable for the commander. Senior warrants provide the commander with the benefit of years of tactical and technical experience.

As warrant officers begin to function at the higher levels, they become "systems-of-systems" experts, rather than specific equipment experts. As such, they must have a firm grasp of the joint and multinational environments and know how to integrate systems they manage into complex operating environments.

C. Army Civilian Leaders
Ref: FM 6-22 Army Leadership, pp. 3-3 to 3-4.

Note: See following page (p. 1-32) for additional discussion of Army civilians.

The Army civilian corps consists of experienced personnel committed to serving the Nation. Army civilians are an integral part of the Army team and are members of the executive branch of the federal government. They fill positions in staff and sustaining base operations that would otherwise be filled by military personnel. They provide mission-essential capability, stability, and continuity during war and peace in support of the Soldier. Army civilians take their support mission professionally. Army civilians are committed to selfless service in the performance of their duties as expressed in the Army Civilian Corps Creed.

The Civilian Corps Creed

I am an Army civilian -- a member of the Army team. I am dedicated to the Army, its Soldiers and civilians. I will always support the mission.

I provide stability and continuity during war and peace. I support and defend the Constitution of the United States and consider it an honor to serve the Nation and its Army. I live the Army Values of loyalty, duty, respect, selfless service, honor, integrity, and personal courage. I am an Army civilian.

Ref: FM 6-22, fig. 3-2, p. 3-4.

The major roles and responsibilities of Army civilians include establishing and executing policy; managing Army programs, projects, and systems; and operating activities and facilities for Army equipment, support, research, and technical work. These roles are in support of the organizational Army as well as warfighters based around the world. The main differences between military and civilian leaders are in the provisions of their position, how they obtain their leadership skills, and career development patterns.

Army civilians' job placement depends on their eligibility to hold the position. Their credentials reflect the expertise with which they enter a position. Proficiency in that position is from education and training they have obtained, prior experiences, and career-long ties to special professional fields. Unlike military personnel, Army civilians do not carry their grade with them regardless of the job they perform. Civilians hold the grade of the position in which they serve. Except for the Commander in Chief (the President of the United States) and Secretary of Defense, civilians do not exercise military command; however, they could be designated to exercise general supervision over an Army installation or activity under the command of a military superior. Army civilians primarily exercise authority based on the position held, not their grade.

C. Army Civilians

Note: See previous page for more detailed discussion of Army civilian leaders.

Civilian personnel do not have career managers like their military counterparts, but there are functional proponents for career fields that ensure provisions exist for career growth. Army civilians are free to pursue positions and promotions as they desire. While mobility is not mandatory in all career fields, there are some (and some grade levels) where mobility agreements are required. Personnel policies generally state that civilians should be in positions that do not require military personnel for reasons of law, training, security, discipline, rotation, or combat readiness. While the career civilian workforce brings a wealth of diversity to the Army team, there is also a wealth of knowledge and experience brought to the Army's sustaining base when retired military join the civilian ranks.

While most civilians historically support military forces at home stations, civilians also deploy with military forces to sustain theater operations. As evidenced by the ever-increasing demands of recent deployments, civilians have served at every level and in every location, providing expertise and support wherever needed.

D. Joint And Multinational Forces

The Army team may also include embedded joint or multinational forces. Members of these groups, when added to an organization, change both the makeup and the capabilities of the combined team. While leaders may exercise formal authority over joint service members attached to a unit, they must exercise a different form of leadership to influence and guide the behavior of members of allied forces that serve with them. Leaders must adapt to the current operating environment and foster a command climate that includes and respects all members of the Army team.

E. Defense Contractors

A subset of the Army team is contractor personnel. Contractors fill gaps in the available military and Army civilian work force. They also provide services not available through military means to include essential technical expertise to many of our newly fielded weapon systems. Contractor personnel can focus on short-term projects; maintain equipment and aircraft for already over-tasked units; or fill positions as recruiters, instructors, and analysts, freeing up Soldiers to perform Soldier tasks. Contractors used as part of sections, teams, or units must use influence techniques to obtain commitment and compliance as they fulfill their duties or deliver services.

Managing contractors requires a different leadership approach since they are not part of the military chain-of-command. Contractor personnel should be managed through the terms and conditions set forth in their contract. They do not normally fall under Uniform Code of Military Justice authority.

E. Shared Roles

Good leaders wear both Army uniforms and business attire. All leaders take similar oaths upon entry to the Army. These groups work together in a superior-subordinate concept for command positions and formal leadership. Leadership draws on the same aspects of character, using the same competencies regardless of category. The military and civilian functions are complementary and highly integrated. While Soldiers focus on actively fighting and winning in war, the civilian workforce supports all warriors by sustaining operations and helping shape the conditions for mission success. Interdependence and cooperation of these leader categories within the Army make it the multifunctional, highly capable force the Nation depends on.

III. Leader Teams

Leaders at all levels recognize the Army is a team as well as a team of teams. These teams interact as numerous functional units, designed to perform necessary tasks and missions that in unison produce the collective effort of all Army components. Everyone belongs to a team, serving as either leader or responsible subordinate. For these teams to function at their best, leaders and followers must develop mutual trust and respect, recognize existing talents, and willingly contribute talents and abilities for the common good of the organization.

Leadership within Teams

 A Legitimate (formal)

 B Influential (informal)

Ref: FM 6-22, p. 3-8.

A. Formal (Legitimate) Leadership

Legitimate or formal leadership is granted to individuals by virtue of assignment to positions of responsibility and is a function of rank and experience. The positions themselves are based on the leader's level of job experience and training. One selection process used for the assignment of legitimate authority is the command selection board. Similar to a promotion board, the selection board uses past performance and potential for success to select officers for command positions. NCOs assume legitimate authority when assigned as a platoon sergeant, first sergeant, or command sergeant major. These positions bring with them the duty to recommend disciplinary actions and advancement or promotion.

The Uniform Code of Military Justice supports military leaders in positions of legitimate authority. Regardless of the quality of leadership exhibited by organizationally appointed leaders, they possess the legal right to impose their will on subordinates, using legal orders and directives.

B. Informal (Influential) Leadership

Informal leadership can be found throughout organizations, and while it can play an important role in mission accomplishment, it should never undermine legitimate authority. All members of the Army could find themselves in a position to serve as a leader at any time. Informal leadership is not based on any particular rank or position in the organizational hierarchy. It can arise from the knowledge gained from experience and sometimes requires initiative on the part of the individual to assume responsibility not designated to his position. Therefore, even the most junior member may be able to influence the decision of the highest organizational authority. As the final decision maker, the formal leader is ultimately responsible for legitimizing an informal leader's course of action.

Implications For Organizational Leaders And Unit Commanders

To be effective team builders, organizational leaders and commanders must be able to identify and interact with both formal and informal teams, including—

- The traditional chain of command
- Chains of coordination directing joint, interagency, and multinational organizations
- Chains of functional support combining commanders and staff officers

Although leading through other leaders is a decentralized process, it does not imply a commander or supervisor cannot step in and temporarily take active control if the need arises. However, bypassing the habitual chain of command should be by exception and focused on solving an urgent problem or guiding an organization back on track with the leader's original guidance.

IV. Team Structures

There are two leader team categories: horizontal and vertical.

1. Horizontal Leader Teams

Horizontal leader teams can also be either formal (headquarters staffs, major commands) or informal (task forces, advisory boards). Vertical leader teams can be both formal (commanders and subordinates) and informal (members of a career field or functional area).

2. Vertical Leader Teams

Vertical leader teams often share a common background and function, such as intelligence analysis or logistical support. Vertical and horizontal teams provide structure to organize team training.

A. Serving As Responsible Subordinates

Most leaders are also subordinates within the context of organizations or the institution called the Army. All members of the Army are part of a larger team. A technical supervisor leading several civilian specialists is not just the leader of that group. That team chief also works for someone else and that team has a place in a larger organization.

Part of being a responsible subordinate implies supporting the chain of command and making sure that the team supports the larger organization and its purpose. Just consider a leader whose team is responsible for handling the pay administration of a large organization. The team chief knows that when the team makes a mistake or falls behind in its work, hard-working Soldiers and civilians pay the price in terms of delayed pay actions. When the team chief introduces a new computer system for handling payroll changes, there is an obligation to try making it succeed, even if the chief initially has doubts that it will work as well as the old one. The team does not exist in a vacuum; it is part of a larger organization, serving many Soldiers, Army civilians, and their families.

Should the team chief strongly disagree with a superior's implementation concept as project failure that could negatively affect the team's mission and the welfare of many, the chief has an obligation to speak up. The team chief must show the moral courage to voice an opinion in a constructive manner. Disagreement does not imply undermining the chain of command or showing disrespect. Disagreement can lead to a better solution, providing the team chief maintains a positive attitude and offers workable alternatives.

Ultimately, the discussion must conclude and the team chief should accept a superior's final decision. From that point on, the team chief must support that decision and execute it to the highest of standards. Just imagine what chaos would engulf an organization if subordinates chose freely which orders to obey and which to ignore. In the end, it is important for all leaders to preserve trust and confidence in the chain of command and the collective abilities of the organization.

B. Leadership Without Authority

Often leadership arises from responsible subordinates who take charge and get the task completed in the absence of clear guidance from superiors. These circumstances arise when situations change or new situations develop for which the leader has not provided guidance or any standing orders for action and cannot be contacted promptly.

Leadership without authority can originate from one's expertise in a technical area. If others, including those of higher rank, consistently seek a Soldier's or civilian's expertise, that person has an implied responsibility to determine when it is appropriate to take the initiative related to that subject. When leading without designated authority, leaders need to appreciate the potential impact and act to contribute to the team's success.

Often leadership without authority arises when one must take the initiative to alert superiors of a potential problem or predict consequences if the organization remains on its current course. Informal leaders without formal authority need to exhibit a leader's image, that of self-confidence and humility.

Leadership is expected from everyone in the Army regardless of designated authority or recognized position of responsibility. Every leader has the potential to assume ultimate responsibility.

C. Empowering Subordinates

Competent leaders know the best way to create a solid organization is to empower subordinates. Give them a task, delegate the necessary authority, and let them do the work. Empowering the team does not mean omitting checks and making corrections when necessary. When mistakes happen, leaders ensure subordinates sort out what happened and why. A quality AAR will help them learn from their mistakes in a positive manner. All Soldiers and leaders err. Good Soldiers and conscientious leaders learn from mistakes.

Because subordinates learn best by doing, leaders should be willing to take calculated risks and accept the possibility that less experienced subordinates will make mistakes. If subordinate leaders are to grow and develop trust, it is best to let them learn through experience. Good leaders allow space so subordinates can experiment within the bounds of intent-based orders and plans.

On the opposite end of the spectrum, weak leaders who have not trained their subordinates sometimes insist, "They can't do it without me." Leaders, used to being the center of the attention, often feel indispensable, their battle cry being, "I can't take a day off. I have to be here all the time. I must watch my subordinates' every move, or who knows what will happen?" The fact is that no Army leader is irreplaceable. The Army will not stop functioning just because one leader, no matter how senior or central, steps aside. In combat, the loss of a leader can be a shock to a unit, but the unit must, and will, continue its mission.

Team Building during the Enrichment Stage

Ref: FM 22-100, app. A, p. 60 - 61 (not included in FM 6-22). See also p. 3-30 for Stages of Team Building from FM 6-22.

Leader Actions

1. Are your soldiers allowed time to get their personal affairs and their families settled before they are put to work?
2. Do you use the new soldier in productive activity as soon as he finishes his initial inprocessing and orientation?
3. Do you take time to listen to your soldiers?
4. Do you retain control and respect of your soldiers as you allow them to express their questions and concerns?
5. Do team members know who is next in line in case of leader casualties?
6. Are all team members involved in the unit goal-setting process?
7. Do you periodically spend time with each soldier to help clarify his expectations of you and the team and to help him understand your expectations of him?
8. Do soldiers trust one another, you, and other leaders?
9. Do your policies and practices communicate trust to the soldier?
10. Do your actions and words encourage acceptance?
11. Do you attempt to protect your unit from taskings beyond available resources?
12. Are you concerned about each soldier's development so that the soldier is best equipped to become a productive team member?

Training

1. Does unit training challenge the soldier? Is he actively involved?
2. Do you productively use lulls in the training scenario?
3. What benefits do your soldiers feel they get from training experiences?
4. When you give missions or tasks, are they unit missions?
5. Do you reward your unit for team accomplishments in training?
6. Does your unit keep training detractors to a minimum?
7. When talking about training, do they view it as "we" and "our" rather than "I"?
8. Do you continually upgrade the training situation to ensure the soldier is challenged?
9. Do you emphasize safety awareness for all training activities?
10. Are you present for training events?
11. Does your unit realistically train for combat?
12. Do you train your soldiers to cope with fear through training?
13. Do you give leadership responsibilities to soldiers during training?
14. Does your unit utilize and reinforce the chain of command in all training exercises?
15. Do your soldiers develop pride in their training accomplishments?
16. Do you reward your soldiers for unit accomplishment in training events?
17. Do your soldiers criticize themselves and seek better ways of doing things?

Development in Combat

1. Do you demonstrate competence that wins the respect of your soldiers?
2. Do you know your soldiers? Do you continuously assess them for ldrship potential?
3. Do you have a plan to pace the new soldier's integration into combat activity?
4. Are your soldiers prepared to receive and assist new soldiers who enter the unit?
5. Do you keep the soldiers informed?
6. Do you make your presence known to your soldiers during combat?
7. Do your soldiers have a realistic picture of the enemy, or do they overestimate?

The Army Leader

Ref: FM 6-22 Army Leadership, part 2, chap 4 through chap 6 and app. A.

The Army Leader: Person of Character, Presence and Intellect

Army leadership doctrine concerns itself with all aspects of leadership, the most important of which is the Army leader. Part Two of FM 6-22 examines that person and highlights critical attributes that all Army leaders can bring to bear, in order to reach their full professional potential on a career path from direct leader to strategic leader. It demonstrates that when Soldiers and Army civilians begin as leaders, they bring certain values and attributes, such as family-ingrained values and the aptitude for certain sports or intellectual abilities, such as learning foreign languages. Army institutional training, combined with education, training, and development on the job, aims at using these existing qualities and potential to develop a well-rounded leader with sets of desired attributes forming the leader's character, presence, and intellect. Development of the desired attributes requires that Army leaders pay attention to them through consistent self-awareness and lifelong learning.

Leadership Requirements Model

Attributes	Core Leader Competencies
What an Army Leader is	*What an Army Leader Does*
A Leader of Character ■ Army Values ■ Empathy ■ Warrior Ethos	**A. Leads** ■ Leads others ■ Extends influence beyond the chain of command ■ Leads by example ■ Communicates
A Leader with Presence ■ Military bearing ■ Physically fit ■ Composed, confident ■ Resilient	**B. Develops** ■ Creates a postive environment ■ Prepares self ■ Develops others
A Leader with Intellectual Capacity ■ Mental agility ■ Sound judgement ■ Innovation ■ Interpersonal tact ■ Domain knowledge	**C. Achieves** ■ Gets results

Ref: FM 6-22, fig. 2-2, p. 2-4.

The core leader competencies stem directly from the Army definition of leadership: Leadership is influencing people by providing purpose, motivation, and direction while operating to accomplish the mission and improve the organization.

The definition contains three basic goals: to lead others, to develop the organization and its individual members, and to accomplish the mission.

The Army Leader 2-1

A. Leader Competencies - Leads

Ref: FM 6-22 Army Leadership, table A-2, app. A. See also pp. 1-24 and 2-14.

Leads Others

Ref: FM 6-22, app. A, fig. A-2

Leaders motivate, inspire, and influence others to take initiative, work toward a common purpose, accomplish critical tasks, and achieve organizational objectives. Influence is focused on compelling others to go beyond their individual interests and tot work for the common good.

Establishes and imparts clear intent and purpose

- Determines goals or objectives
- Determines the course of action necessary to reach objectives and fulfill mission requirements
- Restates the higher headquarters' mission in terms appropriate to the organization
- Communicates instructions, orders and directives to subordinates
- Ensures subordinates understand and accept direction
- Empowers and delegates authority to subordinates
- Focuses on the most important aspects of a situation

Uses appropriate influence techniques to energize others

- Uses techniques ranging from compliance to commitment (pressure, legitimate requests, exchange, personal appeals, collaboration, rational persuasion, apprising, inspiration, participation and relationship building)

Conveys the significance of the work

- Inspires, encourages, and guides others toward mission accomplishment
- When appropriate, explains how tasks support the mission and how missions support organizational objectives
- Emphasizes the importance of organizational goals

Maintains and enforces high professional standards

- Reinforces the importance and role of standards
- Performs individual and collective tasks to standard
- Recognizes and takes responsibility for poor performance and addresses it appropriately

Balances requirements of mission with welfare of followers

- Assess and routinely monitors the impact of mission fulfillment on mental, physical and emotional attributes of subordinates
- Monitors morale, physical condition and safety of subordinates
- Provides appropriate relief when conditions jeopardize success of the mission or present overwhelming risk to personnel

Creates and promulgates vision of the future

- Interprets data about the future environment, tasks and missions
- Forecasts probable situations and outcomes and formulates strategies to prepare for them
- Communicates to others a need for greater understanding of the future environment, challenges and objectives

Extends Influence Beyond the Chain of Command

Ref: FM 6-22, app. A, fig. A-3.

Leaders need to influence beyond their direct lines of authority and beyond chains of command. This influence may extend to joint, interagency, intergovernmental, multinational and other groups. In these situations, leaders use indirect means of influence: diplomacy, negotiation, mediation, arbitration, partnering, conflict resolution, consensus building and coordination.

Understands sphere of influence, means of influence, and limits of influence
- Assesses situations, missions, and assignments to determine the parties involved in decision making, decision support, and possible interference or resistance

Builds trust
- Is firm, fair, and respectful to gain trust
- Identifies areas of commonality
- Engages other members in activities and objectives
- Follows through on actions related to expectations of others
- Keeps people informed of actions and results

Negotiates for understanding, builds consensus, and resolves conflict
- Leverages trust to establish agreements and courses of action
- Clarifies the situation
- Identifies individual and group positions and needs
- Identifies roles and resources
- Facilitates understanding of conflicting positions
- Generates and facilitates generation of possible solutions
- Gains cooperation or support when working with others

Builds and maintains alliances
- Establishes contact and interacts with others who share common interests, such as development, reaching goals, and giving advice
- Maintains friendships, business associations, interest groups and support networks
- Influences perceptions about the organization
- Understands the value of and learns from partnerships, associations, and other cooperative alliances

Leads by Example

Ref: FM 6-22, app. A, fig. A-4.

Leaders constantly serve as role models for others. Leaders will always be viewed as the example, so they must maintain standards and provide examples of effectiveness through all their actions. All Army leaders should model the Army values. Modeling provides tangible evidence of desired behaviors and reinforces verbal guidance through demonstration of commitment and action.

Displays character by modeling the Army Values consistently through actions, attitudes and communications
- Sets the example by displaying high standards of duty performance, personal appearance, military and professional bearing, physical fitness and health, and ethics
- Fosters an ethical climate

– (Continued on next page)

(Continued from previous page)

- Shows good moral judgment and behavior
- Completes individual/unit tasks to standard, on time, and within the cdr's intent
- Is punctual and meets deadlines
- Demonstrates determination, persistence and patience

Exemplifies the Warrior Ethos

- Fights through obstacles, difficulties, and hardships to accomplish the mission
- Demonstrates the will to succeed
- Demonstrates physical and emotional courage
- Communicates how the Warrior Ethos is demonstrated

Demonstrates commitment to the Nation, Army, unit, Soldiers, community, and multinational partners

- Demonstrates enthusiasm for task completion and, if necessary, methods of accomplishing assigned tasks
- Is available to assist peers and subordinates
- Shares hardships with subordinates
- Participates in team task and missions without being asked

Leads with confidence in adverse situations

- Provides leader presence at the right time and place
- Displays self-control, composure, and positive attitude under adverse conditions
- Is resilient
- Remains decisive after discovering a mistake
- Acts in the absence of guidance
- Does not show discouragement when facing setbacks
- Remains positive when the situation becomes confusing or changes
- Encourages subordinates when they show signs of weakness

Demonstrates technical and tactical knowledge and skills

- Meets mission standards, protects resources, and accomplishes the mission with available resources using technical and tactical skills
- Displays appropriate knowledge of equipment, procedures and methods

Understands the importance of conceptual skills and models them to others

- Displays comfort working in open systems
- Makes logical assumptions in the absence of facts
- Identifies critical issues to use as a guide in making decisions and taking advantage of opportunities
- Recognizes and generates innovative solutions
- Relates and compares information from different sources to identify possible cause-and-effect relationships
- Uses sound judgment and logical reasoning

Seeks and is open to diverse ideas and points of view

- Encourages respectful, honest communications among staff and decision makers
- Explores alternative explanations and approaches to accomplishing tasks
- Reinforces new ideas; demonstrates willingness to consider alternative perspectives to resolve difficult problems
- Uses knowledgeable sources and subject matter experts
- Recognizes & discourages individuals seeking to gain favor from tacit agreement

Communicates

Ref: FM 6-22, app A, fig. A-5.

Leaders communicate effectively by clearly expressing ideas and actively listening to others. By understanding the nature and importance of communication and practicing effective communication techniques, leaders will relate better to others and be able to translate goals into actions. Communication is essential to all leader competencies.

Listens actively
- Listens and watches attentively
- Makes appropriate notes
- Tunes into content, emotion and urgency
- Uses verbal and nonverbal means to reinforce with the speaker that you are paying attention
- Reflects on new information before expressing views

Determines information-sharing strategies
- Shares necessary information with others and subordinates
- Protects confidential information
- Coordinates plans with higher, lower and adjacent individuals and affected organizations
- Keeps higher and lower headquarters, superiors and subordinates informed

Employs engaging communication techniques
- States goals to energize others to adopt and act on them
- Speaks enthusiastically and maintains listeners' interest and involvement
- Makes appropriate eye contact when speaking
- Uses gestures that are appropriate but not distracting
- Uses visual aides as needed
- Acts to determine, recognize and resolve misunderstandings

Conveys thoughts and ideas to ensure shared understanding
- Expresses thoughts and ideas clearly to individuals and groups
- Uses correct grammar and doctrinally correct phrases
- Recognizes potential miscommunication
- Uses appropriate means for communicating a message
- Communicates clearly and concisely up, down, across, and outside the organization
- Clarifies when there is some question about goals, tasks, plans, performance expectations, and role responsibilities

Presents recommendations so others understand advantages
- Uses logic and relevant facts in dialogue
- Keeps conversations on track
- Expresses well-thoughout and well-organized ideas

Is sensitive to cultural factors in communication
- Maintains awareness of communication customs, expressions, actions, or behaviors
- Demonstrates respect for others

B. Leader Competencies - Develops

Ref: FM 6-22 Army Leadership, table A-6, app. A. See also pp. 1-24 and 2-14.

Creates a Positive Environment

Ref: FM 6-22, app. A, fig. A-6.

Leaders have the responsibility to establish and maintain positive expectations and attitudes that produce the setting for healthy relationships and effective work behaviors. Leaders are charged with improving the organization while accomplishing missions. They should leave the organization better than it was when they arrived.

Fosters teamwork, cohesion, cooperation and loyalty
- Encourages people to work together effectively
- Promotes teamwork and team achievement to build trust
- Draws attention to the consequences of poor coordination
- Acknowledges and rewards successful team coordination
- Integrates new members into the unit quickly

Encourages subordinates to exercise initiative, accept responsibility and take ownership
- Involves others in decisions and keeps them informed of consequences that affect them
- Allocates responsibility for performance
- Guides subordinate leaders in thinking through problems for themselves
- Allocates decision making to the lowest appropriate level
- Acts to expand and enhance subordinate's competence and self-confidence
- Rewards initiative

Creates a learning environment
- Uses effective assessment and training methods
- Encourages leaders and their subordinates to reach their full potential
- Motivates others to develop themselves
- Express the value of interacting with others and seeking counsel
- Stimulates innovative and critical thinking to others
- Seeks new approaches to problems

Encourages open and candid communications
- Shows others how to accomplish tasks while remaining respectful, resolute, and focused
- Communicates a positive attitude to encourage others and improve morale
- Reinforces the expression of contrary and minority viewpoints
- Displays appropriate reactions to new or conflicting information or opinions
- Guards against groupthink

Encourages fairness and inclusiveness
- Provides accurate evaluations and assessments
- Supports equal opportunity
- Prevents all forms of harassment
- Encourages learning about and leveraging diversity

Expresses and demonstrates care for people and their well-being

- Encourages subordinates and peers to express candid opinions
- Ensures that subordinates and their families are provided for, including their health, welfare and development
- Stands up for subordinates
- Routinely monitors morale and encourages honest feedback

Anticipates people's on-the-job needs

- Recognizes and monitors subordinates' needs and reactions
- Shows concern for the impact of tasks and missions on subordinate morale

Sets and maintains high expectations for individuals and teams

- Clearly articulates expectations
- Creates a climate that expects good performance, recognizes superior performance, and does not accept poor performance
- Challenges others to match the leader's example

Accepts reasonable setbacks and failures

- Communicates the difference between maintaining professional standards and a zero-defects mentality
- Expresses the importance of being competent and motivated but recognizes the occurrence of failure
- Emphasizes learning from one's mistakes

Prepares Self

Ref: FM 6-22, app. A, fig. A-7.

Leaders ensure they are prepared to execute their leadership responsibilities fully. They are aware of their limitations and strengths and seek to develop themselves. Leaders maintain physical fitness and mental well-being. They continue to improve the domain knowledge required of their leadership roles and their profession. Only through continuous preparation for missions and other challenges, being aware of self and situations and practicing lifelong learning and development can an individual fulfill the responsibilities of leadership.

Maintains mental and physical health and well-being

- Recognizes imbalance or inappropriateness of one's own actions
- Removes emotions from decision making
- Applies logic and reason to make decisions or when interacting with emotionally charged individuals
- Recognizes the sources of stress and maintains appropriate levels of challenge to motivate self
- Takes part in regular exercise, leisure activities, and time away from routine work
- Stays focused on life priorities and values

(Continued on next page)

(Continued from previous page)

Maintains self awareness: employs self understanding, and recognizes impact on others
- Evaluates one's strengths and weaknesses
- Learns from mistakes and makes corrections, learns from experience
- Considers feedback on performance, outcomes associated with actions, and actions taken by others to achieve similar goals
- Seeks feedback on how others view one's own actions
- Routinely determines personal goals and makes progress toward them
- Develops capabilities where possible but accepts personal limitations
- Seeks opportunities where capabilities can be used appropriately
- Understands self-motivation under various task conditions

Evaluates and incorporates feedback from others
- Determines areas in need of development
- Judges self with the help of feedback from others

Expands knowledge of technical, technological, and tactical areas
- Keeps informed about developments and policy changes inside and outside the organization
- Seeks knowledge of systems, equipment, capabilities, and situations, particularly information technology systems

Expands conceptual and interpersonal capabilities
- Understands the contribution of concentration, critical thinking (assimilation of information, discriminating relevant cues, question asking), imagination (decentering), and problem solving in different task conditions
- Learns new approaches to problem solving
- Applies lessons learned
- Filters unnecessary information efficiently
- Reserves time for self-development, reflection and personal growth
- Considers possible motives behind conflicting information

Analyzes and organizes information to create knowledge
- Reflects on what has been learned and organizes these insights for future application
- Considers source, quality or relevance and criticality of information to improve understanding
- Identifies reliable sources of data & other resources related to acquiring knowledge
- Sets up systems or procedures to store knowledge for reuse

Maintains relevant cultural awareness
- Learns about issues of language, values, customary behavior, ideas, beliefs, and patterns of thinking that influence others
- Learns about results of previous encounters when culture plays a role in mission success

Maintains relevant geopolitical awareness
- Learns about relevant societies outside the United States experiencing unrest
- Recognizes Army influences on other countries, multinational partners and enemies
- Understands the factors influencing conflict and peacekeeping, peace enforcing, and peacemaking missions

Develops others

Ref: FM 6-22, app. A, fig. A-8.

Leaders encourage and support others to grow as individuals and teams. They facilitate the achievement of organizational goals through assisting others to develop. They prepare others to assume new positions elsewhere in the organization, making the organization more versatile and productive.

Assesses current developmental needs of others

- Observes and monitors subordinates under different task conditions to establish strengths and weaknesses
- Notes changes in proficiency
- Evaluates subordinates in a fair and consistent manner

Fosters job development, job challenge, and job enrichment
- Assesses task and subordinate to consider methods of improving work assignments, when job enrichment would be useful, methods of cross-training on tasks, and methods of accomplishing missions
- Designs tasks to provide practice in areas of subordinate's weaknesses
- Designs ways to challenge subordinates and improve practice
- Encourages subordinates to improve processes

Coaches, counsels, mentors
- Improves subordinate's understanding and proficiency
- Uses experience and knowledge to improve future performance
- Counsels, coaches and mentors subordinates, subordinate leaders, and others

Facilitates ongoing development
- Maintains awareness of existing individual and organizational development programs and removes barriers to development
- Supports opportunities for self-development
- Arranges training opportunities as needed that help subordinates improve self-awareness, confidence and competence

Supports institutional-based development
- Encourages subordinates to pursue institutional learning opportunities
- Provides information about institutional training and career progression to subordinates
- Maintains resources related to development

Builds team or group skills and processes
- Presents challenging assignments for team or group interaction
- Provides resources and support
- Sustains and improves the relationships among team or group members
- Provides realistic, mission-oriented training
- Provides feedback on team processes

C. Leader Competencies - Achieves

Ref: FM 6-22 Army Leadership, table A-9, app. A. See also p. 1-24 and 2-14.

Gets Results

Ref: FM 6-22, app. A, fig. A-9.

A leader's ultimate purpose is to accomplish organizational results. A leader gets results by providing guidance and managing resources, as well as performing other leader competencies. This competency is focused on consistent and ethical task accomplishment through supervising, managing, monitoring, and controlling of the work.

Prioritizes, organizes, and coordinates taskings for teams or other organizational structures/groups.

- Uses planning to ensure each course of action achieves the desired outcome
- Organizes groups and teams to accomplish work
- Plans to ensure that all task can be executed in the time available and that tasks depending on other tasks are executed in the correct sequence
- Limits overspecification and micromanagement

Identifies and accounts for individual and group capabilities and commitment to task

- Considers duty positions, capabilities and developmental needs when assigning tasks
- Conducts initial assessments when beginning a new task or assuming a new position

Designates, clarifies and deconflicts roles

- Establishes and employs procedures for monitoring, coordinating, and regulating subordinates actions and activities
- Mediates peer conflicts and disagreements

Identifies, contends for, allocates and manages resources

- Allocates adequate time for task completion
- Keeps track of people and equipment
- Allocates time to prepare and conduct rehearsals
- Continually seeks improvement in operating efficiency, resource conservation, and fiscal responsibility

Removes work barriers

- Protects organization from unnecessary taskings and distractions
- Recognizes and resolves scheduling conflicts
- Overcomes other obstacles preventing full attention to accomplishing the mission

Recognizes and rewards good performance

- Recognizes individual and team accomplishments; rewards them appropriately
- Credits subordinates for good performance
- Builds on successes
- Explores new reward systems and understands individual reward motivations

Seeks, recognizes and takes advantage of opportunities to improve performance

- Asks incisive questions
- Anticipates need for action
- Analyzes activities to determine how desired end states are achieved or affected
- Acts to improve the organizations collective performance
- Envisions way to improve
- Recommends best methods for accomplishing tasks
- Leverages information and communication technology to improve individual and group effectiveness
- Encourages staff to use creativity to solve problems

Makes feedback part of work processes

- Gives and seeks accurate and timely feedback
- Uses feedback to modify duties, tasks, procedures, requirements, and goals when appropriate
- Uses assessment techniques and evaluation tools (such as AARs) to identify lessons learned and facilitate consistent improvement
- Determines the appropriate setting and timing for feedback

Executes plans to accomplish the mission

- Schedules activities to meet all commitments in critical performance areas
- Notifies peers and subordinates in advance when their support is required
- Keeps track of task assignments and suspenses
- Adjusts assignments, if necessary
- Attends to details

Identifies and adjusts to external influences on the mission or taskings and organization

- Gathers and analyzes relevant information about changing situations
- Determines causes, effects, and contributing factors of problems
- Considers contingencies and their consequences
- Makes necessary, on-the-spot adjustments

II. Leader Attributes

Ref: FM 6-22 Army Leadership, app. A.

The core leader competencies are complemented by attributes that distinguish high performing leaders of character. Attributes are characteristics that are an inherent part of an individual's total core, physical, and intellectual aspects. Attributes shape how an individual behaves in their environment. Attributes for Army leaders are aligned to identity, presence, and intellectual capacity.

A. A Leader of Character (Identify)

Ref: FM 6-22, app. A, fig. A-10. See also pp. 2-15 to 2-22.

Factors internal and central to a leader, that which makes up an individual's core

Army Values
- Values are the principles, standards or qualities considered essential for successful leaders
- Values are fundamental to help people discern right from wrong in any situation
- The Army has set seven values that must be developed in all Army individuals: loyalty, duty, respect, selfless service, honor, integrity, and personal courage

Empathy
- The propensity to experience something from another person's point of view
- The ability to identify with and enter into another person's feeling and emotions
- The desire to care for and take care of Soldiers and others

Warrior Ethos
- The shared sentiment internal to Soldiers that represents the spirit of the profession of arms

B. A Leader with Presence

Ref: FM 6-22, app. A, fig. A-11. See also pp. 2-23 to 2-25.

How a leader is perceived by others based on the leader's outward appearance, demeanor, actions and words

Military Bearing
- Possessing a commanding presence
- Projecting a professional image of authority

Physically Fit
- Having sound health, strength, and endurance that support one's emotional health and conceptual abilities under prolonged stress

Confident
- Projecting self-confidence and certainty in the unit's ability to succeed in whatever it does
- Demonstrating composure and an outward calm through steady control over one's emotions

Resilient
- Showing a tendency to recover quickly from setbacks, shock, injuries, adversity, and stress while maintaining a mission and organizational focus

C. A Leader with Intellectual Capacity

Ref: FM 6-22, app. A, fig. A-12. See also pp. 2-27 to 2-32.

The mental resources or tendencies that shape a leader's conceptual abilities and impact of effectiveness

Agility
- Flexibility of mind

- The tendency to anticipate or adapt to uncertain or changing situations; to think through second- and third-order effects when current decisions or actions are not producing the desired effects

- The ability to break out of mental "sets" or habitual though patterns; to improvise when faced with conceptual impasses

- The ability to quickly apply multiple perspectives and approaches to assessment, conceptualization, and evaluation

Judgment
- The capacity to assess situations or circumstances shrewdly and to draw sound conclusions

- The tendency to form sound opinions and make sensible decisions and reliable guesses

- The ability to make sound decisions when all facts are not available

Innovative
- The tendency to introduce new ideas when the opportunity exists or in the face of challenging circumstances

- Creativity in the production of ideas and objects that are both novel or original and worthwhile or appropriate

Interpersonal Tact
- The capacity to understand interactions with others

- Being aware of how others see you and sensing how to interact with them effectively

- Consciousness of character and motives of others and how that affects interacting with them

Domain Knowledge
- Possessing facts, beliefs, and logical assumptions in relevant areas

- Technical knowledge—specialized information associated with a particular function or system

- Tactical knowledge – understanding military tactics related to securing a designated objective through military means

- Joint knowledge – understanding joint organizations, their procedures, and their roles in national defense

- Cultural and geopolitical knowledge – understanding cultural, geographic, and political differences and sensitivities

I. Leader Core Competencies
Ref: FM 6-22 Army Leadership, app. A. See also p. 1-24.

The core leader competencies stem directly from the Army definition of leadership: Leadership is influencing people by providing purpose, motivation, and direction while operating to accomplish the mission and improve the organization. The core leader competencies emphasize the roles, functions, and activities of what leaders do.

The definition contains three basic goals: to lead others, to develop the organization and its individual members, and to accomplish the mission. These goals are extensions of the Army's strategic goal of remaining relevant and ready through effective leadership. The leadership requirements model outlines the attributes and competencies Army leaders develop to meet these goals.

A. Leads

Leading is all about influencing others. Leaders and commanders set goals and establish a vision, and then must motivate or influence others to pursue the goals. Leaders influence others in one of two ways. Either the leader and followers communicate directly, or the leader provides an example through everyday actions. The key to effective communication is to come to a common or shared understanding. Leading by example is a powerful way to influence others and is the reason leadership starts with a foundation of the Army Values and the Warrior Ethos. Serving as a role model requires a leader to display character, confidence, and competence to inspire others to succeed. Influencing outside the normal chain of command is a new way to view leadership responsibilities. Leaders have many occasions in joint, interagency, intergovernmental, and multinational situations to lead through diplomacy, negotiation, conflict resolution, and consensus building. To support these functions, leaders need to build trust inside and outside the traditional lines of authority and need to understand their sphere, means, and limits of influence.

Note: See also pp. 3-3 to 3-16.

B. Develops

Developing the organization, the second category, involves three competencies: creating a positive environment in which the organization can flourish, preparing oneself, and developing other leaders. The environment is shaped by leaders taking actions to foster working together, encouraging initiative and personal acknowledgment of responsibility, setting and maintaining realistic expectations, and demonstrating care for people—the number one resource of leaders. Preparing self involves getting set for mission accomplishment, expanding and maintaining knowledge in such dynamic topic areas as cultural and geopolitical affairs, and being self-aware. Developing others is a directed responsibility of commanders. Leaders develop others through coaching, counseling, and mentoring—each with a different set of implied processes. Leaders also build teams and organizations through direct interaction, resource management, and providing for future capabilities.

Note: See also pp. 3-17 to 3-32.

C. Achieves

Achieving is the third competency goal. Ultimately, leaders exist to accomplish those endeavors that the Army has prescribed for them. Getting results, accomplishing the mission, and fulfilling goals and objectives are all ways to say that leaders exist at the discretion of the organization to achieve something of value. Leaders get results through the influence they provide in direction and priorities. They develop and execute plans and must consistently accomplish goals to a high ethical standard.

Note: See pp. 3-33 to 3-40.

Chap 2

I. Leader Character

Ref: FM 6-22 Army Leadership, part 2, chap 4. See also p. 2-12 (A).

Character, a person's moral and ethical qualities, helps determine what is right and gives a leader motivation to do what is appropriate, regardless of the circumstances or the consequences. An informed ethical conscience consistent with the Army Values strengthens leaders to make the right choices when faced with tough issues. Since Army leaders seek to do what is right and inspire others to do the same, they must embody these values.

Character is essential to successful leadership. It determines who people are and how they act. It helps determine right from wrong and choose what is right.

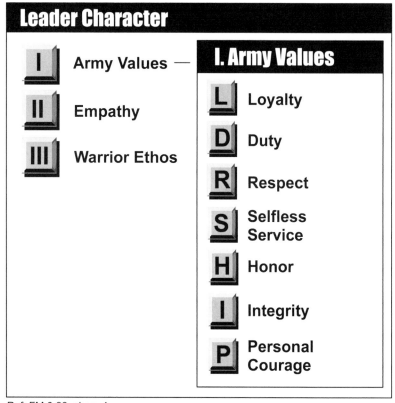

Ref: FM 6-22, chap. 4.

The Army Leader

I. Army Values

Ref: FM 6-22 Army Leadership, pp. 4-2 to 4-9.

Soldiers and Army civilians enter the Army with personal values developed in childhood and nurtured over many years of personal experience. By taking an oath to serve the Nation and the institution, one also agrees to live and act by a new set of values—Army Values. The Army Values consist of the principles, standards, and qualities considered essential for successful Army leaders. They are fundamental to helping Soldiers and Army civilians make the right decision in any situation.

The Army recognizes seven values that must be developed in all Army individuals. It is not coincidence that when reading the first letters of the Army Values in sequence they form the acronym "LDRSHIP":

I. Army Values

L   **Loyalty**

D   **Duty**

R   **Respect**

S   **Selfless Service**

H   **Honor**

I   **Integrity**

P   **Personal Courage**

Ref: FM 6-22, pp. 4-2 to 4-9.

The Army Values firmly bind all Army members into a fellowship dedicated to serve the Nation and the Army. They apply to everyone, in every situation, anywhere in the Army. The trust Soldiers and civilians have for each other and the trust of the American people, all depend on how well a Soldier embodies the Army Values..

L - Loyalty

Bear true faith and allegiance to the U.S. Constitution, the Army, your unit, and other Soldiers. All Soldiers and government civilians swear a sacred oath to support and defend the Constitution of the United States. The Constitution established the legal basis for the existence of our Army. Article I, Section 8, outlines congressional responsibilities regarding America's armed forces. As a logical consequence, leaders as members of the armed forces or government civilians have an obligation to be faithful to the Army and its people.

D - Duty

Fulfill your obligations. Duty extends beyond everything required by law, regulation, and orders. Professionals work not just to meet the minimum standard, but consistently strive to do their very best. Army leaders commit to excellence in all aspects of their professional responsibility.

R - Respect

Treat people as they should be treated. Respect for the individual is the basis for the rule of law—the very essence of what the Nation stands for. In the Army, respect means treating others as they should be treated. This value reiterates that people are the most precious resource and that one is bound to treat others with dignity and respect.

S - Selfless Service

Put the welfare of the Nation, the Army and subordinates before your own. The military is often referred to as "the Service." Members of the Army serve the United States of America. Selfless service means doing what is right for the Nation, the Army, the organization, and subordinates. While the needs of the Army and the Nation should come first, it does not imply family or self-neglect. To the contrary, such neglect weakens a leader and can cause the Army more harm than good.

H - Honor

Live up to all the Army Values. Honor provides the moral compass for character and personal conduct for all members of the Army. Honor belongs to those living by words and actions consistent with high ideals. The expression "honorable person" refers to the character traits an individual possesses that the community recognizes and respects.

I - Integrity

Do what's right -- legally and morally. Leaders of integrity consistently act according to clear principles, not just what works now. The Army relies on leaders of integrity who possess high moral standards and who are honest in word and deed. Leaders are honest to others by not presenting themselves or their actions as anything other than what they are, remaining committed to the truth.

P - Personal Courage

Face fear, danger, or adversity (physical or moral). Physical courage requires overcoming fears of bodily harm and doing one's duty. It triggers bravery that allows a Soldier to take risks in combat in spite of the fear of wounds or even death. One lieutenant serving during World War II displayed such courage despite serving in a time when he and his fellow African-American Soldiers were not fully recognized for their actions.

II. Empathy

Army leaders show a propensity to share experiences with the members of their organization. When planning and deciding, try to envision the impact on Soldiers and other subordinates. The ability to see something from another person's point of view, to identify with and enter into another person's feelings and emotions, enables the Army leader to better care for civilians, Soldiers, and their families.

Competent and empathetic leaders take care of Soldiers by giving them the training, equipment, and all the support they need to keep them alive in combat and accomplish the mission. During wartime and difficult operations, empathetic Army leaders share the hardships with their people to gauge if their plans and decisions are realistic. Competent and empathetic leaders also recognize the need to provide Soldiers and civilians with reasonable comforts and rest periods to maintain good morale and mission effectiveness. When a unit or organization suffers injuries or death, empathetic Army leaders can help ease the trauma and suffering in the organization to restore full readiness as quickly as possible.

Modern Army leaders recognize that empathy also includes nourishing a close relationship between the Army and Army families. To build a strong and ready force, Army leaders at all levels promote self-sufficient and healthy families. Empathy for families includes allowing Soldiers recovery time from difficult missions, protecting leave periods, permitting critical appointments, as well as supporting events that allow information exchange and family teambuilding.

The requirement for leader empathy extends beyond civilians, Soldiers, and their families. Within the larger operational environment, leader empathy may be helpful when dealing with local populations and prisoners of war. Providing the local population within an area of operations with the necessities of life often turns an initially hostile disposition into one of cooperation.

IV. Character Development

People join the Army as Soldiers and Army civilians with their character, pre-shaped by their background, beliefs, education, and experience. An Army leader's job would be simpler if merely checking the team member's personal values against the Army Values and developing a simple plan to align them sufficed. Reality is much different. Becoming a person of character and a leader of character is a career-long process involving day-to-day experience, education, self-development, developmental counseling, coaching, and mentoring. While individuals are responsible for their own character development, leaders are responsible for encouraging, supporting, and assessing the efforts of their people. Leaders of character can develop only through continual study, reflection, experience, and feedback. Leaders hold themselves and subordinates to the highest standards. The standards and values then spread throughout the team, unit, or organization and ultimately throughout the Army.

Doing the right thing is good. Doing the right thing for the right reason and with the right goal is better. People of character must possess the desire to act ethically in all situations. One of the Army leader's primary responsibilities is to maintain an ethical climate that supports development of such character. When an organization's ethical climate nurtures ethical behavior, people will, over time, think, feel, and act ethically. They will internalize the aspects of sound character.

III. Warrior Ethos

Ref: FM 6-22 Army Leadership, pp. 4-10 to 4-12.

The Warrior Ethos refers to the professional attitudes and beliefs that characterize the American Soldier. It echoes through the precepts of the Code of Conduct and reflects a Soldier's selfless commitment to the Nation, mission, unit, and fellow Soldiers. The Warrior Ethos was developed and sustained through discipline, commitment to the Army Values, and pride in the Army's heritage. Lived by Soldiers and supported by dedicated Army civilians, a strong Warrior Ethos is the foundation for the winning spirit that permeates the institution.

U.S Army Soldiers embrace the Warrior Ethos as defined in the Soldier's Creed.

The Warrior Ethos

I will always place the mission first.

I will never accept defeat.

I will never quit.

I will never leave a fallen comrade.

Ref: FM 6-22, fig. 4-1, p. 4-10.

The Warrior Ethos is more than persevering in war. It fuels the fire to fight through any demanding conditions—no matter the time or effort required. It is one thing to make a snap decision to risk one's life for a brief period. It is quite another to sustain the will to win when the situation looks hopeless and shows no indication of getting better, when being away from home and family is already a profound hardship. The Soldier who jumps on a grenade to save comrades is courageous without question—that action requires great mental and physical courage. Pursuing victory over extended periods with multiple deployments requires this deep moral courage, one that focuses on the mission.

The actions of all who have fought courageously in wars past exemplify the essence of the Army's Warrior Ethos. Developed through discipline, commitment to the Army Values, and knowledge of the Army's proud heritage, the Warrior Ethos makes clear that military service is much more than just another job. It is about the warrior's total commitment. It is the Soldiers' absolute faith in themselves and their comrades that makes the Army invariably persuasive in peace and invincible in war. The Warrior Ethos forges victory from the chaos of battle. It fortifies all leaders and their people to overcome fear, hunger, deprivation, and fatigue. The Army wins because it fights hard and with purpose. It fights hard because it trains hard.

The Warrior Ethos is a component of character. It shapes and guides what a Soldier does. It is linked tightly to the Army Values such as personal courage, loyalty to comrades, and dedication to duty.

A. Character and Beliefs

Beliefs matter because they help people understand their experiences. Those experiences provide a start point for what to do in everyday situations. Beliefs are convictions people hold as true. Values are deep-seated personal beliefs that shape a person's behavior. Values and beliefs are central to character.

Army leaders should recognize the role beliefs play in preparing Soldiers for battle. Soldiers often fight and win against tremendous odds when they are convinced of the beliefs for which they are fighting. Commitment to such beliefs as justice, liberty, and freedom can be essential ingredients in creating and sustaining the will to fight and prevail. Warrior Ethos is another special case of beliefs.

Beliefs derive from upbringing, culture, religious backgrounds, and traditions. As a result, different moral beliefs have, and will, continue to be shaped by diverse religious and philosophical traditions. Army leaders serve a Nation that protects the fundamental principle that people are free to choose their own beliefs. America's strength derives and benefits from that diversity. Effective leaders are careful not to require their people to violate their beliefs by ordering or encouraging illegal or unethical actions.

America's Constitution reflects fundamental national principles. One of these principles is the guarantee of freedom of religion. The Army places a high value on the rights of its Soldiers to observe tenets of their respective religious faiths while respecting individual differences in moral background and personal conviction. While religious beliefs and practices remain a decision of individual conscience, Army leaders are responsible for ensuring their Soldiers and civilians have the opportunity to practice their religion. Commanders, in accordance with regulatory guidance, normally approve requests for accommodation of religious practices unless they will have an adverse impact on unit readiness, individual readiness, unit cohesion, morale, discipline, safety, and/or health. At the same time, no leader may apply undue influence, coerce, or harass subordinates with reference to matters of religion. Chaplains are staff officers with specialized training and specific responsibilities for ensuring the free exercise of religion and are available to advise and assist Army leaders at every level.

A common theme expressed by American prisoners of war during the Korean and Vietnam wars was the importance of beliefs instilled by a common American culture. Those beliefs helped them to withstand torture and the hardships of captivity.

B. Character and Ethics

Adhering to the principles that the Army Values embody is essential to upholding high ethical standards of behavior. Unethical behavior quickly destroys organizational morale and cohesion—it undermines the trust and confidence essential to teamwork and mission accomplishment. Consistently doing the right thing forges strong character in individuals and expands to create a culture of trust throughout the organization.

Ethics are concerned with how a person should behave. Values represent the beliefs that a person has. The seven Army Values represent a set of common beliefs that leaders are expected to uphold and reinforce by their actions. The translation from desirable ethics to internal values to actual behavior involves choices.

Ethical conduct must reflect genuine values and beliefs. Soldiers and Army civilians adhere to the Army Values because they want to live ethically and profess the values because they know what is right. Adopting good values and making ethical choices are essential to produce leaders of character.

Ethical Reasoning

Ref: FM 22-100, pp. 4-8 to 4-9 (not included in FM 6-22). See also FM 6-22 Army Leadership, p. 4-15.

Ethical reasoning isn't a separate process you trot out only when you think you're facing an ethical question. It should be part of the thought process you use to make any decision. Your subordinates count on you to do more than make tactically sound decisions. They rely on you to make decisions that are ethically sound as well. You should always consider ethical factors and, when necessary, use Army values to gauge what's right.

1. Define the Problem
Defining the problem is the first step in making any decision. When you think a decision may have ethical aspects or effects, it's especially important to define it precisely. Know who said what—and what specifically was said, ordered, or demanded. Don't settle for secondhand information; get the details. Problems can be described in more than one way. This is the hardest step in solving any problem. It's especially difficult for decisions in the face of potential ethical conflicts. Too often some people come to rapid conclusions about the nature of a problem and end up applying solutions to what turn out to be only symptoms.

2. Know the Relevant Rules
This step is part of fact gathering, the second step in problem solving. Do your homework. Sometimes what looks like an ethical problem may stem from a misunderstanding of a regulation or policy, frustration, or overenthusiasm. Sometimes the person who gave an order or made a demand didn't check the regulation and a thorough reading may make the problem go away. Other times, a difficult situation results from trying to do something right in the wrong way. Also, some regulations leave room for interpretation; the problem then becomes a policy matter rather than an ethical one. If you do perceive an ethical problem, explain it to the person you think is causing it and try to come up with a better way to do the job.

3. Develop and Evaluate Courses of Action
Once you know the rules, lay out possible courses of action. As with the previous steps, you do this whenever you must make a decision. Next, consider these courses of action in view of Army values. Consider the consequences of your courses of action by asking yourself a few practical questions: Which course of action best upholds Army values? Do any of the courses of action compromise Army values? Does any course of action violate a principle, rule, or regulation identified in Step 2? Which course of action is in the best interest of the Army and of the nation? This part will feel like a juggling act; but with careful ethical reflection, you can reduce the chaos, determine the essentials, and choose the best course—even when that choice is the least bad of a set of undesirable options.

4. Choose the COA That Best Represents Army Values
The last step in solving any problem is making a decision and acting on it. Leaders are paid to make decisions. As an Army leader, you're expected—by your bosses and your people— to make decisions that solve problems without violating Army values.

As a values-based organization, the Army uses expressed values—Army values—to provide its fundamental ethical framework. Army values lay out the ethical standards expected of soldiers and DA civilians. Taken together, Army values and ethical decision making provide a moral touchstone and a workable process that enable you to make sound ethical decisions and take right actions confidently.

In combat, ethical choices are not always easy. The right thing may not only be unpopular, but dangerous as well. Complex and dangerous situations often reveal who is a leader of character and who is not.

Army leaders must consistently focus on shaping ethics-based organizational climates in which subordinates and organizations can achieve their full potential. To reach their goal, leaders can use tools such as the Ethical Climate Assessment Survey (GTA 22-06-001) to assess ethical aspects of their own character and actions, the workplace, and the external environment. Once they have done a climate assessment, leaders prepare and follow a plan of action. The plan of action focuses on solving ethical problems within the leader's span of influence, while the higher headquarters is informed of ethical problems that cannot be changed at the subordinate unit's level.

Ethical Orders

Making the right choice and acting on it when faced with an ethical question can be difficult. Sometimes it means standing firm and disagreeing with the boss on ethical grounds. These occasions test character. Situations in which a leader thinks an illegal order is issued can be the most difficult.

Under normal circumstances, a leader executes a superior leader's decision with energy and enthusiasm. The only exception would be illegal orders, which a leader has a duty to disobey. If a Soldier perceives that an order is illegal, that Soldier should be sure the details of the order and its original intent are fully understood. The Soldier should seek immediate clarification from the person who gave it before proceeding.

If the question is more complex, seek legal counsel. If it requires an immediate decision, as may happen in the heat of combat, make the best judgment possible based on the Army Values, personal experience, critical thinking, and previous study and reflection. There is a risk when a leader disobeys what may be an illegal order, and it may be the most difficult decision that Soldier ever makes. Nonetheless, that is what competent, confident, and ethical leaders should do.

While a leader may not be completely prepared for the complex situations, spending time to reflect on the Army Values, studying, and honing personal leadership competencies will help. Talk to superiors, particularly those who have done the same.

Living the Army Values and acting ethically is not just for generals and colonels. There are ethical decisions made every day in military units and in offices on Army installations across the world. They include decisions that can directly affect the lives of Soldiers in the field, innocent noncombatants, Army civilians, as well as American taxpayers. It is up to all Army leaders to make value-based, ethical choices for the good of the Army and the Nation. Army leaders should have the strength of character to make the right choices.

II. Leader Presence

Ref: FM 6-22 Army Leadership, part 2, chap 5. See also p. 2-12 (B).

The impression that a leader makes on others contributes to the success in leading them. How others perceive a leader depends on the leader's outward appearance, demeanor, actions, and words.

Leader Presence

Presence is a critical attribute that leaders need to understand. A leader's effectiveness is dramatically enhanced by understanding and developing the following areas:

 Military and Professional Bearing

 Health Fitness

 Physical Fitness

 Confidence

 Resilience

Ref: FM 6-22 Army Leadership, pp. 5-1 to 5-3.

Followers need a way to size up their leaders, dependent on leaders being where Soldiers and civilians are. Organizational and strategic level leaders who are willing to go everywhere, including where the conditions are the most severe, illustrate through their presence that they care. There is no greater inspiration than leaders who routinely share in team hardships and dangers. Moving to where duties are performed allows the leader to have firsthand knowledge of the real conditions Soldiers and civilians face. Soldiers and civilians who see or hear from the boss appreciate knowing that their unit has an important part to play.

Presence is not just a matter of the leader showing up; it involves the image that the leader projects. Presence is conveyed through actions, words, and the manner in which leaders carry themselves. A reputation is conveyed by the respect that others show, how they refer to the leader, and respond to the leader's guidance.

Leader Presence

Ref: FM 6-22 Army Leadership, pp. 5-1 to 5-3.

Presence is not just a matter of the leader showing up; it involves the image that the leader projects. Presence is conveyed through actions, words, and the manner in which leaders carry themselves. A reputation is conveyed by the respect that others show, how they refer to the leader, and respond to the leader's guidance.

Physical characteristics—military and professional bearing, health and physical fitness—can and must be continuously developed in order to establish presence. Army leaders represent the institution and government and should always maintain an appropriate level of physical fitness and professional bearing.

A. Military and Professional Bearing

Pride in self starts with pride in appearance. Army leaders are expected to look and act like professionals. They must know how to wear the appropriate uniform or civilian attire and do so with pride. Soldiers seen in public with their jackets unbuttoned and ties undone do not send a message of pride and professionalism. Instead, they let down their unit and fellow Soldiers in the eyes of the American people. Meeting prescribed height and weight standards is another integral part of the professional role. How leaders carry themselves when displaying military courtesy and appearance sends a clear signal: I am proud of my uniform, my unit, and my country.

Skillful use of professional bearing—fitness, courtesy, and proper military appearance—can also aid in overcoming difficult situations. A professional presents a decent appearance because it commands respect. Professionals must be competent as well. They look good because they are good.

B. Health Fitness

Disease remains a potent enemy on modern battlefields. Staying healthy and physically fit is important to protect Soldiers from disease and strengthen them to deal with the psychological impact of combat. A Soldier is similar to a complex combat system. Just as a tank requires good maintenance and fuel at regular intervals, a Soldier needs exercise, sufficient sleep, and adequate food and water for peak performance.

Health fitness is everything done to maintain good health. It includes undergoing routine physical exams; practicing good dental hygiene, personal grooming, and cleanliness; keeping immunizations current; as well as considering mental stresses. Healthy and hygiene-conscious Soldiers perform better in extreme operational environments. One sick crewmember on a well-trained flight crew represents a weak link in the chain and makes the entire aircraft more vulnerable and less lethal. Health fitness also includes avoiding things that can degrade personal health, such as substance abuse, obesity, and smoking.

C. Physical Fitness

Unit readiness begins with physically fit Soldiers and leaders, for combat drains physically, mentally, and emotionally. Physical fitness, while crucial for success in battle, is important for all members of the Army team, not just Soldiers. Physically fit people feel more competent and confident, handle stress better, work longer and harder, and recover faster. These attributes provide valuable payoffs in any environment.

The physical demands of leadership, prolonged deployments, and continuous operations can erode more than physical attributes. Physical fitness and adequate rest support cognitive functioning and emotional stability, both essential for sound leadership. Soldiers must be prepared for deprivation; it is difficult to maintain high levels of fitness during fast-paced, demanding operations. If not physically fit before deployment, the effects of additional stress compromise mental and emotional fitness as well. Combat operations in difficult terrain, extreme climates, and high altitude require extensive physical pre-conditioning; once in the area of operations there must be continued efforts to sustain physical readiness.

Preparedness for operational missions must be a primary focus of the unit's physical fitness program. Fitness programs that merely emphasize top scores on the Army physical fitness test do not prepare Soldiers for the strenuous demands of actual combat. The forward-looking leader develops a balanced physical fitness program that enables Soldiers to execute the unit's mission-essential task list. (FM 7-0 discusses the integration of Soldier, leader, and collective training based on the mission-essential task list).

Ultimately, the physical fitness requirements for Army leaders have significant impact on their personal performance and health. Since leaders' decisions affect their organizations' combat effectiveness, health, and safety, it is an ethical as well as a practical imperative for leaders to remain healthy and fit.

D. Confidence

Confidence is the faith that leaders place in their abilities to act properly in any situation, even under stress and with little information. Leaders who know their own capabilities and believe in themselves are confident. Self-confidence grows from professional competence. Too much confidence can be as detrimental as too little confidence. Both extremes impede learning and adaptability. Bluster—loudmouthed bragging or self-promotion—is not confidence. Truly confident leaders do not need to advertise their gift because their actions prove their abilities.

Confidence is important for leaders and teams. The confidence of a good leader is contagious and quickly permeates the entire organization, especially in dire situations. In combat, confident leaders help Soldiers control doubt while reducing team anxiety. Combined with strong will and self-discipline, confidence spurs leaders to do what must be done in circumstances where it would be easier to do nothing.

E. Resilience

Resilient leaders can recover quickly from setbacks, shock, injuries, adversity, and stress while maintaining their mission and organizational focus. Their resilience rests on will, the inner drive that compels them to keep going, even when exhausted, hungry, afraid, cold, and wet. Resilience helps leaders and their organizations to carry difficult missions to their conclusion.

Resilience and the will to succeed are not sufficient to carry the day during adversity. Competence and knowledge guide the energies of a strong will to pursue courses of action that lead to success and victory in battle. The leader's premier task is to instill resilience and a winning spirit in subordinates. That begins with tough and realistic training.

Resilience is essential when pursuing mission accomplishment. No matter what the working conditions are, a strong personal attitude helps prevail over any adverse external conditions. All members of the Army—active, reserve, or civilian—will experience situations when it would seem easier to quit rather than finish the task. During those times, everyone needs an inner source of energy to press on to mission completion. When things go badly, a leader must draw on inner reserves to persevere.

Team Building during the Formation Stage

Ref: FM 22-100, app. A, p. 58 - 59 (not included in FM 6-22). See also p. 3-30 for Stages of Team Building from FM 6-22.

Kind of Leader

1. As a leader, are you sensitive to the personal problems of your soldiers? Do the soldiers feel that you care?

2. Do you know your soldiers? The way the soldier reacts and thinks? Personal data? Strengths and weaknesses? Reliability?

3. Are you fair in the assignment and treatment of all soldiers regardless of race, sex, or religious belief?

4. Are your soldiers confident that you know what you are doing?

5. Do you know enough about the job of your subordinates to teach and guide them as they develop?

Reception

1. Does your soldier reception address the needs of both single and married soldiers?

2. Are sponsors carefully selected to ensure they are good role models?

3. Are your soldiers given adequate time to deal with administrative and personal details?

4. Are you taking action to make the family feel welcomed into the unit?

Orientation

Values and Standards

1. Do you know and live by Army ethical values?

2. Do you know how to communicate appropriate Army and unit values to the soldier?

3. Do you communicate standards of conduct clearly to the soldier during orientation?

4. Do you recognize and reward soldiers for exemplifying unit values and standards?

5. Does your team accept the values and standards of the unit?

6. Do your team members require acceptance of the unit values and standards?

Mission and Goals

1. Do you communicate unit mission/ goals during the orientation period?

2. Do you spend personal time with each of your soldiers to tell him what is expected and to find out what he expects?

Standing Operating Procedure

1. Does your unit have a simple, clear SOP that soldiers are required to read?

2. Do you communicate the way the squad, section, and platoon do business?

Unit Heritage

1. Do you utilize unit patches, colors, crests, and mottoes to develop pride and spirit?

2. Do you teach the unique history of the unit as a source of pride and identification?

3. Are your soldiers required to learn important facts about unit heritage? Are questions about these subjects included on soldier of the month boards, promotion boards, guard mounts, and other prominent places?

4. Do your soldiers talk with pride about successful accomplishments of the recent past?

Team Formation in Combat

1. Do you take care in combat to reassure the new soldier and welcome him to the unit?

2. Is your team prepared to orient the soldier in combat procedures/guidance to survive?

3. Does your unit have a working buddy system to assist the new soldier as he adjusts to the uncertainties of combat?

III. Leader Intelligence

Ref: FM 6-22 Army Leadership, part 2, chap 6. See also p. 2-12.

An Army leader's intelligence draws on the mental tendencies and resources that shape conceptual abilities, which are applied to one's duties and responsibilities. Conceptual abilities enable sound judgment before implementing concepts and plans. They help one think creatively and reason analytically, critically, ethically, and with cultural sensitivity to consider unintended as well as intended consequences. Like a chess player trying to anticipate an opponent's moves three or four turns in advance (action-reaction-counteraction), leaders must think through what they expect to occur because of a decision. Some decisions may set off a chain of events. Therefore, leaders must attempt to anticipate the second- and third-order effects of their actions. Even lower-level leaders' actions may have effects well beyond what they expect.

Leader Intelligence

The conceptual components affecting the Army leader's intelligence include:

 Agility

 Judgment

 Innovation

 Interpersonal Tact

 Domain Knowledge

Ref: FM 6-22 Army Leadership, chap. 6.

I. Mental Agility

Mental agility is a flexibility of mind, a tendency to anticipate or adapt to uncertain or changing situations. Agility assists thinking through second- and third-order effects when current decisions or actions are not producing the desired effects. It helps break from habitual thought patterns, to improvise when faced with conceptual impasses, and quickly apply multiple perspectives to consider new approaches or solutions.

Mental agility is important in military leadership because great militaries adapt to fight the enemy, not the plan. Agile leaders stay ahead of changing environments and incomplete planning to preempt problems. In the operational sense, agility also shows in the ability to create ad hoc and tactically creative units that adapt to changing situations. They can alter their behavior to ease transitioning from full-scale maneuver war to stability operations in urban areas.

The basis for mental agility is the ability to reason critically while keeping an open mind to multiple possibilities until reaching the most sensible solution. Critical thinking is a thought process that aims to find truth in situations where direct observation is insufficient, impossible, or impractical. It allows thinking through and solving problems and is central to decision making. Critical thinking is the key to understanding changing situations, finding causes, arriving at justifiable conclusions, making good judgments, and learning from experience.

Critical thinking implies examining a problem in depth, from multiple points of view, and not settling for the first answer that comes to mind. Army leaders need this ability because many of the choices they face require more than one solution. The first and most important step in finding an appropriate solution is to isolate the main problem. Sometimes determining the real problem presents a huge hurdle; at other times, one has to sort through distracting multiple problems to get to the real issue.

Modern Army training and education focuses on improving leader agility and small unit initiative. Combat deployments in Grenada, Panama, Kosovo, Somalia, Afghanistan, and Iraq have emphasized the demands on mental agility and tactical initiative down to the level of the individual Soldier. Contemporary operational environments call for more agile junior officers and noncommissioned officers, able to lead effectively small and versatile units across the spectrum of conflicts.

II. Sound Judgment

Judgment goes hand in hand with agility. Judgment requires having a capacity to assess situations or circumstances shrewdly and to draw feasible conclusions. Good judgment enables the leader to form sound opinions and to make sensible decisions and reliable guesses. Good judgment on a consistent basis is important for successful Army leaders and much of it comes from experience. Leaders acquire experience through trial and error and by watching the experiences of others. Learning from others can occur through mentoring and coaching by superiors, peers, and even some subordinates (see Part Three for more information). Another method of expanding experience is self-development by reading biographies and autobiographies of notable men and women to learn from their successes and failures. The histories of successful people offer ageless insights, wisdom, and methods that might be adaptable to the current environment or situation.

Often, leaders must juggle facts, questionable data, and gut-level feelings to arrive at a quality decision. Good judgment helps to make the best decision for the situation at hand. It is a key attribute of the art of command and the transformation of knowledge into understanding and quality execution. FM 6-0 discusses how leaders convert data and information into knowledge and understanding.

Good judgment contributes to an ability to determine possible courses of action and decide what action to take. Before choosing the course of action, consider the consequences and think methodically. Some sources that aid judgment are senior leaders' intents, the desired outcome, rules, laws, regulations, experience, and values. Good judgment includes the ability to size up subordinates, peers, and the enemy for strengths, weaknesses, and to create appropriate solutions and action. Like agility, it is a critical part of problem solving and decision making.

III. Innovation

Innovation describes the Army leader's ability to introduce something new for the first time when needed or an opportunity exists. Being innovative includes creativity in the production of ideas that are original and worthwhile.

Sometimes a new problem presents itself or an old problem requires a new solution. Army leaders should seize such opportunities to think creatively and to innovate. The key concept for creative thinking is developing new ideas and ways to challenge subordinates with new approaches and ideas. It also involves devising new ways for their Soldiers and civilians to accomplish tasks and missions. Creative thinking includes using adaptive approaches (drawing from previous similar circumstances) or innovative approaches (coming up with a completely new idea).

All leaders can and must think creatively to adapt to new environments. A unit deployed for stability operations may find itself isolated on a small secure compound with limited athletic facilities and without much room to run. This situation would require its leaders to devise reliable ways to maintain their Soldiers' physical fitness. Innovative solutions might include weight training, games, stationary runs, aerobics, treadmills, and other fitness drills.

Innovative leaders prevent complacency by finding new ways to challenge subordinates with forward-looking approaches and ideas. To be innovators, leaders learn to rely on intuition, experience, knowledge, and input from subordinates. Innovative leaders reinforce team building by making everybody responsible for, and stakeholders in, the innovation process.

IV. Interpersonal Tact

Effectively interacting with others depends on knowing what others perceive. It also relies on accepting the character, reactions, and motives of oneself and others. Interpersonal tact combines these skills, along with recognizing diversity and displaying self-control, balance, and stability in all situations.

A. Recognizing Diversity

Soldiers, civilians, and contractors originate from vastly different backgrounds and are shaped by schooling, race, gender, religion, as well as a host of other influences. Personal perspectives can even vary within societal groups. People should avoid snap conclusions based on stereotypes. It is better to understand individuals by acknowledging their differences, qualifications, contributions, and potential.

Joining the Army as Soldiers and civilians, subordinates agreed to accept the Army's culture. This initial bond holds them together. Army leaders further strengthen the team effort by creating an environment where subordinates know they are valued for their talents, contributions, and differences. A leader's job is not to make everyone the same; it is to take advantage of the different capabilities and talents brought to the team. The biggest challenge is to put each member in the right place to build the best possible team.

Army leaders should keep an open mind about cultural diversity. It is important, because it is unknown how the talents of certain individuals or groups will contribute to mission accomplishment. During World War II, U.S. Marines from the Navajo nation formed a group of radio communications specialists called the Navajo Code Talkers. The code talkers used their native language—a unique talent—to handle command radio traffic. Using the Navajo code significantly contributed to successful ground operations because the best Japanese code breakers could not decipher their messages.

V. Domain Knowledge

Ref: FM 6-22 Army Leadership, pp. 6-5 to 6-9.

Domain knowledge requires possessing facts, beliefs, and logical assumptions in many areas. Tactical knowledge is an understanding of military tactics related to securing a designated objective through military means. Technical knowledge consists of the specialized information associated with a particular function or system. Joint knowledge is an understanding of joint organizations, their procedures, and their roles in national defense. Cultural and geopolitical knowledge is awareness of cultural, geographic, and political differences and sensitivities.

A. Tactical Knowledge

Army leaders know doctrine, tactics, techniques, and procedures. Their tactical knowledge allows them to effectively employ individuals, teams, and larger organizations together with the activities of systems (combat multipliers) to fight and win engagements and battles or to achieve other objectives. While direct leaders usually fight current battles, organizational leaders focus deeper in time, space, and events. This includes a geopolitical dimension.

Tactics is the art and science of employing available means to win battles and engagements. The science of tactics encompasses capabilities, techniques, and procedures that can be codified. The art includes the creative and flexible array of means to accomplish assigned missions, decision making when facing an intelligent enemy, and the effects of combat on Soldiers.

1. Fieldcraft

Fieldcraft describes the skills Soldiers require to sustain themselves in the field. Proficiency in fieldcraft reduces the likelihood of casualties. Understanding and excelling at fieldcraft sets conditions for mission success. Likewise, the requirement that Army leaders make sure their Soldiers take care of themselves and provide them with the means to do so also sets conditions for success.

STP 21-1-SMCT, Soldier's Manual of Common Tasks, lists the individual skills all Soldiers must know to operate effectively in the field. Those skills include everything from staying healthy to digging fighting positions. Some military occupational specialties require proficiency in additional fieldcraft skills. They are listed in Soldiers' manuals for these specialties.

2. Tactical Proficiency

While practicing tactical abilities is generally challenging, competent leaders try to replicate actual operational conditions during battle-focused training (see FM 7-0). Unfortunately, Army leaders cannot always take their entire unit to the field for full-scale maneuvers. They must therefore learn to achieve maximum readiness by training parts of a scenario or a unit on the ground, while exercising larger echelons with simulations. Despite distracters and limitations, readiness-focused leaders train for war as realistically as possible. FM 7-0 and FM 7-1 discuss training principles and techniques.

B. Technical Knowledge

1. Knowing Equipment

Technical knowledge relates to equipment, weapons, and systems—everything from a gun sight to the computer that tracks personnel actions. Since direct leaders are closer to their equipment than organizational and strategic leaders, they have a greater need to know how it works and how to use it. Direct leaders are usually the experts called upon to solve problems with equipment.

2. Operating Equipment

Military and civilian leaders know how to operate their organizations' equipment and ensure their people do as well. They often set an example with a hands-on approach. When new equipment arrives, direct leaders learn how to use it and train their subordinates to do the same. Once individuals are trained, teams, and in turn, whole units train together. Army leaders know understanding equipment strengths and weaknesses are critical. Adapting to these factors is necessary to achieve success in combat.

3. Employing Equipment

Direct, organizational, and strategic level leaders need to know what functional value the equipment has for their operations and how to employ the equipment in their units and organizations. At higher levels, the requirement for technical knowledge shifts from understanding how to operate single items of equipment to how to employ entire systems. Higher-level leaders have a responsibility to keep alert to future capabilities and the impact that fielding will have on their organizations. Some organizational and strategic level leaders have general oversight responsibility for the development of new systems; they should have knowledge of the major features and required capabilities. Their interests are in knowing the technical aspects of how systems affect doctrine, organizational design, training, related materiel, personnel, and facilities. They must ensure that organizations are provided with all necessary resources to properly field, train, maintain, operate, inventory, and turn-in equipment.

C. Joint Knowledge

Joint warfare is team warfare. The 1986 Goldwater-Nichols legislation mandated a higher level of cooperation among America's military Services, based on experiences drawn from previous deployments. Since then, Army leaders from the most junior field leader to the generals serving at the strategic level have embraced the importance of joint warfare. Leaders acquire joint knowledge through formal training in the Joint Professional Military Education program and assignments in joint organizations and staffs.

D. Cultural and Geopolitical Knowledge

Culture consists of shared beliefs, values, and assumptions about what is important. Army leaders are mindful of cultural factors in three contexts:

- Sensitive to the different backgrounds of team members to best leverage their talents
- Aware of the culture of the country in which the organization is operating
- Consider and evaluate the possible implications of partners' customs, traditions, doctrinal principles, and operational methods when working with forces of another nation

Understanding the culture of adversaries and of the country in which the organization is operating is just as important as understanding the culture of a Soldier's own country and organization. Contemporary operational environments, which place smaller units into more culturally complex situations with continuous media coverage, require even greater cultural and geopolitical awareness from every Army leader. Consequently, be aware of current events—particularly those in areas where America has national interests. Before deploying, ensure that Soldiers and the organization are properly prepared to deal with the population of particular areas—either as partners, neutrals, or adversaries. The more that is known about them, including their language, the better off the organization will be.

B. Self-Control

Good leaders control their emotions. Instead of hysterics or showing no emotion at all, leaders should display the right amount of sensitivity and passion to tap into sub-ordinates' emotions. Maintaining self-control inspires calm confidence in the team. Self-control encourages feedback from subordinates that can expand understanding of what is really happening. Self-control in combat is especially important for Army leaders. Leaders who lose their self-control cannot expect those who follow them to maintain theirs.

C. Emotional Factors

An Army leader's self-control, balance, and stability greatly influence his ability to interact with others. People are human beings with hopes, fears, concerns, and dreams. Understanding that motivation and endurance are sparked by emotional energy is a powerful leadership tool. Giving constructive feedback will help mobilize the team's emotional energies to accomplish difficult missions during tough times.

Self-control, balance, and stability also assist making the right ethical choices.

1. Self-Control

An ethical leader successfully applies ethical principles to decision making and retains self-control. Leaders cannot be at the mercy of emotion. It is critical for leaders to remain calm under pressure and expend energy on things they can positively influence and not worry about things they cannot affect.

Emotionally mature and competent leaders are also aware of their own strengths and weaknesses. They spend their energy on self-improvement, while immature leaders usually waste their energy denying that there is anything wrong or analyzing the shortcomings of others. Mature, less defensive leaders benefit from feedback in ways that immature people cannot.

2. Balance

Emotionally balanced leaders are able to display the right emotion for a given situation and can read others' emotional state. They draw on their experience and provide their subordinates the proper perspective on unfolding events. They have a range of attitudes, from relaxed to intense, with which to approach diverse situations. They know how to choose the one appropriate for the circumstances. Balanced leaders know how to convey that things are urgent without throwing the entire organization into chaos. They are able to encourage their people to continue the mission, even in the toughest of moments.

3. Stability

Effective leaders are steady, levelheaded when under pressure and fatigued, and calm in the face of danger. These characteristics stabilize their subordinates who are always looking to their leader's example:

- Model the emotions for subordinates to display
- Do not give in to the temptation to do what personally feels good
- If under great stress, it might feel better to vent—but will that help the organization?
- If subordinates are to be calm and rational under pressure, leaders must display the same stability

Leading, Developing, Achieving

Ref: FM 6-22 Army Leadership, part 3, chap 7 through chap 10 (C).

Competency-Based Leadership for Direct Through Strategic Levels

Leaders serve to provide purpose, direction and motivation. Army leaders work hard to lead people, to develop themselves, their subordinates, and organizations, and to achieve mission accomplishment across the spectrum of conflicts.

Competency-Based Leadership

I Leading

II Developing

III Achieving

Ref: FM 6-22, chap. 7 to chap. 10.

For leadership to be effective in the operational environment, it is important to consider the impact of its dimensions on the members of the organization. Weather and terrain, combined with the day-night cycle, form the basis for all operations. This basic environment is influenced by technology, affecting the application of firepower, maneuver, protection and leadership. A combination of the psychological impact of mortal danger, weapons effects, difficult terrain, and the presence of enemy forces can create chaos and confusion, turning simple tactical and operational plans into the most challenging endeavors.

Continuously building and refining values and attributes, as well as acquiring professional knowledge, is only part of becoming a competent leader. Leadership succeeds when the leader effectively acts and applies the core leader competencies and their subsets. As one moves from direct leadership positions to the organizational and strategic leader levels, those competencies take on different nuances and complexities.

As a direct leader, an example of leading would be providing mission intent. At the organizational level the leader might provide a vision and empower others, while at the strategic level the same leader would lead change and shape an entire insitituion for future success.

Team Building during the Sustainment Stage

Ref: FM 22-100, app. A, p. 62 - 63 (not included in FM 6-22). See also p. 3-30 for Stages of Team Building from FM 6-22.

Leader Actions

1. Are you aware of the effects of change on teamwork? Do you actively work to minimize its impact?

2. Do you periodically check on the progress of each soldier to ensure that personal goals and team goals are compatible?

3. Do your team members use team expectations and standards as a measurement by which they accept new soldiers into the team?

4. Do your team members share a commitment to the team mission?

5. Do you reassess team goals often to ensure timely adjustment to the changing situation of combat?

6. Do you listen for suggestions, concerns, or complaints of soldiers that can assist in maintaining a high level of team work?

7. Does your training program challenge your soldiers and minimize boredom?

8. Is maintenance a day-to-day routine with your soldiers? Do they see its value?

9. Are you continually sensitive to soldiers' personal concerns?

Unit Activities

1. Does your unit plan and utilize activities that build unit spirit and identity?

2. Do you use military ceremonies to build and reinforce soldier spirit, identification and pride?

3. Do your sports teams reinforce the identity and teamwork of the unit? Do your soldiers view their unit teams as "our team"?

4. Does your unit sponsor social events for your soldiers and their families that build identification of the soldier and his family with the unit?

5. Do you encourage the spiritual development of your soldiers and their families?

Sustainment in Combat

1. Do your soldiers observe and learn from actual experiences in combat?

2. Does your unit have a realistic plan for sleep discipline in continuous combat operations?

3. Are your soldiers prepared to react to enemy movement in conjunction with other team members?

4. Do your soldiers spend time talking about immediately prior combat action in order to adjust to and overcome enemy actions?

5. Do team members know what to do in case of a casualty?

6. Are you prepared for team member reactions to injury or death of a team member?

7. Are you prepared to counteract boredom during lulls in combat activity?

8. Are your soldiers aware of stress-reduction techniques?

9. Do you take decisive steps to deal with rumors?

10. Do you discuss aspects of combat, such as fear and panic, with your soldiers?

11. Are your soldiers prepared to deal with fear as a normal reaction to the dangers of combat?

12. Are you alert to critical incidents that might trigger panic among your soldiers?

13. Do you take decisive action to prevent/cope with despair and panic among soldiers?

14. Are you alert to disruptions in your unit that might cause teamwork to suffer?

I. Leading

Ref: FM 6-22 Army Leadership, part 3, chap 7. See also pp. 2-2 to 2-5.

Army leaders apply character, presence, intellect, and abilities to the core leader competencies while guiding others toward a common goal and mission accomplishment. Direct leaders influence others person-to-person, such as a team leader who instructs, recognizes achievement, and encourages hard work. Organizational and strategic leaders influence those in their sphere of influence, including immediate subordinates and staffs, but often guide their organizations using indirect means of influence. At the direct level, a platoon leader knows what a battalion commander wants done, not because the lieutenant was briefed personally, but because the lieutenant understands the commander's intent two levels up. The intent creates a critical link between the organizational and direct leadership levels. At all levels, leaders take advantage of formal and informal processes to extend influence beyond the traditional chain of command.

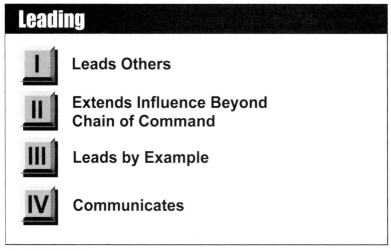

Leading

I   **Leads Others**

II   **Extends Influence Beyond Chain of Command**

III   **Leads by Example**

IV   **Communicates**

Ref: FM 6-22, chap. 7.

The leading category of the core leader competencies includes four competencies. Two competencies focus on who is being led and with what degree of authority and influence: leads others and extends influence beyond the chain of command. The other leading competencies address two ways by which leaders to convey influence: leads by example and communicates.

I. Leads Others

All of the Army's core leader competencies, especially leading others, involve influence. Army leaders can draw on a variety of techniques to influence others. These range from obtaining compliance to building a commitment to achieve. Compliance is the act of conforming to a specific requirement or demand. Commitment is willing dedication or allegiance to a cause or organization. Resistance is the opposite of compliance and commitment. There are many techniques for influencing others to comply or commit, and leaders can use one or more of them to fit to the specifics of any situation.

A. Compliance And Commitment

Lead, Develop, Achieve

Compliance-focused influence is based primarily on the leader's authority. Giving a direct order to a follower is one approach to obtain compliance during a task. Compliance is appropriate for short-term, immediate requirements and for situations where little risk can be tolerated. Compliance techniques are also appropriate for leaders to use with others who are relatively unfamiliar with their tasks or unwilling or unable to commit fully to the request. If something needs to be done with little time for delay, and there is not a great need for a subordinate to understand why the request is made, then compliance is an acceptable approach. Compliance-focused influence is not particularly effective when a leader's greatest aim is to create initiative and high esteem within the team.

Commitment-focused influence generally produces longer lasting and broader effects. Whereas compliance only changes a follower's behavior, commitment reaches deeper—changing attitudes and beliefs, as well as behavior. For example, when a leader builds responsibility among followers, they will likely demonstrate more initiative, personal involvement, and creativity. Commitment grows from an individual's desire to gain a sense of control and develop self-worth by contributing to the organization. Depending on the objective of the influence, leaders can strengthen commitment by reinforcing followers' identification with the Nation (loyalty), the Army (professionalism), the unit or organization (selfless service), the leadership in a unit (respect), and to the job (duty).

1. Influence Techniques

Leaders use several specific techniques for influence that fall along a continuum between compliance and commitment. The ten techniques described below seek different degrees of compliance or commitment ranging from pressure at the compliance end to relations building at the commitment end.

Note: See pp. 3-6 to 3-7 for an overview of ten techniques for influencing.

B. Providing Purpose, Motivation And Inspiration

Leaders influence others to achieve some purpose. To be successful at exerting influence Army leaders have an end or goal in mind. Sometimes the goal will be very specific, like reducing the number of training accidents by one-half over a period of six months. Many goals are less distinct and measurable than this example, but are still valid and meaningful. A leader may decide that unit morale needs to be improved and may set that as a goal for others to join to support.

Purpose provides what the leader wants done, while motivation and inspiration provide the energizing force to see that the purpose is addressed and has the strength to mobilize and sustain effort to get the job done. Motivation and inspiration address the needs of the individual and team. Indirect needs—like job satisfaction, sense of accomplishment, group belonging, and pride—typically have broader reaching effects than formal rewards and punishment, like promotions or nonjudicial actions.

Besides purpose and motivation, leader influence also consists of direction. Direction deals with how a goal, task, or mission is to be achieved. Subordinates do not need to receive guidance on the details of execution in all situations. The skilled leader will know when to provide detailed guidance and when to focus only on purpose, motivation, or inspiration.

Mission command conveys purpose without providing excessive, detailed direction. Mission command is the conduct of military operations through decentralized execution based on mission orders for effective mission accomplishment. Successful mission command rests on four elements:

- Commander's intent
- Subordinates' initiative
- Mission orders
- Resource allocation

Note: Mission command is a basis for Army planning (as described in FM 5-0) and is explained in FM 6-0.

1. Providing Purpose

Leaders in command positions use commander's intent to convey purpose. The commander's intent is a clear, concise statement of what the force must do and the conditions the force must meet to succeed with respect to the enemy, terrain, and desired end state (FM 3-0). When leading in other than command positions or in a nontactical application, leaders also establish tasks and the conditions for successful accomplishment. For leader situations other than command and for Army civilian leaders, enemy and terrain may be substituted by factors such as goals or organizational obstacles. Leaders communicate purpose with implied or explicit instructions so that others may exercise initiative while maintaining focus. This is important for situations when unanticipated opportunities arise or the original solution no longer applies. While direct and organizational level leaders provide purpose or intent, strategic leaders usually provide long-term vision or conceptual models.

2. Motivating and Inspiring

Motivation is the reason for doing something or the level of enthusiasm for doing it. Motivation comes from an inner desire to put effort into meeting a need. People have a range of needs. They include basics, such as survival and security and advanced needs, such as belonging and a sense of accomplishment. Awareness of one's own needs is most acute when needs go unfulfilled.

Army leaders use the knowledge of what motivates others to influence those they lead. Knowing one's Soldiers and others who may be influenced, gives leaders insight into guiding the team to higher levels of performance. Understanding how motivation works provides insight into why people may take action and how strongly they are driven to act.

Influence Techniques

Ref: FM 6-22 Army Leadership, pp. 7-4 to 7-5.

Leaders use several specific techniques for influence that fall along a continuum between compliance and commitment.

Pressure

Pressure is applied when leaders use explicit demands to achieve compliance, such as establishing task completion deadlines with negative consequences imposed for unmet completion. Indirect pressure includes persistent reminders of the request and frequent checking. This technique should be used infrequently since it tends to trigger resentment from followers, especially if the leader-exerted pressure becomes too severe. When followers perceive that pressures are not mission related but originate from their leader's attempt to please superiors for personal recognition, resentment can quickly undermine an organization's morale, cohesion, and quality of performance. Pressure is a good choice when the stakes are high, time is short, and previous attempts at achieving commitment have not been successful.

Legitimate Requests

Legitimate requests occur when leaders refer to their source of authority to establish the basis for a request. In the military, certain jobs must be done regardless of circumstances when subordinate leaders receive legitimate orders from higher headquarters. Reference to one's position suggests to those who are being influenced that there is the potential for official action if the request is not completed.

Exchange

Exchange is an influence technique that leaders use when they make an offer to provide some desired item or action in trade for compliance with a request. The exchange technique requires that the leaders control certain resources or rewards that are valued by those being influenced. A four-day pass as reward for excelling during a maintenance inspection is an example of an exchange influence technique.

Personal Appeals

Personal appeals occur when the leader asks the follower to comply with a request based on friendship or loyalty. This might often be useful in a difficult situation when mutual trust is the key to success. The leader appeals to the follower by highlighting the subordinate leader's special talents and professional trust to strengthen him prior to taking on a tough mission.

Collaboration

Collaboration occurs when the leader cooperates in providing assistance or resources to carry out a directive or request. The leader makes the choice more attractive by being prepared to step in and resolve any problems. A major planning effort prior to a deployment for humanitarian assistance would require possible collaboration with joint, interagency, or multinational agencies.

Rational Persuasion

Rational persuasion requires the leader to provide evidence, logical arguments, or explanations showing how a request is relevant to the goal. This is often the first approach to gaining compliance or commitment from followers and is likely to be effective if the leader is recognized as an expert in the specialty area in which the influence occurs. Leaders often draw from their own experience to give reasons that some task can be readily accomplished because the leader has tried it and done it.

Apprising

Apprising happens when the leader explains why a request will benefit a follower, such as giving them greater satisfaction in their work or performing a task a certain way that will save half the time. In contrast to the exchange technique, the benefits are out of the control of the leader. A commander may use the apprising technique to inform a newly assigned noncommissioned officer that serving in an operational staff position, prior to serving as a platoon sergeant, could provide him with invaluable experience. The commander points out that the additional knowledge may help the NCO achieve higher performance than his peers and possibly lead to an accelerated promotion to first sergeant.

Inspiration

Inspiration occurs when the leader fires up enthusiasm for a request by arousing strong emotions to build conviction. A leader may stress to a fellow officer that without help, the safety of the team may be at risk. By appropriately stressing the results of stronger commitment, a unit leader can inspire followers to surpass minimal standards and reach elite performance status.

Participation

Participation occurs when the leader asks a follower to take part in planning how to address a problem or meet an objective. Active participation leads to an increased sense of worth and recognition. It provides value to the effort and builds commitment to execute the commitment. Invitation to get involved is critical when senior leaders try to institutionalize a vision for long-term change. By involving key leaders of all levels during the planning phases, senior leaders ensure that their followers take stock in the vision.

Relationship Building

Relationship building is a technique in which leaders build positive rapport and a relationship of mutual trust, making followers more willing to support requests. Examples include, showing personal interest in a follower's well-being, offering praise, and understanding a follower's perspective. This technique is best used over time. It is unrealistic to expect it can be applied hastily when it has not been previously used. With time, this approach can be a consistently effective way to gain commitment from followers.

Putting Influence Techniques to Work

To succeed and create true commitment, influencing techniques should be perceived as authentic and sincere. Positive influence comes from leaders who do what is right for the Army, the mission, the team, and each individual Soldier. Negative influence—real and perceived—emanates from leaders who primarily focus on personal gain and lack self-awareness. Even honorable intentions, if wrongly perceived by followers as self-serving, will yield mere compliance.

The critical nature of the mission also determines which influence technique or combination of techniques is appropriate. When influencing their followers, Army leaders should consider that—

- Objectives for the use of influence should be in line with the Army Values, ethics, the Uniform Code of Military Justice, the Warrior Ethos, and the Civilian Creed
- Various influence techniques can be used to obtain compliance and commitment
- Compliance-seeking influence focuses on meeting and accounting for specific task demands
- Commitment-encouraging influence emphasizes empowerment and long-lasting trust

While it is difficult to know others' needs, it helps to consider three parts that define motivation:

- **Arousal:** A need or desire for something that is unfulfilled or below expectations
- **Direction:** Goals or other guides that direct the course of effort and behavior
- **Intensity:** The amount of effort that is applied to meet a need or reach a goal

The arousal, direction, and intensity of motivation produce at least four things that contribute directly to effective task performance. Motivation focuses attention on issues, goals, task procedures, or other aspects of what needs to be done. Motivation produces effort that dictates how hard one tries. Motivation generates persistence in terms of how long one tries. The fourth product of motivation is task strategies that define how a task is performed—the knowledge and skills used to reach a particular goal. Knowing better ways to perform a task can improve performance and lead to success in reaching a desired goal.

Motivation is based on the individual and the situation. Individuals contribute job knowledge and ability, personality and mood, and beliefs and values. The situation is the physical environment, task procedures and standards, rewards and reinforcements, social norms, and organization climate and culture. Leaders can improve individual motivation by influencing the individual and the situation. The influence techniques operate on different parts of motivation.

Self-efficacy is the confidence in one's ability to succeed at a task or reach a goal. Leaders can improve others' motivation by enhancing their self-efficacy by developing necessary knowledge and skills. Certain knowledge and skills may contribute to working smarter and just working harder or longer. An example is learning a more effective way to perform a task without reducing the quality of work.

Emotional inspiration is another way that a leader can enhance motivation. Providing an inspirational vision of future goals can increase the inner desire of a subordinate to achieve that vision. Leaders can inspire through the images when speaking. Inspirational images energize the team to go beyond satisfying individual interests and exceed expectations. Combat and life-threatening situations cause enough arousal as a natural response that leaders in these situations do not need to energize. Instead, they need to moderate too much arousal by providing a steady and calming influence and focus. Creating the right level of emotional arousal takes a careful balancing act. Training under severe and stressful conditions allows individuals the chance to experience different levels of arousal.

Leaders can encourage subordinates to set goals on their own and to set goals together. When goals are accepted they help to focus attention and action, increase the effort that is expended and persistence even in the face of failure, and develop strategies to help in goal accomplishment.

Positive reinforcement in the form of incentives (for example, monetary rewards or time off) as well as internal rewards (for example, praise and recognition) can enhance motivation. Punishment can be used when there is an immediate need to discontinue dangerous or otherwise undesirable behavior. Punishment can also send a clear message to others in the unit about behavioral expectations and the consequences of violating those expectations. In this way, a leader can shape the social norms of a unit. One caution is that punishment should be used sparingly and only in extreme cases because it can lead to resentment.

Effective leaders leverage the values and shared goals of those within their sphere of influence in order to motivate others. Leaders encourage others to reflect on their commitments such as the shared goals in this unit. Additionally, there are often shared values within an organization that form the basis of individual commitments (for example, personal courage, honor, and loyalty). Letting others know how a particular task is related to a larger mission, objective, or goal is often an effective motivational technique.

Individuals can be motivated by the duties they perform. Generally, if someone enjoys performing a task and is internally motivated, the simple acknowledgment of a job well done may be enough to sustain performance. No other rewards or incentives are necessary to motivate continued work on the task. In this case, task enjoyment provides the internal reward that motivates a Soldier to complete a task.

People often want to be given the opportunity to be responsible for their own work and to be creative—they want to be empowered. Empower subordinates by training them to do a job and providing them with necessary task strategies; give them the necessary resources, authority and clear intent; and then step aside to let them accomplish the mission. Empowering subordinates is a forceful statement of trust and one of the best ways of developing them as leaders. It is important to point out that being empowered also implies accepting the responsibility for the freedom to act and create.

Effective motivation is achieved when the team or organization wants to succeed. Motivation involves using words and examples to inspire subordinates to accomplish the mission. It grows from people's confidence in themselves, their unit, and their leaders. That confidence develops through tough and realistic training as well as consistent and fair leadership. Motivation also springs from the person's faith in the organization's larger missions, a sense of being a part of the bigger picture.

3. Building and Sustaining Morale

Military historians describing great armies often focus on weapons and equipment, training, and the National cause. They may mention numbers or other factors that can be analyzed, measured, and compared. Many historians also place great emphasis on one critical factor that cannot be easily measured: the emotional element called morale.

Morale is the human dimension's most important intangible element. It is a measure of how people feel about themselves, their team, and their leaders. High morale comes from good leadership, shared effort, and mutual respect. An emotional bond springs from the Warrior Ethos, common values like loyalty, and a belief that the Army will care for Soldiers' families. High morale results in a cohesive team striving to achieve common goals. Competent leaders know that morale—the essential human element—holds the team together and keeps it going in the face of the terrifying and dispiriting things that occur in war.

Leaders can furthermore boost morale in the face of extreme danger by providing their Soldiers the force protection means and support for successful operations. Units with high morale are usually more effective in combat and deal with hardships and losses better. It does not come as a surprise that these units conduct reunions and maintain close friendships for decades after they have served together in combat.

C. Enforcing Standards

To lead others and gauge if a job has been done correctly, the Army has established standards for military activities. Standards are formal, detailed instructions that can be described, measured, and achieved. They provide a mark for performance to assess how a specific task has been executed. To use standards effectively, leaders know, communicate, and enforce high but realistic standards. Good leaders explain the standards that apply to their organizations, but give subordinates the authority to enforce them.

Note: See facing page (3-11) for further discussion on enforcing standards.

D. Balancing Mission And Welfare Of Soldiers

Consideration of the needs of Soldiers and civilians is a basic function of all Army leaders. Having genuine concern for the well-being of followers goes hand-in-hand with motivation, inspiration, and influence. Soldiers and civilians will be more willing to go the extra mile for leaders who they know look out for them. Sending Soldiers or civilians in harm's way to accomplish the mission seems to contradict all the emphasis on taking care of people. How can a leader truly care for comrades and send them on missions that might get them killed? Similarly, when asking junior officers and NCOs to define what leaders do, the most common response is, "Take care of Soldiers."

Taking care of Soldiers entails creating a disciplined environment where they can learn and grow. It means holding them to high standards when training and preparing them to do their jobs so they can succeed in peace and win in war. Taking care of Soldiers, treating them fairly, refusing to cut corners, sharing hardships, and setting a personal example are crucial.

Taking care of Soldiers also means demanding that Soldiers do their duty—even at risk to their lives. Preparing Soldiers for the brutal realities of actual combat is a direct leader's most important duty. It does not mean coddling or making training easy or comfortable. Training neglect of that kind can get Soldiers killed. Training must be rigorous and simulate combat as much as possible, while keeping safety in mind. Leaders use risk management to ensure safety standards are appropriate. During wartime operations, unit leaders must also recognize the need to provide Soldiers with reasonable comforts to bolster morale and maintain long-term combat effectiveness. Comfort always takes second seat to the mission.

Taking care of others means finding out a Soldier's personal state on a particular day or their attitude about a particular task. The three attributes of a leader—character, presence, and intellectual capacity—can be applied as a leader's mental checklist to check on the welfare and readiness of Soldiers and civilians alike. It is up to the leader to provide the encouragement to push through to task completion or, when relief is required, to prevent unacceptable risk or harm and find other means to accomplish the task.

Many leaders connect at a personal level with their followers so they will be able to anticipate and understand the individual's circumstances and needs. As discussed previously in the chapter, building relationships is one way to gain influence and commitment from followers. Knowing others is the basis that many successful leaders use to treat personnel well. It includes everything from making sure a Soldier has time for an annual dental exam, to finding out about a person's preferred hobbies and pastimes. Leaders should provide an adequate family support and readiness network that assures Soldiers' families will be taken care of, whether the Soldier is working at home station or deployed.

C. Enforcing Standards

Ref: FM 6-22 Army Leadership, pp. 7-9 to 7-10.

To lead others and gauge if a job has been done correctly, the Army has established standards for military activities. Standards are formal, detailed instructions that can be described, measured, and achieved. To use standards effectively, leaders know, communicate, and enforce high but realistic standards. Good leaders explain the standards that apply to their organizations, but give subordinates the authority to enforce them.

When enforcing standards for unit activities, leaders must remain aware that not everything can be a number one priority. Striving for excellence in every area, regardless of how trivial, would work an organization too hard. Leaders must prioritize the tasks without allowing other tasks to drop below established standards. True professionals make sure the standard fits the task's importance.

A leader's ultimate goal is to train the organization to the standards that ensure success in its wartime mission. The leader's daily work includes setting the intermediate goals to prepare the organization to reach the standards. To be successful at this, leaders use the Army training management cycle. The training management process is used to set appropriate training goals and to plan, resource, execute, and evaluate training accordingly (see FM 7-0 for more detail).

1. Performing Checks and Inspections

Proper supervision is essential to ensuring mission accomplishment to standard. It is an integral part of caring for Soldiers. The better they know their unit and subordinates, the more they can strike a balance for finding the details. To foster independence and initiative, direct leaders give instructions and clear mission intent. They allow subordinates to get the work done without constantly looking over their shoulders.

Accomplishing the unit's real-world mission is critically important. This requires that units and individuals are fully prepared. It is why leaders check things—conducting pre-operation checks and formal inspections (FM 6-0). Thorough inspections ensure that Soldiers, units, and systems are as fully capable and ready to execute the mission as time and resources permit.

Focused checking minimizes the chance of neglect or mistakes that may derail a mission or cause unnecessary casualties. Checking also gives leaders a chance to see and recognize subordinates who are doing things right or to make on-the-spot corrections when necessary.

2. Instilling Discipline

Leaders who consistently enforce standards are simultaneously instilling discipline that will pay-off in critical situations. True discipline demands habitual and reasoned obedience, an obedience that preserves initiative and works, even when the leader is not around or when chaos and uncertainty abound.

Discipline does not mean barking orders and demanding instant responses. A good leader gradually instills discipline by training to standard, using rewards and punishment judiciously, instilling confidence, building trust among team members, and ensuring that Soldiers and civilians have necessary technical and tactical expertise. Confidence, trust, and team effort are crucial for success in operational settings.

Individual and collective discipline generally carries the day when organizations are faced with complex and dangerous situations. It usually begins with the resilience, competence, and discipline of one individual who recognizes the need to inspire others to follow an example, turning a negative situation into success.

II. Extends Influence Beyond the Chain of Command

While Army leaders traditionally exert influence within their unit and its established chain of command, multiskilled leaders must also be capable of extending influence to others beyond the chain of command. Extending influence is the second leader competency. In today's politically and culturally charged operational environments, even direct leaders may work closely with joint, interagency, and multinational forces, the media, local civilians, political leaders, police forces, and nongovernmental agencies. Extending influence requires special awareness about the differences in how influence works.

When extending influence beyond the traditional chain, leaders often have to influence without authority designated or implied by rank or position. Civilian and military leaders often find themselves in situations where they must build informal teams to accomplish organizational tasks.

A unique aspect of extending influence is that those who are targets of influence outside the chain may not even recognize or willingly accept the authority that an Army leader has. Often informal teams must be created in situations where there are no official chains of authority. In some cases, it may require leaders to establish their credentials and capability for leading others. At other times, leaders may need to interact as a persuasive force but not from an obvious position and attitude of power.

The key element of extending influence and building teams is the creation of a common vision among prospective team members. At times leaders may need to interact with others as a persuasive influence but not from an obvious position and attitude of power.

Leading without authority requires adaptation to the environment and cultural sensitivities of the given situation. Leaders require cultural knowledge to understand different social customs and belief systems and to address issues in those contexts. When conducting peace operations, for example, even small unit leaders and civilian negotiators must understand that their interaction with locals and their leaders can have dramatic impacts on the overall theater strategy. The manner in which a unit conducts house-to-house searches for insurgents can influence the local population's acceptance of authority, or become a recruiting incentive for the insurgency.

Extending influence includes the following competency subsets:

- Building trust outside lines of military command authority
- Understanding the sphere, means, and limits of influence
- Negotiating, consensus building, and conflict resolution

A. Building Trust Outside Lines of Authority

Forming effective, cohesive teams is often the first challenge of a leader working outside a traditional command structure. These teams usually have to be formed from disparate groups who are unfamiliar with military and Army customs and culture. Without some measure of trust, nothing will work as well. To establish trust, the leader will have to identify areas of common interests and goals. Trust between two people or two groups is based largely on being able to anticipate what the others understand and how they will respond in various situations. Keeping others informed also builds trust. Cementing and sustaining trust depends on following through on commitments.

Successful teams develop an infectious winner's attitude. Problems are challenges rather than obstacles. Cohesive teams accomplish missions much more efficiently than a loose group of individuals. While developing seamless teams is ideal, sometimes it will not be practical to bring disparate groups together.

Building alliances is similar to building teams; the difference being that in alliances the groups maintain greater independence. Trust is a common ingredient in effective alliances. Alliances are groomed over time by establishing contact with others, growing friendships, and identifying common interests.

Whether operating in focused teams or in looser alliances, training and working together builds collective competence and mutual trust. A mutual trust relationship will ultimately permeate the entire organization, embracing every single member, regardless of gender, race, social origin, religion or if permanently assigned or temporarily attached.

The requirements for building trust and cohesion are valid for relationships extending beyond the organization and the chain of command. They apply when working with task-organized organizations; joint, interagency, and multinational forces; and non-combatants. If a special operations team promises critical air support and medical supplies to indigenous multinational forces for an upcoming operation, the personal reputation of the leader, and trust in the United States as a respected, supportive nation, can be at stake.

Lead, Develop, Achieve

B. Understanding Sphere, Means and Limits Of Influence

When operating with an established command structure and common procedures, the provisions and limits of roles and responsibilities are readily apparent. When leading outside an established organization, assessing the parties involved becomes another part of the operation. Identifying who is who, what role they have, over whom they have authority or influence, and how they are likely to respond to the Army leader's influence are all important considerations. Sometimes this is viewed as understanding the limits to the Army's or the leader's influence.

Spanning the boundaries of disparate groups or organizations is a task that requires special attention. The key to influence outside the chain of command is to learn about the people and organizations. By understanding their interests and desires, the leader will know what influence techniques are most likely to work. Leaders can learn some of the art of dealing with disparate interests from business operations that deal with coordinating opposing parties with different interests.

C. Negotiating, Building Consensus and Resolving Conflicts

While operating outside the chain of command, leaders often have to resolve conflicts between Army interests and local populations or others. Conflict resolution identifies differences and similarities among the stances of the various groups. Differences are further analyzed to understand what is behind the difference. Proposals are made for re-interpreting the differences or negotiating compromise to reach common understanding or shared goals. Trust, understanding, and knowing the right influence technique for the situation are the determining factors in negotiating, consensus building, and conflict resolution.

III. Leads By Example

A. Displaying Character

Leaders set an example whether they know it or not. Countless times leaders operate on instinct that has grown from what they have seen in the past. What leaders see others do sets the stage for what they may do in the future. A leader of sound character will exhibit that character at all times. Modeling these attributes of character defines the leaders to the people with whom they interact. A leader of character does not have to worry about being seen at the wrong moment doing the wrong thing.

Living by the Army Values and the Warrior Ethos best displays character and leading by example. It means putting the organization and subordinates above personal self-interest, career, and comfort. For the Army leader, it requires putting the lives of others above a personal desire for self-preservation.

Leading with Confidence in Adverse Conditions

A leader who projects confidence is an inspiration to followers. Soldiers will follow leaders who are comfortable with their own abilities and will question the leader who shows doubt.

Displaying confidence and composure when things are not going well can be a challenge for anyone, but is important for the leader to lead others through a grave situation. Confidence is a key component of leader presence. A leader who shows hesitation in the face of setbacks can trigger a chain reaction among others. A leader who is over-confident in difficult situations may lack the proper degree of care or concern.

Leading with confidence requires a heightened self-awareness and ability to master emotions. Developing the ability to remain confident no matter what the situation involves—

- Having prior opportunities to experience reactions to severe situations
- Maintaining a positive outlook when a situation becomes confusing or changes
- Remaining decisive after mistakes have been discovered
- Encouraging others when they show signs of weakness

Displaying Moral Courage

Projecting confidence in combat and other situations requires physical and moral courage. While physical courage allows infantrymen to defend their ground, even when the enemy has broken the line of defense and ammunition runs critically short, moral courage empowers leaders to stand firm on values, principles, and convictions in the same situation. Leaders who take full responsibility for their decisions and actions display moral courage. Morally courageous leaders are willing to critically look inside themselves, consider new ideas, and change what caused failure.

Moral courage in day-to-day peacetime operations is as important as momentary physical courage in combat. Consider a civilian test board director who has the responsibility to determine whether a new piece of military equipment performs to the established specifications. Knowing that a failed test may cause the possibility of personal pressure and command resistance from the program management office, a morally courageous tester will be prepared to endure that pressure and remain objective and fair in test procedures and conclusions. Moral courage is fundamental to living the Army Values of integrity and honor, whether a civilian or military team member.

B. Demonstrating Competence

It does not take long for followers to become suspicious of a leader who acts confident but does not have the competence to back it up. Having the appropriate levels of domain knowledge is vital to prepare competent leaders who can in turn display confidence through their attitudes, actions, and words.

When examining the majority of small unit military operations, many often were uncertain until competent and confident leaders made the difference. At the right time, the competent leaders apply the decisive characteristics to influence the tactical or operational situation. Their personal presence and indirect influences help mobilize the will and morale in their people to achieve final victory.

Leading by example demands that leaders stay aware of how their guidance and plans are executed. Direct and organizational leaders cannot remain in safe, dry headquarters, designing complex plans without examining what their Soldiers and civilians are experiencing. They must have courage to get out to where the action is, whether the battlefield or the shop floor. Good leaders connect with their followers by sharing hardships and communicating openly to clearly see and feel what goes on from a subordinate's perspective.

IV. Communicates

Competent leadership that gets results depends on good communication. Although communication is usually viewed as a process of providing information, communication as a competency must ensure that there is more than the simple transmission of information. Communication needs to achieve a new understanding. Communication must create new or better awareness. Communicating critical information in a clear fashion is an important skill to reach a shared understanding of issues and solutions. It is conveying thoughts, presenting recommendations, bridging cultural sensitivities and reaching consensus. Leaders cannot lead, supervise, build teams, counsel, coach, or mentor without the ability to communicate clearly.

A. Listening Actively

An important form of two-way communication to reach a shared understanding is active listening. Although the most important purpose of listening is to comprehend the sender's thoughts, listeners should provide an occasional indication to the speaker that they are still attentive. Active listening involves avoiding interruption and keeping mental or written notes of important points or items for clarification. Good listeners will be aware of the content of the message, but also the urgency and emotion of how it is spoken.

It is critical to remain aware of barriers to listening. Do not formulate a response while it prevents hearing what the other person is saying. Do not allow distraction by anger, disagreement with the speaker, or other things to impede. These barriers prevent hearing and absorbing what is said.

B. Stating Goals for Action

The basis for expressing clear goals for action resides in the leader's vision and how well that vision is explained. Before stating goals, objectives, and required tasks for the team, unit, or organization, it is important for the leader to visualize a desired end state. Once the goals are clear, leaders communicate them in a way that motivates them to understand the message and to accept and act on the message.

Speaking to engage listeners can improve by being aware of what styles of communication energize the leader when the leader is the listener. The speaker should be open to cues that listeners give and adapt to ensure that his message is

received. The speaker needs to be alert to recognize and resolve misunderstandings. Since success or failure of any communication is the leader's responsibility, it is
important to ensure the message has been received. Leaders can use backbriefs or
ask a few focused questions to do so.

C. Ensuring Shared Understanding

Competent leaders know themselves, the mission, and the message. They owe it
to their organization and their subordinates to share information that directly applies
to their duties. They should also provide information that provides context for what
needs to be done. Generous sharing of information also provides information that
may be useful in the future.

Leaders keep their organizations informed because it builds trust. Shared information helps relieve stress and control rumors. Timely information exchange allows
team members to determine what needs to be done to accomplish the mission and
adjust to changing circumstances. Informing subordinates of a decision, and the
overall reasons for it, shows they are appreciated members of the team and conveys
that support and input are needed. Good information flow also ensures the next
leader in the chain can be sufficiently prepared to take over, if required. Subordinates must clearly understand the leader's vision. In a tactical setting, all leaders
must fully understand their commanders' intent two levels up.

Leaders use a variety of means to share information: face-to-face talks, written and
verbal orders, estimates and plans, published memos, electronic mail, websites, and
newsletters. When communicating to share information, the leader must acknowledge two critical factors:

- A leader is responsible for making sure the team understands the message
- A leader must ensure that communication is not limited to the traditional chain
  of command but often includes lateral and vertical support networks

When checking the information flow for shared understanding, a team leader should
carefully listen to what supervisors, platoon sergeants, platoon leaders, and company commanders say. A platoon sergeant who usually passes the message through
squad leaders or section chiefs should watch and listen to the troops to verify that
the critical information makes it to where it will ultimately be translated into action.

Communicating also flows from bottom to top. Leaders find out what their people are
thinking, saying, and doing by listening. Good leaders keep a finger on the pulse of
their organizations by getting out to coach, to listen, and to clarify. They then pass
relevant observations to their superiors who can assist with planning and decision
making.

Often, leaders communicate more effectively with informal networks than directly
with superiors. Sometimes that produces the desired results but can lead to misunderstandings and false judgments. To run an effective organization and achieve
mission accomplishment without excessive conflict, leaders must figure out how to
reach their superiors when necessary and to build a relationship of mutual trust.

To prepare organizations for inevitable communication challenges, leaders create
training situations where they are forced to act with minimum guidance or only the
commander's intent. Leaders provide formal or informal feedback to highlight the
things subordinates did well, what they could have done better, and what they should
do differently next time to improve information sharing and processing.

Open communication does more than share information. It shows that leaders care
about those they work with. Competent and confident leaders encourage open dialogue, listen actively to all perspectives, and ensure that others can voice forthright
and honest opinions, without fear of negative consequences.

I. Developing

Ref: FM 6-22 Army Leadership, part 3, chap 8. See also pp. 2-6 to 2-9.

Good leaders strive to leave an organization better than they found it and expect other leaders throughout the Army do the same. Leaders can create a positive organizational climate, prepare themselves to do well in their own duties, and help others to perform well. Good leaders look ahead and prepare talented Soldiers and civilians to assume positions with greater leadership responsibility in their own organization and in future assignments. They also work on their own development to prepare for new challenges.

To have future focus and maintain balance in the present, Army leaders set priorities and weigh competing demands. They carefully steer their organizations' efforts to address short- and long-term goals, while continuing to meet requirements that could contribute directly to achieving those goals. Accounting for the other demands that vie for an organization's time and resources, a leader's job becomes quite difficult. Guidance from higher headquarters may help, but leaders have to make the tough calls to keep a healthy balance.

Developing people and the organization with a long-term perspective requires the following:

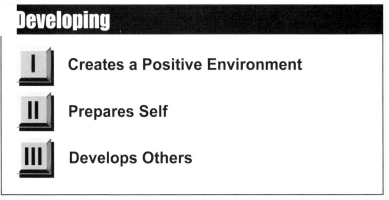

Developing

I	Creates a Positive Environment
II	Prepares Self
III	Develops Others

Ref: FM 6-22, chap. 8.

I. Creates a Positive Environment

Climate and culture describe the environment in which a leader leads. Culture refers to the environment of the Army as an institution and of major elements or communities within it. While strategic leaders maintain the Army's institutional culture, climate refers to the environment of units and organizations, primarily shaped by organizational and direct leaders.

Culture is a longer lasting and more complex set of shared expectations than climate. While climate is a reflection about how people think and feel about their organization right now, culture consists of the shared attitudes, values, goals, and practices that characterize the larger institution over time. It is deeply rooted in long-held beliefs, customs, and practices. Leaders must establish a climate consistent with the culture of the enduring institution. They also use the culture to let their people know they are part of something bigger than just themselves, that they have responsibilities not only to the people around them but also to those who have gone before and those who will come after.

Soldiers draw strength from knowing they are part of a long-standing tradition. Most meaningful traditions have their roots in the institution's culture. Many of the Army's everyday customs and traditions exist to remind Soldiers they are the latest addition to a long line of Soldiers. Army culture and traditions connect Soldiers to the past and to the future. The uniforms, the music played during official ceremonies, the way Soldiers salute, military titles, the organization's history, and the Army Values all are reminders of a place in history. This sense of belonging lives in many veterans long after they have left the service. For most, service to the Nation remains the single most significant experience of their lives.

Soldiers join the Army to become part of a values and tradition based culture. While the Army Values help deepen existing personal values, such as family bonds, work ethic, and integrity, it is tradition that ties Soldiers and their families into military culture. Unit history is an important factor for that bonding, since Soldiers want to belong to organizations with distinguished service records. Unit names, such as the Big Red One, Old Ironsides, All Americans, and Spearhead carry an extensive history. To sustain tradition, leaders must teach Soldiers the history that surrounds unit crests, military greetings, awards, decorations, and badges. Through leading by example, teaching, and upholding traditions, leaders ensure that the Army's culture becomes an integral part of every member of the Army team and adds purpose to their lives.

The Army Learning Environment

The Army, as a learning organization, harnesses the experience of its people and organizations to improve the way it operates. Based on their experiences, learning organizations adopt new techniques and procedures that get the job done more efficiently or effectively. Likewise, they discard techniques and procedures that have outlived their purpose. Learning organizations create a climate that values and supports learning in its leaders and people. Opportunities for training and education are actively identified and supported. Leaders have direct impact on creating a climate that values learning across everyone's entire Army career. This corresponds to the same goal as lifelong learning.

Lifelong learning is the individual lifelong choice to actively and overtly pursue knowledge, the comprehension of ideas, and the expansion of depth in any area in order to progress beyond a known state of development and competency (FM 7-0).

Leaders who learn look at their experience and find better ways of doing things. It takes courage to create a learning environment. Leaders dedicated to a learning environment cannot be afraid to challenge how they and their organizations operate. When leaders question, "why do we do it this way" and find out the only reason is, "because we've always done it that way", it is time for a closer look at this process. Teams that have found a way that works may not be doing things the best way. Unless leaders are willing to question how things operate now, no one will ever know what can be done.

A. Setting Conditions for Positive Climate

Ref: FM 6-22 Army Leadership, pp. 8-2 to 8-3.

Taking care of people and maximizing their performance is influenced by how well the leader shapes the organization's climate. Climate is how members feel about the organization and comes from shared perceptions and attitudes about the unit's daily functioning. These things have a great impact on their motivation and the trust they feel for their team and their leaders. Climate is generally a short-term experience, depending on a network of the personalities in a small organization. The organization's climate changes as people come and go. When a Soldier says, "My last platoon sergeant was pretty good, but this new one is great," the Soldier is pinpointing one of the many elements that affect an organization's climate.

Climate and culture are the context in which leaders and followers interact. Each element has an effect on the other. Research in military, government, and business organizations shows that a positive environment leads to workers who feel better about themselves, have stronger commitments, and produce better work. If leaders set the tone for a positive climate, others will respond in kind.

Good leaders are concerned with establishing a climate that can be characterized as fair, inclusive, and ethical. Fairness means that treatment is equitable and no one gets preferential treatment for arbitrary reasons. Inclusive means that everyone, regardless of any difference, is integrated into the organization. Ethical means that actions throughout the organization conform to the Army Values and moral principles.

Lead, Develop, Achieve

Fairness and Inclusiveness

A leader who uses the same set of policies and the same viewpoint in treatment of others is on the right path to building a positive climate. Although leaders should be consistent and fair in how they treat others, not everyone will be treated exactly alike. People have different capabilities and different needs, so leaders should consider some differences while ignoring irrelevant differences. Leaders need to judge certain situations according to what is important in each case. While not everyone will receive the same treatment, fair leaders will use the same set of principles and values to avoid arbitrary treatment of others.

All leaders are responsible for adhering to equal opportunity policies and preventing all forms of harassment. Creating a positive climate begins with encouraging diversity and inclusiveness.

Open and Candid Communications

Through the example they set and the leadership actions they take, good leaders will encourage open communications and candid observations. A leader who is as interested in getting others' input in advocating a position needs to encourage an environment where others feel free to contribute. An open and candid environment is a key ingredient in creating a unit that is poised to recognize and adapt to change. Approachable leaders show respect for others' opinions, even when it may represent contrary viewpoints or viewpoints out of the mainstream of thought. Some leaders specifically recognize others to provide a critical viewpoint to guard against groupthink. An open leader does not demean others and encourages input and feedback. A positive leader also remains calm and objective when receiving potentially bad news.

Ethics and Climate

Ref: FM 6-22 Army Leadership, pp. 8-3 to 8-4.

Lead, Develop, Achieve

A leader is the ethical standard-bearer for the organization, responsible for building an ethical climate that demands and rewards behavior consistent with the Army Values. Other staff specialists—the chaplain, staff judge advocate, inspector general, and equal employment opportunity specialist—assist in shaping and assessing the organization's ethical climate. Regardless of all the available expert help, the ultimate responsibility to create and maintain an ethical climate rests with the leader.

Setting a good ethical example does not necessarily mean subordinates will follow it. Some may feel that circumstance justifies unethical behavior. Therefore, the leader must constantly monitor the organization's ethical climate and take prompt action to correct any discrepancies between the climate and the standard. To effectively monitor organizational climates, leaders can use a periodic Ethical Climate Assessment Survey combined with a focused leader plan of action as follows:

- **Begin the plan of action by assessing the unit.** Observe, interact, and gather feedback from others, or conduct formal assessments of the workplace.

- **Analyze gathered information to identify what needs improvement.** After identifying what needs improvement, begin developing courses of action to make the improvements.

- **Develop a plan of action.** First, develop and consider several possible courses of action to correct identified weaknesses. Gather important information, assess the limitations and risks associated with the various courses, identify available key personnel and resources, and verify facts and assumptions. Attempt to predict the outcome for each possible course of action. Based on predictions, select several leader actions to deal with target issues.

- **Execute the plan of action** by educating, training, or counseling subordinates; instituting new policies or procedures; and revising or enforcing proper systems of rewards and punishment. The organization moves towards excellence by improving substandard or weak areas and maintaining conditions that meet or exceed the standard. Finally, periodically reassess the unit to identify new matters of concern or to evaluate the effectiveness of the leader actions.

Use this process for many areas of interest and concern within the organization. It is important for subordinates to have confidence in the organization's ethical environment because much of what is necessary in war goes against the grain of societal values that individuals bring into the Army. A Soldier's conscience may say it is wrong to take human life while the mission calls for exactly that. A strong ethical climate helps Soldiers define their duty, preventing a conflict of values that may sap a Soldier's will to fight at tremendous peril to the entire team.

Leaders who make it a priority to improve their Soldiers and civilians, and the way the teams work, lead a learning organization. They use effective assessment and training methods, encourage others to reach their full potential, motivate others to develop themselves, and help others obtain training and education. An upbeat climate encourages Soldiers and civilians to recognize the need for organizational change and supports a willing attitude of learning to deal with change.

Assessing Climate

Some very definite actions and attitudes can determine climate. The members' collective sense of the group—its organizational climate—is directly attributable to the leader's values, skills, and actions. Army leaders shape the climate of the organization, no matter what the size. Conducted within 90 days of taking company command, Command Climate Surveys assist leaders in understanding the unit's climate. (See DA Pam 600-69 for information.) Answering the following questions can help assess organizational climate:

- Are clear priorities and goals set?
- Does a system of recognition, rewards, and punishments exist? Does it work?
- Do leaders know what they are doing?
- Do leaders have the courage to admit when they are wrong?
- Do leaders actively seek input from subordinates?
- Do leaders act on the feedback they have provided?
- In the absence of orders, do junior leaders have authority to make decisions when they are consistent with the commander's intent or guidance?
- Do leaders perceive high levels of internal stress and negative competition in the organization? If so, what are the options to change that situation??
- Do leaders lead by example and serve as good role models?
- Is leader behavior consistent with the Army Values?
- Do leaders lead from the front, sharing hardship when things get rough?
- Do leaders talk to the organization on a regular basis and keep people informed?

The leader's behavior has significant impact on the organizational climate. Army leaders who do the right things for the right reasons will create a healthy organizational climate. Leader behavior signals to every member of the organization what is or is not tolerated.

B. Building Teamwork and Cohesion

Teamwork and cohesion are measures of climate. Willingness to engage in teamwork is the opposite of selfishness. Selfless service is a requirement for effective teamwork. To operate effectively, teams, units, and organizations need to work together for common Army Values and task and mission objectives. Leaders encourage others to work together, while promoting group pride in accomplishments. Teamwork is based on commitment to the group, which in turn is built on trust. Trust is based on expecting that others will act for the team and keep its interests ahead of their own. Leaders have to do the hard work of dealing with breaches in trust, poor team coordination, and outright conflicts. Leaders should take special care in quickly integrating new members into the team with this commitment in mind.

Leaders can shape teams to be cohesive by setting and maintaining high standards. Positive climate exists where good, consistent performance is the norm. This is very different from a climate where perfectionism is the expectation. Team members should feel that a concentrated, honest effort is appreciated even when the results are incomplete. They should feel that their leader recognizes value in every opportunity as a means to learn and to get better.

Good leaders recognize that reasonable setbacks and failures occur whether the team does everything right or not. Leaders should express the importance of being competent and motivated, but understand that weaknesses exist. Mistakes create opportunities to learn something that may not have been brought to mind.

Soldiers and Army civilians expect to be held to high but realistic standards. In the end, they feel better about themselves when they accomplish their tasks successfully. They gain confidence in leaders who help them achieve standards and lose confidence in leaders who do not know the standards or who fail to demand quality performance.

C. Encouraging Initiative

One of the greatest challenges for a leader is to encourage subordinates to exercise initiative. Soldiers and civilians who are not in leadership positions are often reluctant to recognize that a situation calls for them to accept responsibility and step forward. This could involve speaking up when the Soldier has technical knowledge or situational information that his commander does not.

Climate is largely determined by the degree to which initiative and input is encouraged from anyone with an understanding of the relevancy of the point. Leaders can set the conditions for initiative by guiding others in thinking through problems for themselves. They can build confidence in the Soldier's, or Army civilian's, competence and ability to solve problems.

D. Demonstrating Care for People

The care that leaders show for others affects climate. Leaders who have the well-being of their subordinates in mind create greater trust. Leaders who respect those they work with will likely be shown respect in return. Respect and care can be demonstrated by simple actions such as listening patiently or ensuring that Soldiers or civilians who are deploying have their families' needs addressed. Regular sensing of morale and actively seeking honest feedback about the health of the organization also indicate care.

II. Prepares Self

To prepare for increasingly more demanding operational environments, Army leaders must invest more time on self-study and self-development than before. Besides becoming multiskilled, Army leaders have to balance the demands of diplomat and warrior. Acquiring these capabilities to succeed across the spectrum of conflicts is challenging, but critical. In no other profession is the cost of being unprepared as unforgiving, often resulting in mission failure and unnecessary casualties.

A. Being Prepared for Expected and Unexpected Changes

Ref: FM 6-22 Army Leadership, pp. 8-6 to 8-7.

Successful self-development concentrates on the key components of the leader: character, presence, and intellect. While continuously refining their ability to apply and model the Army Values, Army leaders know that in the physical arena, they must maintain high levels of fitness and health, not only to earn continuously the respect of subordinates, peers, and superiors, but also to withstand the stresses of leading and maintaining their ability to think clearly.

While physical self-development is important, leaders must also exploit every available opportunity to sharpen their intellectual capacity and knowledge in relevant domains. The conceptual components affecting the Army leader's intelligence include agility, judgment, innovation, interpersonal tact, and domain knowledge. A developed intellect helps the leader think creatively and reason analytically, critically, ethically, and with cultural sensitivity.

When faced with diverse operational settings, a leader draws on intellectual capacity, critical thinking abilities, and applicable domain knowledge. Leaders create these capabilities by frequently studying doctrine, tactics, techniques, and procedures, and by putting the information into context with personal experiences, military history, and geopolitical awareness. Here, self-development should include taking the time to learn languages, customs, belief systems, motivational factors, operational principles, and the doctrine of multinational partners and those of potential adversaries. Leaders can gain additional language skills and geopolitical awareness by seeking language schooling and assignments in specific regions of interest.

Self-development is continuous and must be pursued during both institutional and operational assignments. Successful self-development begins with the motivated individual, supplemented by a concerted team effort. Part of that team effort is quality feedback from multiple sources, including peers, subordinates, and superiors. Trust-based mentorship can also help focus self-development efforts to achieve specific professional objectives. It is important to understand that this feedback leads to establishing self-development goals and self-improvement courses of action. These courses of action are designed to improve performance by enhancing previously acquired skills, knowledge, behaviors, and experience. They further determine the potential for progressively more complex and higher-level assignments.

Generally, self-development for junior leaders is more structured and focused. The focus broadens as individuals identify their own strengths and weaknesses, determine individual needs, and become more independent. While knowledge and perspective increase with age, experience, institutional training, and operational assignments, goal-oriented self-development actions can greatly accelerate and broaden skills and knowledge. Soldiers and civilians can expect their leaders to assist in their self-development.

Civilian and military education is another important part of self-development. Army leaders never stop learning and seek out education and training opportunities beyond what is offered in required schooling or during duty assignments. To prepare for future responsibilities, Army leaders should explore off-duty education, such as available college courses that teach additional skills and broaden perspectives on life, as well as distributed learning courses on management principles or specific leadership topics.

B. Expanding Knowledge

Leaders prepare themselves for leadership positions through lifelong learning. Lifelong learning involves study and reflection to acquire new knowledge and to learn how to apply it when needed. Some leaders readily pick up strategies about how to learn new information faster and more thoroughly. Becoming a better learner involves several purposeful steps:

- Plan the approach to use to learn
- Focus on specific, achievable learning goals
- Set aside time to study
- Organize new information as it is encountered
- Track how learning is proceeding

Good learners will focus on new information, what it means in relation to other information, and how it might be applied. To solidify new knowledge, try to apply it and experience what it means. Leaders need to develop and extend knowledge of tactics and operational art, technical equipment and systems, diverse cultures, and geopolitical situations. (Chapter 6 describes these domains.)

C. Developing Self-Awareness

Self-awareness is a component of preparing self. It is being prepared, being actively engaged in a situation and interacting with others. Self-awareness has the potential to help all leaders become better adjusted and more effective. Self-awareness is relevant for contemporary operations requiring cultural sensitivity and for a leader's adaptability to inevitable environmental change.

Self-awareness enables leaders to recognize their strengths and weaknesses across a range of environments and progressively leverage strengths to correct these weaknesses. To be self-aware, leaders must be able to formulate accurate self-perceptions, gather feedback on others' perceptions, and change their self-concept as appropriate. Being truly self-aware ultimately requires leaders to develop a clear, honest picture of their capabilities and limitations.

Self-awareness is being aware of oneself, including one's traits, feelings, and behaviors.

As a given situation changes, so must a leader's assessment of abilities and limitations in order to adapt. Every leader has the ability to be self-aware. Competent leaders understand the importance of self-awareness and work to develop it.

In contrast, leaders who lack self-awareness are often seen as arrogant and disconnected from their subordinates. They may be technically competent but lack of awareness as to how they are seen by subordinates. This may also obstruct learning and adaptability, which in turn, keeps them from creating a positive work climate and a more effective organization. Self-aware leaders understand the variety of Soldiers and civilians on their team. They sense how others react to their actions, decisions, and image.

Self-aware leaders are open to feedback and actively seek it. A leader's goal in obtaining feedback is to develop an accurate self-perception by understanding other people's perceptions. Many leaders have successfully used a multisource assessment and feedback method to gain insight. A multisource assessment is a formal measure of peer, subordinate, superior, and self-impressions of a single individual. It may provide critical feedback and insights that are otherwise not apparent.

The Army's after-action review (AAR) process is a well-used awareness tool. Its purpose is to help units and individuals identify their strengths and weaknesses. A productive self-review occurs when one examines his or her self and becomes conscious of one's own behavior and interactions with others.

Leaders should also seek out others to help them make sense of their experiences. Talking with coaches, friends, or other trusted individuals can provide valuable information. Most, but not all Army leaders, find a mentor whom they trust to provide honest feedback and encouragement.

It is important to realize that feedback does not have to be gathered in formal counseling, survey, or sensing sessions. Some of the best feedback comes from simply sitting down and informally talking with Soldiers and civilians. Many commanders have gained valuable information about themselves from merely eating a meal in the dining facility with a group of Soldiers and asking about unit climate and training.

Self-aware leaders analyze themselves and ask hard questions about experiences, events, and their actions. They should examine their own behavior seriously. Competent and confident leaders make sense of their experience and use it to learn more about themselves. Journals and AARs are valuable tools to help gain an understanding of one's past experiences and reactions to the changes in the environment. Self-critique can be as simple as posing questions about one's own behavior, knowledge, or feelings. It can be as formal as answering a structured set of questions about a high profile event. Critical questions include—

- What happened?
- How did I react?
- How did others react and why?
- What did I learn about myself based on what I did and how I felt?
- How will I apply what I learned?

In the rapidly changing environment of both the current and future force, leaders are faced with unfamiliar and uncertain situations. For any leader, self-awareness is a critical factor in making accurate assessments of the changes in the environment and their personal capabilities and limitations to operate in that environment. Self-awareness helps leaders translate prior training to a new environment and seek out new information when the situation requires. Self-aware leaders are better informed and able to determine what needs to be learned and what assistance they need to seek out to handle a given situation.

Adjusting one's thoughts, feelings, and actions based on self-awareness is called self-regulation. It is the proactive and logical follow-up to self-awareness. When leaders determine a gap from actual "self" to desired "self," they should take steps to close the gap. Leaders can seek new perspectives about themselves and turn those perspectives into a leadership advantage. Because leaders cannot afford to stop learning, they seek to improve and grow. Becoming more self-aware is not something that happens automatically. Competent and confident leaders seek input and improvements over the entire span of their careers.

III. Develops Others

Leader development is a deliberate, continuous, sequential, and progressive process grounded in the Army Values. It grows Soldiers and civilians into competent and confident leaders capable of directing teams and organizations to execute decisive action. Leader development is achieved through the lifelong synthesis of the knowledge, skills, and experiences gained through institutional training and education, organizational training, operational experience, and self-development.

Leader development takes into consideration that military leaders are inherently Soldiers first and must be technically and tactically proficient as well as adaptive to change. Army training and leader development therefore centers on creating trained and ready units, led by competent and confident leaders. The concept acknowledges an important interaction that trains Soldiers now and develops leaders for the future.

The three core domains that shape the critical learning experiences throughout Soldiers' and leaders' careers are—

- Institutional training
- Training, education, and job experience gained during operational assignments
- Self-development

These three domains interact by using feedback and assessment from various sources and methods. Although leader development aims at producing competent leadership at all levels, it recognizes small unit leaders must reach an early proficiency to operate in widely dispersed areas in combined arms teams. The Army increasingly requires proficient small unit leaders capable of operating in widely dispersed areas and/or integrated with joint, multinational, special operations forces as well as nongovernmental agencies. These leaders must be self-aware and adaptive, comfortable with ambiguity, able to anticipate possible second- and third-order effects, and be multifunctional to exploit combined arms integration.

To that end, the Army leverages leader development education (professional military education and the Civilian Education System), ensuring the best mix of experiences and operational assignments supported by resident and distributed education. The effort requires improved individual assessment and feedback and increased development efforts at the organizational level in the form of mentoring, coaching, and counseling, as well as picking the right talent for specific job assignments. The purpose of the increased developments efforts is to instill in all Soldiers and leaders the desire and drive to update their professional knowledge and competencies, thus improving current and future Army leaders' abilities to master the challenges of full spectrum operations.

Leader development also requires organizational support. A commander or other designated leader has the responsibility to develop others for better performance in their current and future positions. There are specific actions that leaders can take to personalize leader development in their organization.

A. Assessing Developmental Needs

The first step in developing others is to understand how they may be developed best; what areas are already strong and what areas should be stronger. Leaders who know their subordinates will have an idea where to encourage them to develop. New subordinates can be observed under different task conditions to identify strengths and weaknesses to see how quickly they pick up new information and skills.

Leaders often conduct an initial assessment before they take over a new position. They ask themselves questions: how competent are new subordinates? what is expected in the new job? Leaders review the organization's standing operating procedure and any regulations that apply as well as status reports and recent inspection results. They meet with the outgoing leader and ask for an assessment and meet with key people outside the organization. Leaders listen carefully as everyone sees things through personal filters. .They reflect and realize initial that their impressions may still be off base. Good leaders update in-depth assessments with assumption of new duty positions since a thorough assessment assists in implementing changes gradually and systematically without causing damaging organizational turmoil.

To objectively assess subordinates, leaders do the following:

- Observe and record subordinates' performance in the core leader competencies
- Determine if the performances meet, exceed, or fall below expected standards
- Tell subordinates what was observed and give an opportunity to comment
- Help subordinates develop an individual development plan (IDP) to improve performance

Good leaders provide honest feedback to others, discussing strengths and areas for improvement. Effective assessment results in an IDP designed to correct weaknesses and sustain strengths. Here is what is required to move from planning to results:

- Design the individual development plan together, but let the subordinate take the lead
- Agree on the required actions to improve leader performance in the core leader competencies. Subordinates must buy into this plan if it is going to work.
- Review the plan frequently, check progress, and modify the plan if necessary

B. Developing On the Job

The best development opportunities often occur on the job. Leaders who have an eye for developing others will encourage growth in current roles and positions. How a leader assigns tasks and duties can serve as a way to direct individual Soldiers or civilians to extend their capabilities. The Army civilian intern program is an excellent example of this type of training. Feedback from a leader during routine duty assignments can also direct subordinates to areas where they can focus their development. Some leaders constantly seek new ways to re-define duties or enrich a job to prepare subordinates for additional responsibilities in their current position or next assignment. Cross training on tasks provides dual benefits of building a more robust team and expanding the skill set of team members. Challenging subordinates with different job duties is a good way to keep them interested in routine work.

C. Supporting Professional and Personal Growth

Preparing self and subordinates to lead aims at the goal of developing multiskilled leaders—leader pentathletes. The adaptable leader will more readily comprehend the challenges of a constantly evolving strategic environment, demanding not only warfighting skills, but also creativity and a degree of diplomacy combined with multicultural sensitivity. To achieve this balance, the Army creates positive learning environments at all levels to support its lifelong learning strategy.

As a lifelong learning institution, the Army addresses the differences between operations today and in the future and continuously develops enhanced training and leader development capabilities. Army leaders who look at their experiences and learn from them will find better ways of doing things. It takes openness and imagination to create an effective organizational learning environment. Do not be afraid to make mistakes. Instead, stay positive and learn from those mistakes. Leaders must remain confident in their own and their subordinates' ability to make learning the profession of arms a lifelong commitment. This attitude will allow growth into new responsibilities and adapt to inevitable changes.

Leaders who have the interest of others and the organization in mind will fully support available developmental opportunities, nominate and encourage subordinates for those opportunities, help remove barriers to capitalize on opportunities, and see that the new knowledge and skills can be reinforced once they are back on the job.

D. Helping People Learn

In any developmental relationship, the leader can adopt special ways to help others learn. It is the leader's responsibility to help subordinates to learn. Certain instructions clearly help people learn. Explain why a subject is important. Leaders show how it will help individuals and the organization perform better and actively involve subordinates in the learning process. For instance, never try to teach someone how to drive a vehicle with classroom instruction alone. Ultimately, the person has to get behind the wheel. To keep things interesting, keep lectures to a minimum and maximize hands-on training.

Learning from actual experience is not always possible. Leaders cannot have every experience in training. They substitute for that by taking advantage of what others have learned and getting the benefit without having the personal experience. Leaders should also share their experiences with subordinates during counseling, coaching, and mentoring, such as combat veterans sharing experiences with Soldiers who have not been to war.

E. Counseling, Coaching and Mentoring

Leaders have three principal ways of developing others. They can provide others with knowledge and feedback through counseling, coaching, and mentoring:

- **Counseling**—occurs when a leader, who serves as a subordinate's designated rater, reviews with the subordinate his demonstrated performance and potential, often in relation to a programmed performance evaluation.
- **Coaching**—the guidance of another's person's development in new or existing skills during the practice of those skills.
- **Mentoring**—a leader with greater experience than the one receiving the mentoring provides guidance and advice; it is a future-oriented developmental activity focused on growing in the profession.

Note: Counseling, Coaching and Mentoring are covered in detail in Chap. 4, pp. 4-1 to 4-24.

F. Building Team Skills and Processes

The national cause, the purpose of the mission, and many other concerns may not be visible from the Soldier's perspective on the battlefield. Regardless of larger issues, Soldiers perform for the other people in the squad or section, for others on the team or crew, for the person on their right or left. It is a fundamental truth, born from the Warrior Ethos. Soldiers get the job done because they do not want to let their friends down. Similarly, Army civilians feel part of the installation and organizational team and want to be winners.

Developing close teams takes hard work, patience, and interpersonal skill on the part of the leader. It is a worthwhile investment because good teams complete missions on time with given resources and a minimum of wasted effort. In combat, cohesive teams are the most effective and take the fewest casualties.

Characteristics of Teams
The hallmarks of close teams include—

- Trusting each other and being able to predict what each other will do
- Working together to accomplish the mission
- Executing tasks thoroughly and quickly
- Meeting and exceeding the standard
- Thriving on demanding challenges
- Learning from their experiences and developing pride in their accomplishments

The Army as a team includes many members who are not Soldiers. The contributions made by countless Army civilians, contractors, and multinational personnel in critical support missions during Operation Desert Storm, the Balkans, and the War on Terrorism are often forgotten. In today's logistic-heavy operational environments, many military objectives could not be achieved without the dedicated support of the Army's hard-working civilian team members.

Within a larger team, smaller teams may be at different stages of development. For instance, members of First Squad may be accustomed to working together. They trust one another and accomplish the mission, usually exceeding the standard without wasted effort. Second Squad in the same platoon just received three new Soldiers and a team leader from another company. As a team, Second Squad is less mature and it will take them some time to get up to the level of First Squad. Second Squad's new team members have to learn how things work. First, they have to feel like members of the team. Subsequently, they must learn the standards and the climate of their new unit and demonstrate competence before other members really accept them. Finally, they must practice working together. Leaders can best oversee the integration process if they know what to expect.

Competent leaders are sensitive to the characteristics of the team and its individual members. Teams develop differently and the boundaries between stages are not hard and fast. The results can help determine what to expect of the team and what is needed to improve its capabilities.

Stages of Team Building

Ref: FM 6-22 Army Leadership, pp. 8-16 to 8-18.

Teams do not come together by accident. Leaders must guide them through three developmental stages:

Developing

1 **The Formation Stage**

2 **The Development Stage**

3 **The Sustainment Stage**

Ref: FM 6-22, p. 8-16.

1. Formation Stage (see also p. 2-26)

Teams work best when new members quickly feel a part of the team. The two critical steps of the formation stage—reception and orientation—are dramatically different in peace and war. In combat, a good sponsorship process can literally make the difference between life and death for new arrivals and to the entire team.

Reception is the leader's welcome to the organization. Time permitting; it should include a handshake and personal introduction. The orientation stage begins with meeting other team members, learning the layout of the workplace, learning the schedule, and generally getting to know the environment. In combat, leaders may not have much time to spend with new members. In this case, a sponsor is assigned to new arrivals. That person will help them get oriented until they "know the ropes." In combat, Army leaders have countless things to worry about and the mental state of new arrivals might seem low on the list. If Soldiers cannot fight, the unit will suffer needless casualties and may ultimately fail to complete the mission. Discipline and shared hardships pull people together in powerful ways.

2. Enrichment Stage (see also p. 1-36)

New teams and new team members gradually move from questioning everything to trusting themselves, their peers, and their leaders. Leaders learn to trust by listening, following up on what they hear, establishing clear lines of authority, and setting standards. By far the most important thing a leader does to strengthen the team is training. Training takes a group of individuals and molds them into a team while preparing them to accomplish their missions. Training occurs during all three stages of team building, but is particularly important during enrichment. It is at this point that the team is building collective proficiency.

3. Sustainment Stage (see also p. 3-2)

During this stage, members identify with "their team." They own it, have pride in it, and want the team to succeeed. At this stage, team members will do what is necessary without being told. Every new mission gives the leader a chance to strengthen the bonds and challenge the team to reach for new heights of accomplishment. The leader develops his subordinates because he knows they will be tomorrow's team leaders. The team should continuously train so that it maintains proficiency in the collective and individual tasks it must perform to accomplish its missions.

Formation Stage

Stage	Subordinate Actions	Leader/Organization Actions
General Team Building	■ Learn about team purpose, tasks and standards ■ Learn about leaders and other members ■ Achieve belonging and acceptance	■ Design effective reception and orientation ■ Create learning experiences ■ Communicate expectations ■ Listen to and care for subordinates ■ Reward positive contributions ■ Set example
General Team Building	■ Adjust to uncertainty across the spectrum of conflict ■ Cope with fear of unknown injury and death ■ Adjust to separation from home and family	■ Talk with each Soldier ■ Reassure with calm presence ■ Communicate vital safety tips ■ Provide stable situation ■ Establish buddy system ■ Help Soldiers deal with immediate problems

Enrichment Stage

Stage	Subordinate Actions	Leader/Organization Actions
General Team Building	■ Trust leaders and other members ■ Cooperate with team members ■ Share information ■ Accept the way things are done ■ Adjust to feelings about how things ought to be done	■ Trust and encourage trust ■ Reinforce desired group norms ■ Establish clear lines of authority ■ Establish individual and unit goals ■ Identify and grow leaders ■ Train as a unit for mission ■ Build pride through accomplishment
Team Building for Deployments	■ Demonstrate competence ■ Become a team member ■ Learn about the threat ■ Learn about the area of operations ■ Avoid life-threatening mistakes	■ Demonstrate competence ■ Prepare as a unit for operations ■ Know the Soldiers ■ Provide stable unit climate ■ Emphasize safety for improved readiness

Sustainment Stage

Stage	Subordinate Actions	Leader/Organization Actions
General Team Building	■ Trust others ■ Share ideas and feelings freely ■ Assist other team members ■ Sustain trust and confidence ■ Share missions and values	■ Demonstrate trust ■ Focus on teamwork, training and maintaining ■ Respond to subordinate problems ■ Devise more challenging training ■ Build pride and spirt
Team Building for Deployments	■ Adjust to continuous operations ■ Cope with casualties ■ Adjust to enemy actions ■ Overcome boredom ■ Avoid rumors ■ Control fear, anger, despair and panic	■ Observe and enforce sleep discipline ■ Sustain safety awareness ■ Inform Soldiers ■ Know and deal with Soldiers' perceptions ■ Keep Soldiers productively busy ■ Use in-process reviews (IPRs) and after action reviews (AARs) ■ Act decisively in face of panic

Ref: FM 6-22, fig. 8-1, p. 8-17.

Lead, Develop, Achieve

Leader Training and Leader Development Action Plan

Ref: FM 7-1 Battle Focused Training, app. A, pp. A-6 to A-8.

The leader training and leader development action plan consists of three phases: reception and integration, basic competency development, and leader development and sustainment.

1. Reception and Integration Phase

Prior to the arrival of new leaders, the commander or key NCOs review the officer record brief (ORB) or the enlisted record brief (ERB) and DA Form 2-1 (Personnel Qualification Record-Part II). The commander or CSM/1SG interviews the new leader as soon as the leader arrives to define the training and developmental requirements clearly. They discuss the leader's assigned duty position, previous experience, training, education, personal desires, and possible future assignments.

In addition to the records review and interview, the commander or CSM/1SG may use a diagnostic test to identify the new leader's strengths and weaknesses. Units also use training programs to ensure that leaders are trained to the Army standard to serve in potentially hazardous and high-impact leadership positions. An example is certifying a leader to perform the duties of a range OIC or NCOIC. The information gathered is used to design a formal training and developmental program tailored to the individual.

2. Basic Competency Training Phase

The leader then progresses to the second phase of the program, the basic competency training phase. This phase occurs within the first few months. It ensures that the new leader attains a minimum acceptable level of competency in the critical skills and tasks necessary to perform the mission. The responsibility for this phase lies with the rater, assisted by other key officers and NCOs in the unit.

3. Leader Development and Training Sustainment Phase

The last phase is the leader development and training sustainment phase. This phase involves sustaining those tasks already mastered and developing proficiency in new competencies. The commander develops the leader by using additional duty assignments, and technical and professional courses to broaden the leader's perspective and skills for future duties.

Also during this phase, the leader starts a self-development program. It is designed with the assistance of the commander and senior NCOs. Together, they prioritize self-development goals and determine courses of action to improve individual performance. Self-development starts with a competency-based assessment of previously acquired skills, knowledge, and experience. The leader then identifies his or her strengths, weaknesses, and development needs. Goals are categorized into near-term, short-range, and long-range actions and efforts. Near-term goals are remedial and focus on correcting weaknesses that adversely affect performance of current duty assignment requirements. Short-range goals focus on acquiring skills, knowledge, and experience needed for the next operational assignment. Long-range goals focus on preparing soldiers and leaders for more complex duties beyond their next operational assignment.

Future assignments are important in a leader's action plan. The commander uses assigned duties to assess performance and provide junior leaders with the experience and feedback required for professional and personal development. The commander should know his or her leaders so well that the commander can identify when they have mastered their current assignment responsibilities and either increase their responsibilities, expose them to developmental activities, or move them to positions of greater responsibility, as appropriate.

III. Achieving

Ref: FM 6-22 Army Leadership, part 3, chap 9.

Leadership builds effective organizations. Effectiveness is most directly related to the core leader competency of getting results. From the definition of leadership, achieving is focused on accomplishing the mission. Mission accomplishment is a goal that must co-exist with an extended perspective towards maintaining and building up the organization's capability for the future. Achieving begins in the short term by setting objectives. In the long term, achieving based on clear vision requires getting results in pursuit of those objectives. Getting results is focused on structuring what needs to be done so results are consistently produced. This competency focuses on the organization of how to achieve those results.

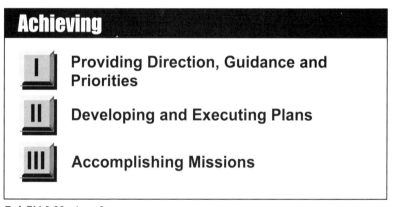

Achieving

I — **Providing Direction, Guidance and Priorities**

II — **Developing and Executing Plans**

III — **Accomplishing Missions**

Ref: FM 6-22, chap. 9.

I. Providing Direction, Guidance & Priorities

As leaders operate in larger organizations, their purpose, direction, guidance, and priorities typically become forward-looking and wider in application. Direct level leaders and small unit commanders usually operate with less time for formal planning than organizational and strategic level leaders. Although leaders use different techniques for guidance depending on the amounts of time and staff available, the basics are the same.

Whether operating with an infantry squad, a finance section, or an engineer team, leaders will match their teams, units, or organizations to the work required. Most work is defined by standard operating procedures and tasks assigned to groups. As new tasks develop and priorities change, assignments will differ. In higher-level positions, commanders and directors have others to help perform these assignment and prioritization functions. Higher-level organizations also have procedures such as running estimates and the military decisionmaking process.

Leaders should provide guidance from both near-term and long-term perspectives. Good leaders make thoughtful trade-offs between providing too much or too little guidance. A near-term focus is based on critical actions that must be accomplished immediately. In contrast, by delegating as much as possible, leaders prepare others to handle future tasks competently and are available for higher-level coordination.

When tasks are difficult, adaptive leaders identify and account for the capabilities of the team. Some tasks will be routine and will require little clarification from the leader, while others will present new challenges for the knowledge and experience that the team has. When a new task is undertaken for the first time working with a new group, leaders are alert to group organization, their capabilities, and their commitment to the task.

Leaders should provide frequent feedback as an embedded, natural part of the work. While it is important to have set periods for developmental performance counseling, it is also important to provide feedback on a regular basis. Making feedback part of the normal performance of work is a technique leaders use to guide how duties are accomplished.

Often the most challenging of the leader's jobs is to identify and clarify conflicts in followers' roles and responsibilities. Good communication techniques with brief backs are useful for identifying conflicts. Role differences may arise during execution and should be resolved by the leader as they occur.

Good guidance depends on understanding how tasks are progressing, so the leader knows if and when to provide clarification. Most workers have a desire to demonstrate competence in their work, so leaders need to be careful that they do not reduce this drive.

II. Developing and Executing Plans

A plan is a proposal for executing a command decision or project. Planning is the means by which the leader or commander envisions a desired outcome and lays out effective ways of achieving it. In the plan, the leader communicates his vision, intent and decisions and focuses his subordinates on the results he expects to achieve (FM 3-0).

In daily peacetime or combat training and operations, a leader's primary responsibility is to help the organization function effectively. The unit must accomplish the mission despite any surrounding chaos. This all begins with a well thought out plan and thorough preparation.

A. Planning

Leaders use planning to ensure that an approach for reaching goals will be practical. Planning reduces confusion, builds subordinates' confidence in themselves and their organization, and allows flexibility to adjust to changing situations. Good planning boosts shared understanding and ensures that a mission is accomplished with a minimum of wasted effort and fewer casualties in combat. FM 6-0 discusses the different types of plans in more detail.

Note: See facing page (3-35) for further discussion on planning.

B. Preparing

Preparation complements planning. Doctrinally, preparation for combat includes plan refinement, rehearsals, reconnaissance, coordination, inspections, and movement. See FM 3-0 and FM 6-0 for more information. In all cases, preparation includes detailed coordination with other organizations involved or affected by the operation or project. In the case of a nontactical requirement, preparation may include ensuring the necessary facilities (for example, hospitals, labs, maintenance shops) and other resources (for example, firefighters, police, and other first responders) are available to support the mission.

Planning

Ref: FM 6-22 Army Leadership, pp. 9-2 to 9-3.

Leaders use planning to ensure that an approach for reaching goals will be practical. Planning reduces confusion, builds subordinates' confidence in themselves and their organization, and allows flexibility to adjust to changing situations. Good planning boosts shared understanding and ensures that a mission is accomplished with a minimum of wasted effort and fewer casualties in combat. FM 6-0 discusses the different types of plans in more detail.

Considering Intended and Unintended Consequences

Plans and the actions taken in those plans will most likely have unintended, as well as intended, consequences. Leaders should think through what they can expect to happen because of a plan or course of action. Some decisions may set off a chain of events that are contrary to the desired effects. Intended consequences are the anticipated results of a leader's decisions and actions. Unintended consequences arise from unplanned events that affect the organization or accomplishment of the mission. Intended and unintended consequences can best be addressed during wargaming and rehearsals that are critical during planning. The aim of wargaming and rehearsals is to reduce the unintended consequences to as few as possible.

Even lower-level leaders' actions may have effects well beyond what they expect. Thinking ahead about intended consequences and beyond to unintended consequences serves to sharpen what is important in the planning process. In this checkpoint example, the intended consequences of conducting an effective and secure operation might be foiled if vehicle drivers are not properly warned of the checkpoint. Are there signs in the appropriate language to demand a slow approach speed? Are there speed bumps to force a slow-go approach? Is the traffic properly funneled to prevent a bypass or escape? If these and other measures are not considered and implemented, the unintended consequences could include accidentally engaging vehicles carrying innocent civilians because of possible driver reactions that might be misinterpreted as hostile behavior.

Sometimes consequences are not direct and immediate. These types of consequences are referred to as second- and third-order effects. These effects can be intended or unintended. However, second- and third-order effects should not be the basis for hindering initiative or doing the right thing.

Reverse Planning

Reverse planning is a specific technique used to ensure that a concept leads to the intended end state. It begins with the goal or desired mission outcome in mind. The start point is the question: "Where do I want to end up?" From there, think and work the plan backwards to the current situation. While following the thought process from projected goal to current position, establish the basics steps along the way and determine the who, what, when, where, and why to accomplish the goal.

While planning, leaders consider the amount of time needed to coordinate and conduct each step. After determining what must happen on the way to the goal, leaders put the tasks in logical sequence, set clear priorities, and determine a realistic time line. They examine all steps required in the order they will occur and if time permits solicit input from subordinates. Experienced subordinates can often provide a valuable reality check for the plan. Subordinates' input also shows their part-ownership of the plan. Positively contributing builds trust while boosting their self-confidence and will to succeed.

A rehearsal is a critical element of preparation. It allows everyone involved in a mission to develop a mental picture of responsibilities and what should happen. It helps the team synchronize operations at times and places critical to successful mission accomplishment. FM 6-0 features a detailed appendix on rehearsals. Rehearsing key combat actions allows subordinates to see how things are supposed to work and builds confidence in the plan. Even a simple walk-through helps leaders visualize who is supposed to be at a specific location to perform a coordinated action at a certain time. Leaders can see how things might unfold, what might go wrong, and how the plan could change to adjust for intended or unintended consequences.

C. Executing

Successful execution of a plan is based on all the work that has gone before. Executing for success requires situational understanding, supervising task completion, assessing progress, and implementing required execution or adjustment decisions (FM 6-0).

Executing in combat means putting a plan into action by applying combat power to accomplish the mission and using situational understanding to assess progress and make execution and adjustment decisions. In combat, leaders strive to effectively integrate and synchronize all elements of the joint and combined arms team as well as nonmilitary assets. The goal is to assign specific tasks or objectives to the most capable organization and empowering its leaders to execute and exercise initiative within the given intent.

Planning execution involves awareness of whether critical tasks are being accomplished on the way to mission completion. Good leaders know which of the most important parts of the mission to check. Knowing from actual experience what makes missions difficult or unsuccessful aids in tracking mission progress. Guiding progress toward mission accomplishment involves scheduling activities, tracking tasks and suspenses, alerting others when their support will be required, and making adjustments as required.

Adapting to Changes

Competent and realistic leaders also keep in mind that friction and uncertainty can and will always affect plans; generally, no plan survives initial contact with the enemy. The leader must therefore be prepared to replace portions of the original plan with new ideas and initiatives. Leaders must have the confidence and resilience to fight through setbacks, staying focused on the intent two levels up and the mission. Leaders preserve freedom of action by adapting to changing situations. They should be in a position to keep their people mission-focused, motivated, and able to react with agility to changes while influencing the team to accomplish the mission as envisioned in the plan.

Adjustments are needed when facing obstacles that were not anticipated. In increasingly busy times, leaders need to provide an environment in which subordinates can focus and accomplish critical tasks. Minimizing and preventing distractions allows subordinates to pay full attention to mission accomplishment. Leaders need to ensure that additional taskings are within the capabilities of the unit or organization. If they are not, the leader needs to seek relief by going to superiors and clarify the impact that the additional workload has on the unit. Experienced leaders anticipate cyclical workloads and schedule accordingly. Competent leaders will make good decisions about when to press Soldiers and civilians and when to ease back and narrow focus on the one or two most important tasks if performance is in decline.

Leaders constantly scan what is going on in the work environment and the mission. With this awareness of the situation, the leader will recognize when the situation has changed or when the plan is not achieving the desired effects. If the situation changes significantly, leaders will consider options for proceeding, including the review of any contingencies that were developed to deal with new circumstances. Leaders make on-the-spot adjustments in the course of action to keep moving toward designated goals.

Managing Resources

A main responsibility of leaders—whether officers, NCOs, or Army civilians—is to accomplish the assigned mission, which includes making the best use of available resources. Some Army leaders specialize in managing single categories of re-sources, such as ammunition, food, personnel, and finances, but all leaders have an interest in overseeing that all categories of resources are provided and used wisely by their teams.

Managing resources consists of multiple steps that require different approaches and even different skills. In many cases, Army leaders need to acquire needed resources for themselves or others. Resources can take the form of money, materiel, person-nel, and time. The acquisition process can be a relatively straightforward process of putting in a request through proper channels. Other times a leader may need to be more creative and resourceful. In such cases, the effective use of influence tactics (see Chapter 7) will likely be instrumental in successfully acquiring needed resources.

After resources have been acquired, leaders are responsible for allocating them in an impartial manner that recognizes different needs and priorities. A leader may have multiple requests for limited resources and will need to make decisions about the best distribution of resources. Doing so in a way that recognizes and resolves potential ethical dilemmas requires a firm grounding in the Army Values. Ultimately, a leader must decide how to best allocate resources in ways to meet the Army's mis-sion. Leaders need to deal openly and honestly with their allocation decisions and be prepared to handle reactions from those who may feel that their requests were not handled fairly or effectively.

Leaders should evaluate if the limited resources were used wisely and effectively. Do the resources advance the mission of the Army and the organization? Conversely, were the resources squandered or used in ways that did not enhance the effective-ness of the individual, unit, or the Army as a whole? In cases in which resources were not used wisely, a leader should follow this evaluation with appropriate coun-seling for those who are accountable for the resources in question.

III. Accomplishing Missions

A critical element of getting results is adopting measures that support a capability for consistent accomplishment. Achieving consistent results hinges on doing all the right things addressed by the other competencies—having a clear vision, taking care of people, setting the right example, building up the organization, encouraging leader growth, and so on. Consistent performance can be achieved by using techniques to—

- Monitor collective performance
- Reinforce good performance
- Implement systems to improve performance

A. Monitoring Performance

The ability to assess a situation accurately and reliably against desired outcomes, established values, and ethical standards is a critical tool for leaders to achieve consistent results and mission success. Assessment occurs continually during planning, preparation, and execution; it is not solely an after-the-fact evaluation. Accurate assessment requires instinct and intuition based on experience and learning. It also demands a feel for the reliability and validity of information and its sources. Periodic assessment is necessary to determine organizational weaknesses and prevent mishaps. Accurately determining causes is essential to training management, developing subordinate leadership, and initiating quality improvements.

1. Assessment Techniques

There are many different ways to gather information for assessment purposes. These include asking team members questions to find out if information is getting to them, meeting people to inquire if tasks and objectives are appropriate, and checking for plan synchronization. Assessing can also involve researching and analyzing electronic databases. No matter which techniques the leader explores, it is important that information be verified as accurate.

Although staff and key subordinates manage and process information for organizational and strategic leaders, this does not relieve them from the responsibility of analyzing information as part of the decision-making process. Often, leaders draw information from various sources to be able to compare the information and create a multidimensional picture. Often, leaders accomplish this by sending out liaison officers thoroughly familiar with their commander's intent as their eyes and ears.

While personal presence and the eyes and ears deliver much useful information, leaders can also exploit technologies for the purpose of timely assessment. In the world of digital command and control, commanders can set various command and control systems to monitor the status of key units, selected enemy parameters, and critical planning and execution time lines. They may establish prompts in the information systems that warn of selected critical events. Information systems may provide alerts about low fuel levels in maneuver units, tight management time lines among aviation crews, or massing enemy artillery. Management information systems in institutional settings may track the amount of email or new documents created.

It is sometimes dangerous to be too analytical when dealing with automated information or limited amounts of time. When analyzing information, leaders should guard against rigidity, impatience, or overconfidence that may bias their analysis.

2. Designing an Effective Assessment System

The first step in designing an effective assessment system is to determine the purpose of the assessment. While purposes vary, most fall into one of the following categories:

- Evaluate progress toward organizational goals, such as using an emergency deployment readiness exercise to check unit readiness or monitoring progress of units through stages of reception, staging, onward movement, and integration

- Evaluate the efficiency of a system: the ratio of the resources expended to the results gained, such as comparing the amount of time spent performing maintenance to the organization's readiness rate

- Evaluate the effectiveness of a system: the quality of the results it produces, such as analyzing the variation in Bradley gunnery scores
- Compare the relative efficiency or effectiveness against standards
- Compare the behavior of individuals in a group with the prescribed standards, such as Army physical fitness test or gunnery scores
- Evaluate systems supporting the organization, such as following up "no pay dues" to see what the NCO support channel did about them

While systems and leader proxies can greatly assist in assessing organizational performance, the leader remains central by spot-checking people, performance, equipment, and resources. Leaders adopt best business practices, use performance indicators to check things, and ensure the organization meets standards while moving toward the goals the leader has established.

While assessing, good leaders find opportunities to engage in impromptu coaching. Junior leaders can learn spot-checking by watching experienced first sergeants or command sergeants major observe daily training or conduct uniform inspections. Pay attention to how these experienced leaders' eyes sweep across Soldiers, weapons, and equipment and note discrepancies and successes. It demonstrates how experience makes supervising, inspecting, and correcting becomes a routine part of daily duties.

B. Reinforcing Good Performance

To accomplish missions consistently leaders need to maintain motivation among the team. One of the best ways to do this is to recognize and reward good performance. Leaders who recognize individual and team accomplishments will shape positive motivation and actions for the future. Recognizing individuals and teams in front of superiors and others gives those contributors an increased sense of worth. Soldiers and civilians who feel their contributions are valued are encouraged to sustain and improve performance.

Leaders should not overlook giving credit to subordinates. Sharing credit has enormous payoffs in terms of building trust and motivation for future actions. A leader who understands how individuals feel about team accomplishments will have a better basis for motivating individuals based on their interests.

C. Improving Organizational Performance

High performing units are learning organizations that take advantage of opportunities to improve performance. Leaders need to encourage a performance improvement mindset that allows for conformity but goes beyond meeting standards to strive for increased efficiencies and effectiveness. Several actions are characteristic of performance improvement:

- Ask incisive questions about how tasks can be performed better
- Anticipate the need for change and action
- Analyze activities to determine how desired end states are achieved or affected
- Identify ways to improve unit or organizational procedures
- Consider how information and communication technologies can improve effectiveness
- Model critical and creative thinking and encourage it from others

Too often, leaders unknowingly discourage ideas. As a result, subordinates become less inclined to approach leaders with new ideas for doing business. From their viewpoint leaders respond to subordinates' ideas with reactions about what is and is not desired. This can be perceived as closed-mindedness and under-appreciation of the Soldier's or civilian's insight. "We've tried that before." "There's no budget for that." "You've misunderstood my request." "Don't rock the boat." These phrases can kill initiative and discourage others from even thinking about changes to improve the organization. Leaders need to encourage a climate of reflection about the organization and encourage ideas for improvement. The concept of lifelong learning applies equally to the collective organization as well as to the individual.

IV. Competencies Applied for Success

Lead, Develop, Achieve

Army history has many examples of units succeeding in accomplishing their mission consistently and ethically because of competent, multiskilled leaders. Achieving results consistently and ethically does not merely pertain to combat or military leadership. Competent military and civilian leaders pursue excellence wherever and whenever possible.

Competent leaders ensure that all organization members know the important roles they play every day. They look for everyday examples occurring under ordinary circumstances: how a Soldier digs a fighting position, prepares for guard duty, fixes a radio, or lays an artillery battery; or how an Army civilian improves maintenance procedures, processes critical combat supplies, and supports the families of deploying service members. Competent leaders know each of these people is contributing in an important way to the Army mission. They appreciate the fact that to accomplish the Army's mission with consistency and ethics, it requires a collection of countless teams, performing countless small tasks to standard every day.

Competent leaders are also realists. They understand that excellence in leadership does not mean perfection. On the contrary, competent leaders allow subordinates room to learn from their mistakes as well as their successes. In an open and positive work climate, people excel to improve and accept calculated risks to learn. It is the best way to improve the force and the only way to develop confident leaders for the future. Competent and confident leaders tolerate honest mistakes that do not result from negligence, because achieving organizational excellence is not a game to reach perfection. It involves trying, learning, trying again, and getting better each time. However, even the best efforts and good intentions cannot take away an individual's responsibility for their own actions.

At the end of the day or a career, Soldier and Army civilian leaders can look back confidently that their efforts have created an Army of consistent excellence. Whether they commanded an invasion force of thousands or supervised a technical support section of three people, they made a positive difference.

IV. Influences on Leadership

Ref: FM 6-22 Army Leadership, part 3, chap 10.

Each day as a leader brings new challenges. Some of these challenges are predictable based on experiences. Some are unpredictable, surfacing because of a situation or place in time in which Soldiers find themselves. Leaders must be prepared to face the effects of stress, fear in combat, external influences from the media, the geopolitical climate, and the impact of changing technology.

Some of these factors are mitigated through awareness, proper training, and open and frank discussion. The Army must consider these external influences and plan accordingly. An effective leader recognizes the tools needed to adapt in changing situations.

I. Challenges of the Operating Environment

A. Adapting to Evolving Threats

America's Army of the 21st century must adapt to constantly evolving threats while taking advantage of the latest technological innovations and adjusting to societal changes.

The National Military Strategy

As part of the United States Armed Forces, the Army is guided by a broader National Military Strategy outlining how to—

- Protect the United States
- Prevent conflict and surprise attacks
- Prevail against adversaries threatening our homeland, deployed forces, or allies and friends

The National Military Strategy also sets priorities for success and changes with each administration and addresses new challenges our country faces. The uncertain nature of the threat will always have major impact on Army leadership. For the Army, a new era began in 1989 with the fall of the Berlin Wall and the subsequent collapse of the Soviet Union. Since 11 September 2001, the War on Terrorism has become America's main effort and long-term security focus. In addition to adapting to evolving issues, U.S. forces must also remain capable to conduct full spectrum operations. This mandates that the Army, as an essential component of America's war effort, be fully capable of seamless shifts across the spectrum of conflict. This blurring of the lines between war and peace make the challenges that leaders face constant and unpredictable.

Agility and adaptability at all leadership levels of Army organizations are becoming more important to address situations that cannot be fully anticipated. In the new operational environment, the importance of direct leaders— noncommissioned officers and junior officers—making the right decisions in stressful situations has taken on a new significance. Decisions and actions taken by direct-level leaders—the sergeants and lieutenants carrying out the missions—can easily have major strategic-level and political implications.

U.S. forces in Afghanistan and Iraq have experienced many situations requiring a balanced application of tactical and diplomatic measures. In most of these tactical confrontations, junior leaders ensure mission accomplishment by reacting appropriately and within the bounds of their commanders' intent.

B. The Influence of the Media

Another influence on leadership is the media. The media can be both an asset and impediment to the leader. Embedded media, like those during Operation Iraqi Freedom, can tell the story from the Soldier's perspective to an anxious Nation back home. The media can provide real-time information, sometimes unfiltered and raw, which the enemy could exploit as a means to change the regional political climate.

Leaders must ensure subordinate leaders and Soldiers are trained to deal with the media and understand the long-term effects of specific stories and images. The morale of those serving and the Nation may be affected if the overall view presented by the media is overly negative or that military actions are in vain. These can adversely impact recruiting, retention, and the treatment of veterans for years to follow. Leaders can counter-act negatives by using media opportunities to explain how the Army mission serves national interests and how Soldiers dedicate themselves to accomplishing the mission.

C. Multicomponent and Joint Environment

Soldiers find themselves serving with members of other Services, the Reserve Components, and other countries' forces more than ever before. Understanding the unique cultures and subcultures of these various groups can be essential to success in a volatile and changing world.

Leaders must be aware that while most of the policies and regulations for Soldiers apply across the board, specific differences apply in the promotion, pay, benefit, and retirement systems of the Reserve Components. Knowledge of the differences is essential for effectively employing all components.

Within the Army, leaders should recognize the existence of subcultures such as the special operations, law enforcement, medical, and branch-specific communities. Members of these subcultures cross components and Services during their careers for specific assignments. Consequently, leaders involved in conducting operations need to understand how members of these specialized units train and work. Often, they approach missions from a different perspective and sometimes use unconventional methods to accomplish them. Special operations forces usually operate in small, independent teams and frequently interface with local civilians and members of other governmental agencies. For operational reasons, they may not be required to disclose routine information about their units like conventional forces. Logisticians and operations planners may need innovative solutions to provide special operations forces autonomy while allowing the joint task force or other commanders to maintain visibility and control over these assets and to provide the special operators the logistical support necessary.

Other subcultures, such as law enforcement, follow norms established by their branches and share experiences developed through specific assignments and schools. These functional subcultures can be useful as a means to exchange knowledge and provide corporate solutions when the Army needs answers from subject matter experts.

D. The Geopolitical Situation

Though the world continues to become more connected by technology and economic growth, it remains very diverse and divided by religions, cultures, living conditions, education, and health. Within the political sphere of influence, maintaining our presence in foreign countries through a careful mix of diplomatic and military arrangements remains an important challenge. Leaders must be aware that the balance between diplomacy and military power is fragile. Army leaders must consistently consider the impact on local civilians, as well as on cultural and religious treasures, prior to committing firepower.

Tomorrow's leaders will be expected to operate in many different environments worldwide. While most Soldiers speak English as their first language, continued deployments and global interaction will require an understanding of other languages and cultures. Forecasts predict the Chinese, Hindu, Arabic, and Spanish languages will gain speakers in the years to come. Leaders will need to become multilingual and study the cultures and histories of other regions of interest. A vehicle for gaining this knowledge of the geopolitical situation is technology.

E. Changing with Technology

While the stresses of combat have been constant for centuries, another aspect of the human dimension has assumed increasing importance: the effect of rapid technological advances on organizations and people. Although military leaders have always dealt with the effect of technological changes, these changes are different from before. It is forcing the Army and its leaders to rethink and redesign itself.

Modern Army leaders must stay abreast of technological advances and learn about their applications, advantages, and requirements. Together with technical specialists, leaders can make technology work for the warrior. The right technology, properly integrated, will increase operational effectiveness, battlefield survivability, and lethality.

Technological challenges facing the Army leadership include—

- Learning the strengths and vulnerabilities of different technologies that support the team and its mission
- Thinking through how the organization will operate with other organizations that are less or more technologically complex, such as operating with joint, inter-Service, and multinational forces
- Considering the effect of technology on the? time available to analyze problems, make a decision, and act. Events happen faster today, and the stress encountered as an Army leader is correspondingly greater
- Leveraging technology to influence virtual teams given the increasing availability and necessity to use reach-back and split-based operations
- Virtual team refers to any team whose interactions are mediated by time, distance, or technology

Technology can also lead to operational issues. A growing reliance on the new global positioning system (GPS) navigation technology since the Desert Storm era decreased emphasis on manual land navigation skills in training, thus rendering forces more vulnerable if the technology fails or is wrongly programmed. Part of the leadership challenge became to determine how to exploit GPS technology while guarding against its weaknesses. The answer was improved training. It included reintroducing essential back-up land navigation training, emphasizing the availability of adequate battery supplies, and detailed instructions on the maintenance and operation of the GPS receiver equipment.

Leaders not on-site with the Soldiers must not discount the fear the Soldiers may be experiencing. A leader who does not share the same risks could easily fall into the trap of making a decision that could prove unworkable given the psychological state of the Soldiers. Army leaders with command and control over a distributed or virtual team should ask for detailed input from the Soldiers or subordinate commanders who are closer to the action and can provide the most accurate information about the situation.

Technology is changing the leadership environment in many aspects, especially the amount of information available for decision makers. Although advances in electronic data processing allow the modern leader to handle large amounts of information easier than ever before, a possible second-order effect of enhanced technology is information overload.

Too much information is as bad as not enough. Leaders must be able to sift through the information provided to them, analyze and synthesize it, and forward only the important data up the chain of command. Senior leaders rely on their subordinates to process information for them, isolating critical information to expedite decisions. Leaders owe it to their subordinates to design information gathering and reporting procedures that do not create more work for already stretched staffs and units.

F. Synchronizing Systems

Today's Army leaders require systems understanding and more technical and tactical knowledge than ever before. Leaders must be aware of the fine line between a healthy questioning of new systems' capabilities and an unreasonable hostility that rejects the advantages technology offers. The adaptable leader remains aware of the capabilities and shortcomings of advanced technology and ensures subordinates do as well.

All leaders must consider systems in their organization—how they work together, how using one affects the others, and how to get the best performance from the whole. They must think beyond their own organizations and consider how the actions of their organization can influence other organizations and the team as a whole.

Technology is also changing battlefield dispersal and the speed of operations. Instant global communications are accelerating the pace of military actions. GPS and night vision capabilities mean the Army can fight at night and during periods of limited visibility—conditions that used to slow things down. Additionally, nonlinear operations make it more difficult for commanders to determine critical points on the battlefield. (FM 3-0 discusses continuous operations.)

II. Stress in Combat

Combat is sudden, intense, and life threatening. It is the Soldier's job to kill in combat. Unfortunately, combat operations may involve the accidental killing of innocent men, women, and children. Soldiers are unsure how they will perform in combat until that moment comes. The stresses experienced in combat and even the stress preparing for, waiting for, and supporting combat can be substantial.

Leaders must understand this human dimension and anticipate Soldiers' reactions to stress. It takes mental discipline and resilience to overcome the plan going wrong, Soldiers becoming wounded or dying, and the enemy attacking unexpectedly.

Note: See pp. 3-46 to 3-47 for further discussion on stress in combat.

III. Stress in Training

It is still valid for the complex combat environment of the War on Terrorism: Training to high standards—using scenarios that closely resemble the stresses and effects of the real battlefield—is essential to victory and survival in combat.

Merely creating a situation for subordinates and having them react does not induce the kind of stress required for combat training. A meaningful and productive mission with detailed constraints and limitations and high standards of performance induces a basic level of stress. To reach a higher level of reality, leaders must add unanticipated conditions to the basic stress levels of training to create a demanding learning environment.

IV. Dealing with the Stress of Change

Since the end of the Cold War, the Army has gone through many changes—dramatic decreases in the number of Soldiers and Army civilians in all components, changes in assignment policies, base closings, new organizational structures, and a host of other shifts that put stress on Soldiers, Army civilians, and their families. Despite the Army's reduced personnel strength, deployments to conduct stability operations and to fight the spread of terrorism have increased considerably. While adapting to the changes, Army leaders continuously have to sustain the force and prepare the Soldiers of all components for the stresses of combat.

To succeed in an environment of continuous change, Army leaders emphasize the constants of the Army Values, teamwork, and discipline while helping their people anticipate change, adapt to change, and seek new ways to improve. Competent leadership implies managing change, adapting, and making it work for the entire team. Leaders determine what requires change. Often, it is better to build on what already exists to limit stress.

Stress will be a major part of the leadership environment, both in peace and war. Major sources of stress include an ever-changing geopolitical situation, combat stress and related fears, the rapid pace of change, and the increasing complexity of technology. A leader's character and professional competence are important factors in mitigating stress for the organization and achieving mission accomplishment, despite environmental pressures and changes. When dealing with these factors, adaptability is essential to success.

V. Tools for Adaptability

Adaptability is an individual's ability to recognize changes in the environment, identify the critical elements of the new situation, and trigger changes accordingly to meet new requirements. Adaptability is an effective change in behavior in response to an altered situation.

Adaptable leaders scan the environment, derive the key characteristics of the situation, and are aware of what it will take to perform in the changed environment. Leaders must be particularly observant for evidence that the environment has changed in unexpected ways. They recognize that they face highly adaptive adversaries, and operate within dynamic, ever-changing environments. Sometimes what happens in the same environment changes suddenly and unexpectedly from a calm, relatively safe operation to a direct fire situation. Other times environments differ (from a combat deployment to a humanitarian one) and adaptation is required for mind-sets and instincts to change.

Note: See p. 3-48, "Tools for Adaptability."

Stress in Combat

Ref: FM 6-22 Army Leadership, pp. 10-4 to 10-7.

Combat is sudden, intense, and life threatening. It is the Soldier's job to kill in combat. Unfortunately, combat operations may involve the accidental killing of innocent men, women, and children. Soldiers are unsure how they will perform in combat until that moment comes. The stresses experienced in combat and even the stress preparing for, waiting for, and supporting combat can be substantial.

Leaders must understand this human dimension and anticipate Soldiers' reactions to stress. It takes mental discipline and resilience to overcome the plan going wrong, Soldiers becoming wounded or dying, and the enemy attacking unexpectedly.

When preparing for war, leaders must thoroughly condition their Soldiers to deal with combat stress during all phases of operations—mobilization, deployment, sustainment, and redeployment. (See FM 6-22.5 for more on combat stress and FM 3-0 for descriptions of specific deployment phases.) The most potent countermeasures to confront combat stress and to reduce psychological breakdown in combat are—

- Admit that fear exists when in combat
- Ensure communication lines are open between leaders and subordinates
- Do not assume unnecessary risks
- Provide good, caring leadership
- Treat combat stress reactions as combat injuries
- Recognize the limits of a Soldier's endurance
- Openly discuss moral implications of behavior in combat
- Reward and recognize Soldiers and their families for personal sacrifices

Units are stabilized during mobilization and in preparation for deployment. Stabilization allows leaders and Soldiers to build a trust relationship while the unit undergoes rigorous combat skills certification or theater-specific training. Confidence in leaders, comrades, training, and equipment are key factors for combat success.

During initial deployment, units should be eased into the mission. A daytime operation could precede a night raid, for example. Training and drill can continue while leaders deepen a personable leader-to-led relationship with their Soldiers based on trust and not fear of rank and duty position.

During sustaining operations, units at all levels should discuss and absorb critical operations experiences and help individuals cope with initial combat stress. Soldiers can be encouraged to reveal their true feelings within their circle of warrior comrades. If the unit suffered casualties, leaders should openly discuss their status. In this phase, it is important to keep people informed about wounded and evacuated team members and to weigh the unit's losses and successes. Memorial services should be held to honor the fallen. Soldiers and leaders who do not succeed during operations should be retrained, counseled, or reassigned. The unit should be allocated appropriate rest periods between missions. Ensure Soldiers with serious issues have access to mental health professionals if necessary.

When preparing to redeploy, Soldiers should talk about their experiences. Leaders and commanders should be available first and refer or bring in backup like psychologists or chaplains when needed. During this phase, leaders must emphasize that Soldiers have an obligation to remain disciplined, just as they were during deployment. Soldiers must participate in provided reintegration screening and counseling. Leaders should stress that it is acceptable, and not shameful, to seek appropriate psychological help.

Once returned to their home station, organizations and units generally remain stabilized to further share common experiences before the individuals are released to new assignments. This can be difficult for returning Reserve Component forces that are often released very soon after redeployment.

When possible, Soldiers should have unfettered access to medical experts and chaplains to continue their physical and psychological recovery. Experts helping and treating the psychologically wounded must work hand-in-hand with the unit chain of command to stress the importance of maintaining good order and discipline. Aggressive or criminal behavior to compensate for wartime experiences is not tolerated.

The Army has implemented a comprehensive mental health recovery plan for all returning Soldiers to counter post-traumatic stress disorder. Sound leadership, unit cohesion, and close camaraderie are essential to assure expeditious psychological recovery from combat experiences.

A. Overcoming Fear in Battle

Leaders need to understand that danger and fear will always be a part of their job. Battling the effects of fear does not mean denying them. It means recognizing fear and effectively dealing with it. Fear is overcome by understanding the situation and acting with foresight and purpose to overcome it. Army leaders must expect fear to take hold when setbacks occur, the unit fails to complete a mission, or there are casualties. Fear can paralyze a Soldier. Strong leaders share the same risks with their Soldiers, but use competence and extensive training to gain their Soldiers' trust and loyalty. The sights and sounds of the modern battlefield are terrifying. So is fear of the unknown. Soldiers who see their friends killed or wounded suddenly have a greater burden—they become aware of their own mortality.

Combat leadership is a different type of leadership where leaders must know their profession, their Soldiers, and the tools of war. Direct leaders have to be strong tacticians and be able to make decisions and motivate Soldiers under horrific conditions. They must be able to execute critical warrior tasks and drills amidst noise, dust, explosions, confusion, and screams of the wounded and dying. They have to know how to motivate their Soldiers in the face of adversity.

B. The Warrior Mindset

It is important for Soldiers to acquire and maintain a warrior mindset when serving in harm's way. Resilience and the Warrior Ethos apply in more situations than those requiring physical courage. Sometimes leaders will have to carry on for long periods in very difficult situations. The difficulties Soldiers face may not only be ones of physical danger, but of great physical, emotional, and mental strain.

An essential part of the warrior mindset is discipline. Discipline holds a team together, while resilience, the Warrior Ethos, competence, and confidence motivate Soldiers to continue the mission against all odds. Raw physical courage causes Soldiers to charge a machine gun but resilience, discipline, and confidence backed by professional competence help them fight on when they are hopelessly outnumbered and living under appalling conditions.

Tools for Adaptability

Ref: FM 6-22 Army Leadership, pp. 10-8 to 10-9.

Adaptability is an individual's ability to recognize changes in the environment, identify the critical elements of the new situation, and trigger changes accordingly to meet new requirements.

Deciding when to adapt is as important as determining how to adapt. Adaptation does not produce certainty that change will improve results. Sometimes, persistence on a given course of action may have merit over change.

Adaptable leaders are comfortable with ambiguity. They are flexible and innovative—ready to face the challenges at hand with the resources available. The adaptable leader is most likely a passionate learner, able to handle multiple demands, shifting priorities and rapid change smoothly. Adaptable leaders see each change thrust upon them as an opportunity rather than a liability.

Adaptability has two key components:

- The ability of a leader to identify the essential elements critical for performance in each new situation
- The ability of a leader to change his practices or his unit by quickly capitalizing on strengths and minimizing weaknesses

Like self-awareness, adaptability takes effort. To become adaptable, leaders must challenge their previously held ideas and assumptions by seeking out situations that are novel and unfamiliar. Leaders who remain safely inside their comfort zone provided by their current level of education, training, and experience will never learn to recognize change or understand the inevitable changes in their environment. Adaptability is encouraged by a collection of thought habits. These include open-mindedness, ability to consider multiple perspectives, not jumping to conclusions about what a situation is or what it means, willingness to take risks, and being resilient to setbacks. To become more adaptable, leaders should—

- **Learn to adapt by adapting.** Leaders must go beyond what they are comfortable with and must get used to experiencing the unfamiliar through diverse and dynamic challenges. For example, the Army's best training uses thinking like an enemy to help leaders recognize and accept that no plan survives contact with the enemy. This encourages adaptive thinking. Adaptive training involves variety, particularly in training that may have become routine.

- **Lead across cultures.** Leaders must actively seek out diverse relationships and situations. Today's joint, interagency, and multinational assignments offer challenging opportunities to interact across cultures and gain insight into people who think and act differently than most Soldiers or average U.S. citizens. Leaders can grow in their capacity for adaptability by seizing such opportunities rather than avoiding them.

- **Seek challenges.** Leaders must seek out and engage in assignments that involve major changes in the operational environment. Leaders can be specialists, but their base of experience should still be broad. As the breadth of experience accumulates, so does the capacity to adapt. Leaders who are exposed to change and embrace new challenges will learn the value of adaptation. They carry forward the skills to develop adaptable Soldiers, civilians, units, and organizations.

While adaptability is an important tool, leaders at all levels must leverage their cognitive abilities to counteract the challenges of the operational environment through logical problem solving processes. FM 5-0 discusses these in detail.

Counseling, Coaching, Mentoring

Ref: FM 6-22 Army Leadership, pp. 8-11 to 8-15.

Leaders have three principal ways of developing others. They can provide others with knowledge and feedback through counseling, coaching, and mentoring:

Counseling-Coaching-Mentoring

Leaders have three principal ways of developing others. They can provide others with knowledge and feedback through counseling, coaching, and mentoring:

 Counseling

 Coaching

 Mentoring

Ref: FM 6-22, pp. 8-11 to 8-15.

I. Counseling

Counseling is central to leader development. Leaders who serve as designated raters have to prepare their subordinates to be better Soldiers or civilians. Good counseling focuses on the subordinate's performance and problems with an eye toward tomorrow's plans and solutions. The subordinate is expected to be an active participant who seeks constructive feedback. Counseling cannot be an occasional event but should be part of a comprehensive program to develop subordinates. With effective counseling, no evaluation report—positive or negative—should be a surprise. A consistent counseling program includes all subordinates, not just the people thought to have the most potential.

Counseling is the process used by leaders to review with a subordinate the subordinate's demonstrated performance and potential.

During counseling, subordinates are not passive listeners but active participants in the process. Counseling uses a standard format to help mentally organize and isolate relevant issues before, during, and after the counseling session. During counseling, leaders assist subordinates to identify strengths and weaknesses and create plans of action. To make the plans work, leaders actively support their subordinates throughout the implementation and assessment processes. Subordinates invest themselves in the process by being forthright in their willingness to improve and being candid in their assessment and goal setting.

Approaches to Counseling

Inexperienced leaders are sometimes uncomfortable when confronting a subordinate who is not performing to standard. Counseling is not about leader comfort; it is about correcting the performance or developing the character of a subordinate. To be effective counselors, Army leaders must demonstrate certain qualities: respect for subordinates, self-awareness, cultural awareness, empathy, and credibility.

One challenging aspect of counseling is selecting the proper approach for a specific situation. To counsel effectively, the technique used must fit the situation. Some cases may only require giving information or listening. A subordinate's improvement may call for just a brief word of praise. Other situations may require structured counseling followed by specific plans for actions. An effective leader approaches each subordinate as an individual. Counseling includes nondirective, directive, and combined approaches. The major difference between the approaches is the degree to which the subordinate participates and interacts during a counseling session.

The nondirective approach is preferred for most counseling sessions. Leaders use their experiences, insight and judgment to assist subordinates in developing solutions. Leaders partially structure this type of counseling by telling the subordinate about the counseling process and explaining expectations.

The directive approach works best to correct simple problems, make on-the-spot corrections, and correct aspects of duty performance. When using the directive style, the leader does most of the talking and tells the subordinate what to do and when to do it. In contrast to the nondirective approach, the leader directs a course of action for the subordinate.

In the combined approach, the leader uses techniques from both the directive and nondirective approaches, adjusting them to articulate what is best for the subordinate. The combined approach emphasizes the subordinate's planning and decision-making responsibilities.

II. Coaching

While a mentor or counselor generally has more experience than the person being supported does, coaching relies primarily on teaching and guiding to bring out and enhance the capabilities already present. From its original meaning, coaching refers to the function of helping someone through a set of tasks. Those being coached may, or may not, have appreciated their potential. The coach helps them understand their current level of performance and instructs them how to reach the next level of knowledge and skill.

When compared to counseling and mentoring, coaching is a development technique that tends to be used for a skill and task-specific orientation. Coaches should possess considerable knowledge in the specific area in which they coach others.

An important aspect of coaching is identifying and planning for short- and long-term goals. The coach and the person being coached discuss strengths, weaknesses, and courses of action to sustain or improve.

Note: See p. 4-5 for a discussion of coaching tools.

Types of Counseling

Ref: FM 6-22 Army Leadership, p. 8-12. (See pp. 4-7 to 4-10 for further discussion).

Counseling is central to leader development. Leaders who serve as designated raters have to prepare their subordinates to be better Soldiers or civilians. Good counseling focuses on the subordinate's performance and problems with an eye toward tomorrow's plans and solutions. The subordinate is expected to be an active participant who seeks constructive feedback. Counseling cannot be an occasional event but should be part of a comprehensive program to develop subordinates.

Types of Counseling

 A Event Counseling

 B Performance Counseling

 C Performance Growth Counseling

Ref: FM 6-22, p. 8-12.

1. Event Counseling

Event counseling covers a specific event or situation. It may precede events such as going to a promotion board or attending a school. It may also follow events such as an exceptional duty performance, a performance problem, or a personal problem. Event counseling is also recommended for reception into a unit or organization, for crises, and for transition from a unit or separation from the Army.

2. Performance Counseling

Performance counseling is the review of a subordinate's duty performance during a specified period. The leader and the subordinate jointly establish performance objectives and clear standards for the next counseling period. The counseling focuses on the subordinate's strengths, areas to improve, and potential. Effective counseling includes providing specific examples of strengths and areas needing improvement and providing guidance on how subordinates can improve their performance. Performance counseling is required under the officer, noncommissioned officer (NCO), and Army civilian evaluation reporting systems.

3. Professional Growth Counseling

Professional growth counseling includes planning for the accomplishment of individual and professional goals. It has a developmental orientation and assists subordinates in identifying and achieving organizational and individual goals. Professional growth counseling includes a review to identify and discuss the subordinate's strengths and weaknesses and the creation of an IDP. The plan builds on existing strengths to overcome weaknesses.

A part of professional growth counseling is a discussion characterized as a "pathway to success." It establishes short- and long-term goals for the subordinate. These goals may include opportunities for civilian or military schooling, future duty assignments, special programs, or reenlistment options.

III. Mentoring

Future battlefield environments will place additional pressures on developing leaders at a rapid pace. To help these leaders acquire the requisite abilities, the Army relies on a leader development system that compresses and accelerates development of professional expertise, maturity, and conceptual and team building skills. Mentoring is a developmental tool that can effectively support many of these learning objectives. It is a combat multiplier because it boosts positive leadership behaviors on a voluntary basis.

It is usually unnecessary for leaders to have the same occupational or educational background as those they are coaching or counseling. In comparison, mentors generally specialize in the same specific area as those being mentored. Mentors have likely experienced what their protégés and mentees are experiencing, or are going to experience. Consequently, mentoring relationships tend to be occupation and/or domain specific, with the mentor having expertise in the particular areas they are assisting in, but without the requirement to have the same background. Mentoring focuses primarily on developing a less experienced leader for the future.

Mentorship is the voluntary developmental relationship that exists between a person of greater experience and a person of lesser experience that is characterized by mutual trust and respect (AR 600-100).

The focus of mentorship is the voluntary mentoring that goes beyond the chain of command. Mentorship is generally characterized by the following:

- Mentoring takes place when the mentor provides a less experienced leader with advice and counsel over time to help with professional and personal growth
- The developing leader often initiates the relationship and seeks counsel from the mentor. The mentor takes the initiative to check on the well-being and development of that person.
- Mentorship affects both personal development (maturity, interpersonal, and communication skills) as well as professional development (technical and tactical knowledge and career path knowledge)
- Mentorship helps the Army maintain a highly competent set of leaders
- The strength of the mentoring relationship is based on mutual trust and respect. The mentored carefully consider assessment, feedback, and guidance; these considerations become valuable for the growth that occurs.

Contrary to common belief, mentoring relationships are not confined to the superior-subordinate relationship. They may also be found between peers and notably between senior NCOs and junior officers. This relationship can occur across many levels of rank. In many circumstances, this relationship extends past the point where one or the other has left the chain of command.

Supportive mentoring occurs when a mentor does not outrank the person being mentored, but has more extensive knowledge and experience. Early in their careers, young officers are paired with senior experienced NCOs. The relationship that frequently comes from this experience tends to be instrumental in the young officer's development. Often, officers will recognize that the noncommissioned officer in their first or second assignment was a critical mentor with a major impact on their development.

Coaching Tools

Ref: FM 6-22 Army Leadership, pp. 8-13 to 8-14.

An important aspect of coaching is identifying and planning for short- and long-term goals. The coach and the person being coached discuss strengths, weaknesses, and courses of action to sustain or improve.

Coaches use the following guidelines:

Focus Goals
This requires the coach to identify the purpose of the coaching session. Expectations of both the person being coached and the coach need to be discussed. The coach communicates to the individual the developmental tasks for the coaching session, which can incorporate the results of the individual's multisource assessment and feedback survey.

Clarify the Leader's Self-Awareness
The coach works directly with the leader to define both strengths and developmental needs. During this session, the coach and the leader communicate perceived strengths, developmental needs, and focus areas to improve leader performance. Both the coach and the individual agree on areas of developmental needs.

Uncover Potential
The coach facilitates self-awareness of the leader's potential and the leader's developmental needs by guiding the discussion with questions. The coach actively listens to how the leader perceives his potential. The aim is to encourage the free flow of ideas. The coach also assesses the leader's readiness to change and incorporates this into the coaching session.

Eliminate Developmental Barriers
The coach identifies developmental needs with the leader and communicates those areas that may hinder self-development. It is during this step that the coach helps the individual determine how to overcome barriers to development and how to implement an effective individual development plan to improve the leader's overall performance. The coach helps the leader identify potential sources of support for implementing an action plan.

Develop Action Plans and Commitment
The coach and the individual develop an action plan defining specific actions that can improve the leader's performance within a given period. The coach utilizes a developmental action guide to communicate those self-directed activities the leader can accomplish on his own to improve his performance within a particular competency.

Follow-Up
After the initial coaching session, there should be a follow up as part of a larger transition. After the initial coaching, participants should be solicited for their feedback concerning the effectiveness of the assessment, the usefulness of the information they received, and their progress towards implementing their IDP. The responsibility for follow-up coaching, further IDP development, and IDP execution is usually the responsibility of the unit chain of command. Leaders in the chain of command who provide coaching have a profound impact on the development of their subordinate leaders. They are the role models and present subordinates with additional information and incentives for self-development. Leaders who coach provide frequent informal feedback and timely, proactive, formal counseling to regularly inspire and improve their subordinates.

Individuals must be active participants in their developmental process. They must not wait for a mentor to choose them but have responsibility to be proactive in their own development. Every Army officer, NCO, Soldier, and civilian should identify specific personal strengths, weaknesses, and areas in need of improvement. Each individual should then determine a developmental plan to correct these deficiencies. Some strategies that may be used are to—

- Ask questions and pay attention to experts
- Read and study
- Watch those in leadership positions
- Find educational opportunities (civilian, military, and correspondence)
- Seek and engage in new and varied opportunities

Soldiers can increase their chances of being mentored by actively seeking performance feedback and by adopting an attitude of lifelong learning. These self-development actions help set the stage for mentoring opportunities. Soldiers who seek feedback to focus their development, coupled with dedicated, well-informed mentors, will be the foundation for embedding the concepts of lifelong learning, self-development, and adaptability into the Army's culture.

While mentoring is generally associated with improving duty-related performance and growth, it does not exclude a spiritual dimension. A chaplain or other spiritually trained or enlightened individual may play a significant role in helping individuals cope with stress and find better professional balance and purpose.

I. Developmental Counseling

Ref: FM 6-22 Army Leadership, appendix B.

Counseling is the process used by leaders to review with a subordinate the subordinate's demonstrated performance and potential.

Counseling is one of the most important leadership development responsibilities for Army leaders. The Army's future and the legacy of today's Army leaders rests on the shoulders of those they help prepare for greater responsibility.

I. Types of Developmental Counseling

Developmental counseling is categorized by the purpose of the session. The three major categories of developmental counseling include:

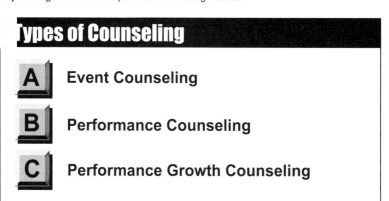

Types of Counseling

A Event Counseling

B Performance Counseling

C Performance Growth Counseling

Ref: FM 6-22, p. 8-12.

A. Event Counseling

Note: See pp. 4-16 to 4-17 for discussion on event counseling.

Event-oriented counseling involves a specific event or situation. It may precede events such as appearing before a promotion board or attending training. It can also follow events such as noteworthy duty performance, a problem with performance or mission accomplishment, or a personal issue. Examples of event-oriented counseling include—

- Instances of superior or substandard performance
- Reception and integration counseling
- Crisis counseling
- Referral counseling
- Promotion counseling
- Separation counseling
- Counseling for Specific Instances

A. Event Counseling
Ref: FM 6-22 Army Leadership, app. B.

Event-oriented counseling involves a specific event or situation. It may precede events such as appearing before a promotion board or attending training. It can also follow events such as noteworthy duty performance, a problem with performance or mission accomplishment, or a personal issue.

1. Instances of superior or substandard performance

Sometimes counseling is tied to specific instances of superior or substandard duty performance. The leader uses the counseling session to convey to the subordinate whether or not the performance met the standard and what the subordinate did right or wrong. Successful counseling for specific performance occurs as close to the event as possible. Leaders should counsel subordinates for exceptional as well as substandard duty performance. The key is to strike a balance between the two. To maintain an appropriate balance, leaders keep track of counseling for exceptional versus substandard performance.

Although good leaders attempt to balance their counseling emphasis, leaders should always counsel subordinates who do not meet the standard. If the Soldier or civilian's performance is unsatisfactory because of a lack of knowledge or ability, leader and subordinate can develop a plan for improvement. Corrective training helps ensure that the subordinate knows and consistently achieves the standard. When counseling a subordinate for a specific performance, take the following actions:

- Explain the purpose of the counseling—what was expected, and how the subordinate failed to meet the standard
- Address the specific unacceptable behavior or action—do not attack the person's character
- Explain the effect of the behavior, action, or performance on the rest of the organization
- Actively listen to the subordinate's response
- Remain neutral
- Teach the subordinate how to meet the standard
- Be prepared to do some personal counseling, since a failure to meet the standard may be related to or be the result of an unresolved personal problem
- Explain to the subordinate how an individual development plan will improve performance and identify specific responsibilities in implementing the plan. Continue to assess and follow up on the subordinate's progress. Adjust the plan as necessary.

2. Reception and Integration Counseling

Caring and empathic Army leaders should counsel all new team members when they join the organization. Reception and integration counseling serves two important purposes:

- It identifies and helps alleviate any problems or concerns that new members may have, including any issues resulting from the new duty assignment.
- It familiarizes new team members with the organizational standards and how they fit into the team. It clarifies roles and assignments and sends the message that the chain of command cares.

Reception and integration counseling should among others include the following discussion points:

- Chain of command familiarization
- Organizational standards
- Security and safety issues
- Noncommissioned officer (NCO) support channel (who is in it and how it is used)
- On- and off-duty conduct
- Personnel/personal affairs/initial and special clothing issue
- Organizational history, structure, and mission
- Soldier programs within the organization, such as Soldier of the Month/Quarter/Year, and educational and training opportunities
- Off limits and danger areas
- Functions and locations of support activities
- On- and off-post recreational, educational, cultural, and historical opportunities
- Foreign nation or host nation orientation
- Other areas the individual should be aware of as determined by the leader

3. Crisis Counseling

Crisis counseling includes getting a Soldier or employee through a period of shock after receiving negative news, such as the notification of the death of a loved one. It focuses on the subordinate's immediate short-term needs. Assisting can also mean referring the subordinate to a support activity or coordinating for external agency support, such as obtaining emergency funding for a flight ticket or putting them in contact with a chaplain.

4. Referral Counseling

Referral counseling helps subordinates work through a personal situation. It may or may not follow crisis counseling. Referral counseling aims at preventing a problem from becoming unmanageable if the empathic Army leader succeeds in identifying the problem in time and involves appropriate resources, such as Army Community Services, a chaplain, or an alcohol and drug counselor.

5. Promotion Counseling

Army leaders must conduct promotion counseling for all specialists and sergeants who are eligible for advancement without waivers but not recommended for promotion to the next higher grade. Army regulations require that Soldiers within this category receive initial (event-oriented) counseling when they attain full promotion eligibility and then periodic (performance/personal growth) counseling thereafter.

6. Adverse Separation Counseling

Adverse separation counseling may involve informing the Soldier of the administrative actions available to the commander in the event substandard performance continues and of the consequences associated with those administrative actions.

Developmental counseling may not apply when an individual has engaged in serious acts of misconduct. In those situations, leaders should refer the matter to the commander and the servicing staff judge advocate. When rehabilitative efforts fail, counseling with a view towards separation is required. It is an administrative prerequisite to many administrative discharges, while sending a final warning to the Soldier: improve performance or face discharge. In many situations, it is advisable to involve the chain of command as soon as it is determined that adverse separation counseling might be required. A unit first sergeant or the commander should inform the Soldier of the notification requirements outlined in AR 635-200.

7. Counseling for Specific Instances

B. Performance Counseling

During performance counseling, leaders conduct a review of a subordinate's duty performance over a certain period. Simultaneously, leader and subordinate jointly establish performance objectives and standards for the next period. Rather than dwelling on the past, focus on the future: the subordinate's strengths, areas of improvement, and potential.

Performance counseling is required under the officer, NCO, and Army civilian evaluation reporting systems. The officer evaluation report (OER) (DA Form 67-9) process requires periodic performance counseling as part of the OER Support Form requirements. Mandatory, face-to-face performance counseling between the rater and the rated NCO is required under the noncommissioned officer evaluation reporting system. (See AR 623-3). Performance evaluation for civilian employees also includes both of these requirements.

Counseling at the beginning of and during the evaluation period ensures the subordinate's personal involvement in the evaluation process. Performance counseling communicates standards and is an opportunity for leaders to establish and clarify the expected values, attributes, and competencies. The OER support form's coverage of leader attributes and competencies is an excellent tool for leader performance counseling. For lieutenants and junior warrant officers, the major performance objectives on the OER Support Form (DA Form 67-9-1) are used as the basis for determining the developmental tasks on the Developmental Support Form (DA Form 67-9-1A). Quarterly face-to-face performance and developmental counseling is required for these junior officers as outlined in AR 623-3. Army leaders ensure that performance objectives and standards are focused and tied to the organization's objectives and the individual's professional development. They should also echo the objectives on the leader's support form as a team member's performance contributes to mission accomplishment.

C. Professional Growth Counseling

Professional growth counseling includes planning for the accomplishment of individual and professional goals. During the counseling, leader and subordinate conduct a review to identify and discuss the subordinate's strengths and weaknesses and to create an individual development plan that builds upon those strengths and compensates for (or eliminates) weaknesses.

As part of professional growth counseling, leader and subordinate may choose to develop a "pathway to success" with short- and long-term goals and objectives. The discussion of the pathway includes opportunities for civilian or military schooling, future duty assignments, special programs, and reenlistment options. An individual development plan is a requirement for all Soldiers and Army civilians as every person's needs and interests are different.

Career field counseling is required for lieutenants and captains before they are considered for promotion to major. Raters and senior raters in conjunction with the rated officer need to determine where the officer's skills and talents best fit the needs of the Army. The rated officer's preference and abilities (both performance and intellectual) must be considered. The rater and senior rater should discuss career field designation with the officer prior to making a recommendation on the rated officer's OER.

While these categories can help organize and focus counseling sessions, they should not be viewed as separate or exhaustive. For example, a counseling session that focuses on resolving a problem may also address improving duty performance. A session focused on performance often includes a discussion on opportunities for professional growth. Regardless of the topic of the counseling session, leaders should follow a basic format to prepare for and conduct it. The Developmental Counseling Form, DA Form 4856, discussed at the end of this appendix provides a useful framework to prepare for almost any type of counseling. Use it to help mentally organize the relevant issues to cover during counseling sessions.

II. The Leader as a Counselor

To be effective, developmental counseling must be a shared effort. Leaders assist their subordinates in identifying strengths and weaknesses and creating plans of action. Once an individual development plan is agreed upon, they support their Soldiers and civilians throughout the plan implementation and continued assessment. To achieve success, subordinates must be forthright in their commitment to improve and candid in their own assessments and goal setting.

Army leaders evaluate Army civilians using procedures prescribed under civilian personnel policies. DA Form 4856 is appropriate to counsel Army civilians on professional growth and career goals. DA Form 4856 is not adequate to address civilian counseling concerning Army civilian misconduct or poor performance. The servicing Civilian Personnel Office can provide guidance for such situations.

Caring and empathic Army leaders conduct counseling to help subordinates become better team members, maintain or improve performance, and prepare for the future. While it is not easy to address every possible counseling situation, leader self-awareness and an adaptable counseling style focusing on key characteristics will enhance personal effectiveness as a counselor. These key characteristics include—

- **Purpose:** Clearly define the purpose of the counseling
- **Flexibility:** Fit the counseling style to the character of each subordinate and to the relationship desired
- **Respect:** View subordinates as unique, complex individuals, each with a distinct set of values, beliefs, and attitudes
- **Communication:** Establish open, two-way communication with subordinates using spoken language, nonverbal actions, gestures, and body language. Effective counselors listen more than they speak
- **Support:** Encourage subordinates through actions while guiding them through their problems

III. The Qualities of the Counselor

Army leaders must demonstrate certain qualities to be effective counselors. These qualities include respect for subordinates, self-awareness and cultural awareness, empathy, and credibility.

One challenging aspect of counseling is selecting the proper approach to a specific situation. To counsel effectively, the technique used must fit the situation, leader capabilities, and subordinate expectations. Sometimes, leaders may only need to give information or listen, while in other situations a subordinate's improvement may call for just a brief word of praise. Difficult circumstances may require structured counseling followed by definite actions, such as referrals to outside experts and agencies.

Self-aware Army leaders consistently develop and improve their own counseling abilities. They do so by studying human behavior, learning the kinds of problems that affect their followers, and developing their interpersonal skills. The techniques needed to provide effective counseling vary from person to person and session to session. However, general skills that leaders will need in almost every situation include active listening, responding, and questioning.

A. Active Listening

Note: See facing page (p. 4-13) for a discussion of key elements of active listening.

Active listening helps communicate reception of the subordinate's message verbally and nonverbally. To capture the message fully, leaders listen to what is said and observe the subordinate's manners.

B. Responding

A leader responds verbally and nonverbally to show understanding of the subordinate. Verbal responses consist of summarizing, interpreting, and clarifying the subordinate's message. Nonverbal responses include eye contact and occasional gestures such as a head nod.

C. Questioning

Although focused questioning is an important skill, counselors should use it with caution. Too many questions can aggravate the power differential between a leader and a subordinate and place the subordinate in a passive mode. The subordinate may also react to excessive questioning as an intrusion of privacy and become defensive. During a leadership development review, ask questions to obtain information or to get the subordinate to think deeper about a particular situation. Questions should evoke more than a yes or no answer. Well-posed questions deepen understanding, encourage further explanation, and help the subordinate perceive the counseling session as a constructive experience.

IV. Counseling Errors

Dominating the counseling by talking too much, giving unnecessary or inappropriate advice, not truly listening, and projecting personal likes, dislikes, biases, and prejudices all interfere with effective counseling. Competent leaders avoid rash judgments, stereotyping, losing emotional control, inflexible counseling methods, or improper follow-up.

To improve leader counseling skills, follow these general guidelines:

- To help resolve the problem or improve performance, determine the subordinate's role in the situation and what the subordinate has done
- Draw conclusions based on more factors than the subordinate's statement
- Try to understand what the subordinate says and feels; listen to what is said and how it is said
- Display empathy when discussing the problem
- When asking questions, be sure the information is needed
- Keep the conversation open-ended and avoid interrupting
- Give the subordinate your full attention
- Be receptive to the subordinate's emotions, without feeling responsible to save the subordinate from hurting
- Encourage the subordinate to take the initiative and to speak aloud

Active Listening
Ref: FM 6-22 Army Leadership, app. B.

Active listening helps communicate reception of the subordinate's message verbally and nonverbally. To capture the message fully, leaders listen to what is said and observe the subordinate's manners. Key elements of active listening include—

Eye contact
Maintaining eye contact without staring helps show sincere interest. Occasional breaks of eye contact are normal and acceptable, while excessive breaks, paper shuffling, and clock-watching may be perceived as a lack of interest or concern.

Body posture
Being relaxed and comfortable will help put the subordinate at ease. However, a too-relaxed position or slouching may be interpreted as a lack of interest.

Head nods
Occasionally head nodding indicates paying attention and encourages the subordinate to continue.

Facial expressions
Keep facial expressions natural and relaxed to signal a sincere interest.

Verbal expressions
Refrain from talking too much and avoid interrupting. Let the subordinate do the talking, while keeping the discussion on the counseling subject.

Active listening implies listening thoughtfully and deliberately to capture the nuances of the subordinate's language. Stay alert for common themes. A subordinate's opening and closing statements as well as recurring references may indicate his priorities. Inconsistencies and gaps may indicate an avoidance of the real issue. Certain inconsistencies may suggest additional questions by the counselor.

Pay attention to the subordinate's gestures to understand the complete message. By watching the subordinate's actions, leaders identify the emotions behind the words. Not all actions are proof of a subordinate's feelings but they should be considered. Nonverbal indicators of a subordinate's attitude include—

- **Boredom**. Drumming on the table, doodling, clicking a ballpoint pen, or resting the head in the palm of the hand
- **Self-confidence**. Standing tall, leaning back with hands behind the head, and maintaining steady eye contact
- **Defensiveness**. Pushing deeply into a chair, glaring at the leader, and making sarcastic comments as well as crossing or folding arms in front of the chest
- **Frustration**. Rubbing eyes, pulling on an ear, taking short breaths, wringing the hands, or frequently changing total body position
- **Interest, friendliness, and openness**. Moving toward the leader while sitting
- **Anxiety**. Sitting on the edge of the chair with arms uncrossed and hands open

Leaders consider each indicator carefully. Although each may reveal something about the subordinate, do not judge too quickly. When unsure look for reinforcing indicators or check with the subordinate to understand the behavior, determine what is underlying it, and allow the subordinate to take responsibility.

- Avoid interrogating
- Keep personal experiences out of the counseling session, unless you believe your experiences will really help
- Listen more and talk less
- Remain objective
- Avoid confirming a subordinate's prejudices
- Help the subordinates help themselves
- Know what information to keep confidential and what to present to the chain of command, if necessary

V. Accepting Limitations

Army leaders cannot help everyone in every situation. Recognize personal limitations and seek outside assistance, when required. When necessary, refer a subordinate to the agency more qualified to help.

Various agencies can assist in solving problems. Although it is generally in an individual's best interest to begin by seeking help from their first-line leaders, caring leaders should respect an individual's preference to contact any of these agencies on their own.

Note: See facing page (p. 4-15) for a partial listing of support activities.

VI. Adaptive Approaches to Counseling

An effective leader approaches each subordinate as an individual. Different people and different situations require different counseling approaches. Three approaches to counseling include nondirective, directive, and combined. These approaches differ in specific techniques, but all fit the definition of counseling and contribute to its overall purpose. The major difference between the approaches is the degree to which the subordinate participates and interacts during a counseling session.

Counseling Approaches

	Advantages	Disadvantages
Nondirective	▪ Encourages maturity ▪ Encourages open communication ▪ Develops personal responsibility	▪ More time-consuming ▪ Requires greatest counselor skills
Directive	▪ Quickest method ▪ Good for people who need clear, concise direction Allows counselors to use their experience	▪ Does not encourage subordinate to be part of solution ▪ Tends to treat symptons, not problems ▪ Tends to discourage subordinates from talking freely ▪ Solution is the counselor's, not the subordinates
Combined	▪ Moderately quick ▪ Encourages maturity ▪ Encourages open communication ▪ Allows counselors to use their experience	▪ May take too much time for some situations

Ref: FM 6-22, fig. B-2, p. B-8.

Support Activities

Ref: FM 6-22, fig. B-1, p. B-7.

Activity	Description
Adjutant General	Provides personnel and administrative services support such as orders, ID cards, retirement assistance, deferments, and in- and out-processing.
American Red Cross	Provides communications support between soldiers and families and assistance during or after emergency or compassionate situations.
Army Community Service	Assists military families through their information and referral services, budget and indebtedness counseling, household item loan closet, information on other military posts, and welcome packets for new arrivals.
Army Substance Abuse Program	Provides alcohol and drug abuse prevention and control programs for DA civilians.
Better Opportunities to Single Soldiers (BOSS)	Serves as a liaison between upper levels of command and single soldiers.
Army Education Center	Provides services for continuing education and individual learning.
Army Emergency Relief	Provides financial assistance and personal budget counseling; coordinates student loans through Army Emergency Relief education loan programs.
Career Counselor	Explains reenlistment options and provides current information on prerequisites for reenlistment and selective reenlistment bonuses.
Chaplain	Provides spiritual and humanitarian counseling to soldiers and DA civilians.
Claims Section, SJA	Handles claims for and against the government, most often those for the loss and damage of household goods.
Legal Assistance Office	Provides legal information or assistance on matters of contracts, citizenship, adoption, marital problems, taxes, wills, and powers of attorney.
Community Counseling Center	Provides alcohol& drug abuse prevention and control programs for soldiers.
Community Health Nurse	Provides preventive health care services.
Community Mental Health	Provides assistance and counseling for mental health problems.
Employees Assistance Program	Provides health nurse, mental health and social work services for DA Civilians.
Equal Opportunity Office	Provides assistance for matters involving discrimination in race, color, national origin, gender, and religion. Provides, information on procedures
Family Advocacy Office	Coordinates programs supporting children and families including abuse and neglect investigation, counseling, and educational programs.
Finance and Accouting Office	Handles inquiries for pay, allowances, and allotments.
Housing Referral Office	Provides assistance with housing on and off post.
Inspector General	Renders assistance to soldiers and DA civilians. Corrects injustices affecting individuals and eliminates conditions determined to be detrimental to the efficiency, economy, morale, and reputation of the Army. Investigates fraud, waste & abuse.
Social Work Office	Provides services dealing with social problems: crisis intervention, family therapy, marital counseling, and parent or child management assistance.

VII. Counseling Techniques

The Army leader can select from several techniques when counseling subordinates. These techniques may cause subordinates to change behavior and improve upon their performance. Counseling techniques leaders may explore during the nondirective or combined approaches include—

- **Suggesting alternatives**. Discuss alternative actions that the subordinate may take. Leader and subordinate together decide which course of action is most appropriate.
- **Recommending**. Recommend one course of action, but leave the decision to accept it to the subordinate.
- **Persuading**. Persuade the subordinate that a given course of action is best, but leave the final decision to the subordinate. Successful persuasion depends on the leader's credibility, the subordinate's willingness to listen, and mutual trust.
- **Advising**. Advise the subordinate that a given course of action is best. This is the strongest form of influence not involving a command.

Techniques to use during the directive approach to counseling include—

A. Corrective training
Teach and assist the subordinate in attaining and maintaining the required standard. A subordinate completes corrective training when the standard is consistently attained.

B. Commanding
Order the subordinate to take a given course of action in clear, precise words. The subordinate understands the order and will face consequences for failing to carry it out.

III. The Four-Stage Counseling Process

Chap 4

Ref: FM 6-22 Army Leadership, appendix B.

Effective Army leaders make use of a four-stage counseling process:

The Four-Stage Counseling Process

1 **Identify the need for counseling**

2 **Prepare for counseling**
1. Select a suitable place
2. Schedule the time
3. Notify the subordinate well in advance
4. Organize information
5. Outline the counseling session
6. Plan counseling strategy
7. Establish the right atmosphere

3 **Conduct the counseling session**
1. Open the session
2. Discuss the issue
3. Develop plan of action
4. Record and close the session

4 **Follow Up**
1. Support plan of action implementation
2. Assess the plan of action

Ref: FM 6-22, app. B.

Counsel, Coach, Mentor

STAGE 1: Identify the Need for Counseling

Usually organizational policies—such as counseling associated with an evaluation or command directed counseling—focus a counseling session. However, leaders may also conduct developmental counseling whenever the need arises for focused, two-way communication aimed at subordinate's development. Developing subordinates consists of observing the subordinate's performance, comparing it to the standard, and then providing feedback to the subordinate in the form of counseling.

STAGE 2: Prepare for Counseling

Successful counseling requires preparation in the following seven areas:

- Select a suitable place
- Schedule the time
- Notify the subordinate well in advance
- Organize information
- Outline the counseling session components
- Plan the counseling strategy
- Establish the right atmosphere

1. Select a Suitable Place
Conduct the counseling in an environment that minimizes interruptions and is free from distracting sights and sounds.

2. Schedule the Time
When possible, counsel a subordinate during the duty day. Counseling after duty hours may be rushed or perceived as unfavorable. Select a time free from competition with other activities. Consider that important events occurring after the session could distract a subordinate from concentrating on the counseling. The scheduled time for counseling should also be appropriate for the complexity of the issue at hand. Generally, counseling sessions should last less than an hour.

3. Notify the Subordinate Well in Advance
Counseling is a subordinate-centered, two-person effort for which the subordinate must have adequate time to prepare. The person to be counseled should know why, where, and when the counseling takes place. Counseling tied to a specific event should happen as closely to the event as possible. For performance or professional development counseling, subordinates may need at least a week or more to prepare or review specific documents and resources, including evaluation support forms or counseling records.

4. Organize Information
The counselor should review all pertinent information, including the purpose of the counseling, facts, and observations about the person to be counseled, identification of possible problems, and main points of discussion. The counselor can outline a possible plan of action with clear obtainable goals as a basis for the final plan development between counselor and the Soldier or civilian.

5. Outline the Components of the Counseling Session
Using the available information, determine the focus and specific topics of the counseling session. Note what prompted the counseling requirement, aims, and counselor role. Identify possible key comments and questions to keep the counseling session subordinate-centered and which can help guide the subordinate through the session's stages. As subordinates may be unpredictable during counseling, a written outline can help keep the session on track and enhances the chance for focused success.

6. Plan the Counseling Strategy
There are many different approaches to counseling. The directive, nondirective, and combined approaches offer a variety of options that can suit any subordinates and situation.

Counseling Outline (Sample)

Ref: FM 6-22 Army Leadership, fig. B-3, p. B-10.

Type of counseling

Initial NCOER counseling for SFC Taylor, a recently promoted new arrival to the unit.

Place and time

The platoon office, 1500 hours, 9 October.

Time to notify the subordinate

Notify SFC Taylor one week in advance of the counseling session.

Subordinate preparation

Instruct SFC Taylor to put together a list of goals and objectives he would like to complete over the next 90 to 180 days. Review the values, attributes, and competencies of FM 6-22.

Counselor preparation

Review the NCO Counseling Checklist/Record

Update or review SFC Taylor's duty description and fill out the rating chain and duty description on the working copy of the NCOER.

Review each of the values and responsibilities in Part IV of the NCOER and the values, attributes, and competencies in FM 6-22. Think of how each applies to SFC Taylor's duties as platoon sergeant.

Review the actions necessary for a success or excellence rating in each value and responsibility.

Make notes in blank spaces on relevant parts of the NCOER to assist in counseling.

Role as a counselor

Help SFC Taylor to understand the expectations and standards associated with the platoon sergeant position. Assist SFC Taylor in developing the values, attributes, and competencies that enable him to achieve his performance objectives consistent with those of the platoon and company. Resolve any aspects of the job that SFC Taylor does not clearly understand.

Session outline

Complete an outline following the counseling session components listed in STAGE 3 and based on the draft duty description on the NCOER. This should happen two to three days prior to the actual counseling session.

7. Establish the Right Atmosphere

The right atmosphere promotes open, two-way communication between a leader and subordinate. To establish a more relaxed atmosphere, offer the subordinate a seat or a cup of coffee. If appropriate, choose to sit in a chair facing the subordinate since a desk can act as a barrier.

Some situations require more formal settings. During counseling to correct substandard performance, leaders seated behind a desk may direct the subordinate to remain standing. This reinforces the leader's role and authority and underscores the severity of the situation.

STAGE 3: Conduct the Counseling Session

Caring Army leaders use a balanced mix of formal and informal counseling and learn to take advantage of everyday events to provide subordinates with feedback. Counseling opportunities often appear when leaders encounter subordinates in their daily activities in the field, motor pool, barracks, and wherever else Soldiers and civilians perform their duties. Even during ad-hoc counseling, leaders should address the four basic components of a counseling session:

- Opening the session
- Discussing the issues
- Developing a plan of action
- Recording and closing the session

1. Open the Session

In the session opening, the leader counselor states the purpose and establishes a subordinate-centered setting. The counselor establishes an atmosphere of shared purpose by inviting the subordinate to speak. An appropriate purpose statement might be "SFC Taylor, the purpose of this counseling is to discuss your duty performance over the past month and to create a plan to enhance performance and attain performance goals." If applicable, start the counseling session by reviewing the status of the current plan of action.

2. Discuss the Issues

Leader and counseled individual should attempt to develop a mutual and clear understanding of the counseling issues. Use active listening and invite the subordinate to do most of the talking. Respond and ask questions without dominating the conversation but help the subordinate better understand the subject of the counseling session: duty performance, a problem situation and its impact, or potential areas for growth.

To reduce the perception of bias or early judgment, both leader and subordinate should provide examples or cite specific observations. When the issue is substandard performance, the leader must be clear why the performance did not meet the standard. During the discussion, the leader must clearly establish what the subordinate must do to meet the standard in the future. It is very important that the leader frames the issue at hand as substandard performance and prevents the subordinate from labeling the issue as an unreasonable standard. An exception would be when the leader considers the current standard as negotiable or is willing to alter the conditions under which the subordinate can meet the standard.

3. Develop a Plan of Action

A plan of action identifies a method and pathway for achieving a desired result. It specifies what the subordinate must do to reach agreed-upon goals set during the counseling session. The plan of action must be specific, showing the subordinate how to modify or maintain his or her behavior.

4. Record and Close the Session

Although requirements to record counseling sessions vary, a leader always benefits from documenting the main points of a counseling session, even the informal ones. Documentation serves as a ready reference for the agreed-upon plan of action and helps the leader track the subordinate's accomplishments, improvements, personal preferences, or problems. A good record of counseling enables the leader to make proper recommendations for professional development, schools, promotions, and evaluation reports.

Army regulations require specific written records of counseling for certain person- nel actions, such as barring a Soldier from reenlisting, processing an administrative separation, or placing a Soldier in the overweight program. When a Soldier faces involuntary separation, the leader must maintain accurate counseling records. Docu- mentation of substandard actions often conveys a strong message to subordinates that a further slip in performance or discipline could require more severe action or punishment.

When closing the counseling session, summarize the key points and ask if the sub- ordinate understands and agrees with the proposed plan of action. With the subordi- nate present, establish any follow-up measures necessary to support the successful implementation of the plan of action. Follow-up measures may include providing the subordinate with specific resources and time, periodic assessments of the plan, and additional referrals. If possible, schedule future meetings before dismissing the subordinate.

STAGE 4: Follow-Up

1. Support Plan of Action Implementation

The counseling process does not end with the initial counseling session. It continues throughout the implementation of the plan of action, consistent with the observed re- sults. Sometimes, the initial plan of action will require modification to meet its goals. Leaders must consistently support their subordinates in implementing the plan of action by teaching, coaching, mentoring, or providing additional time, referrals, and other appropriate resources. Additional measures may include more focused follow- up counseling, informing the chain of command, and taking more severe corrective measures.

2. Assess the Plan of Action

During assessment, the leader and the subordinate jointly determine if the desired results were achieved. They should determine the date for their initial assessment during the initial counseling session. The plan of action assessment provides useful information for future follow-up counseling sessions.

The Developmental Counseling Form

Guidelines on completing DA Form 4856 developmental counseling form (front):

DEVELOPMENTAL COUNSELING FORM
For use of this form see FM 6-22; the proponent agency is TRADOC

DATA REQUIRED BY THE PRIVACY ACT OF 1974

AUTHORITY: 5 USC 301, Departmental Regulations; 10 USC 3013, Secretary of the Army and E.O. 9397 (SSN)
PRINCIPAL PURPOSE: To assist leaders in conducting and recording counseling data pertaining to subordinates.
ROUTINE USES: For subordinate leader development IAW FM 6-22. Leaders should use this form as necessary.
DISCLOSURE: Disclosure is voluntary.

PART I - ADMINISTRATIVE DATA

Name (Last, First, MI)	Rank / Grade	Social Security No.	Date of Counseling
Organization		Name and Title of Counselor	

PART II - BACKGROUND INFORMATION

Purpose of Counseling: (Leader states the reason for the counseling, e.g. Performance/Professional or Event-Oriented counseling and includes the leaders facts and observations prior to the counseling):

See Paragraph B-53 Open the Session

The leader should annotate pertinent, specific, and objective facts and observations made. If applicable, the leader and subordinate start the counseling session by reviewing the status of the previous plan of action.

PART III - SUMMARY OF COUNSELING
Complete this section during or immediately subsequent to counseling.

Key Points of Discussion:

See paragraph B-54 and B-55 Discuss the Issues.

The leader and subordinate should attempt to develop a mutual understanding of the issues. Both the leader and the subordinate should provide examples or cite specific observations to reduce the perception that either is unnecessarily biased or judgmental.

OTHER INSTRUCTIONS
This form will be destroyed upon: reassignment (other than rehabilitative transfers), separation at ETS, or upon retirement. For separation requirements and notification of loss of benefits/consequences see local directives and AR 635-200.

DA FORM 4856, MAR 2006   EDITION OF JUN 99 IS OBSOLETE

Ref: FM 6-22 Army Leadership, fig. B-10, p. B-19.

Guidelines on completing DA Form 4856 developmental counseling form (reverse):

Plan of Action: *(Outlines actions that the subordinate will do after the counseling session to reach the agreed upon goal(s). The actions must be specific enough to modify or maintain the subordinate's behavior and include a specific time line for implementation and assessment (Part IV below):*

See paragraph B-56 Develop a Plan of Action

The plan of action specifies what the subordinate must do to reach the goals set during the counseling session. The plan of action must be specific and should contain the outline, guideline(s), and time line that the subordinate follows. A specific and achievable plan of action sets the stage for successful subordinate development.

Session Closing: *(The leader summarizes the key points of the session and checks if the subordinate understands the plan of action. The subordinate agrees/disagrees and provides remarks if appropriate):*
Individual counseled: ☐ I agree ☐ disagree with the information above
Individual counseled remarks:

See paragraph B-57 through B-59 Close the Session
Signature of Individual Counseled: _____ Date: _____

Leader Responsibilities: *(Leader's responsibilities in implementing the plan of action):*

See paragraph B-60 Leader's Responsibilities

To accomplish the plan of action, the leader must list the resources necessary and commit to providing them to the Soldier.
Signature of Counselor: _____ Date: _____

PART IV - ASSESSMENT OF THE PLAN OF ACTION

Assessment: *(Did the plan of action achieve the desired results? This section is completed by both the leader and the individual counseled and provides useful information for follow-up counseling):*

See paragraph B-61 Assess the Plan of Action

The assessment of the plan of action provides useful information for future follow-up counseling. This block should be completed prior to the start of a follow-up counseling session. During an event-oriented counseling session, the counseling session is not complete until this block is completed.

During performance/professional growth counseling, this block serves as the starting point for future counseling sessions. Leaders must remember to conduct this assessment based on resolution of the situation or the established time line discussed in the plan of action block above.

Counselor: _____ Individual Counseled: _____ Date of Assessment: _____

Note: Both the counselor and the individual counseled should retain a record of the counseling.

REVERSE, DA FORM 4856, MAR 2006

Ref: FM 6-22 Army Leadership, fig. B-11, p. B-20.

Example Counseling Session

Ref: FM 6-22 Army Leadership, fig. B-4, p. B-11.

1. Open the Session

- To establish a relaxed environment for an open exchange, explain to SFC Taylor that the more one discusses and comprehends the importance of the Army Values, leader attributes, and competencies, the easier it is to develop and incorporate them for success into an individual leadership style.
- State the purpose of the counseling session and stress that the initial counseling is based on what SFC Taylor needs to do to be a successful platoon sergeant in the unit. Come to an agreement on the duty description and the specific performance requirements. Discuss related values, competencies, and the standards for success. Explain that subsequent counseling will address his developmental needs as well as how well he is meeting the jointly agreed upon performance objectives. Urge a thorough self-assessment during the next quarter.
- Ensure that SFC Taylor knows the rating chain and resolve any questions he has about his duty position and associated responsibilities. Discuss the close team relationship that must exist between a platoon leader and a platoon sergeant, including the importance of honest, two-way communication.

2. Discuss the Issue

- Jointly review the duty description as spelled out in the NCOER, including all associated responsibilities, such as maintenance, training, and taking care of Soldiers. Relate the responsibilities to leader competencies, attributes, and values. Revise the duty description, if necessary. Highlight areas of special emphasis and additional duties.
- Clearly discuss the meaning of value and responsibility on the NCOER. Discuss the values, attributes, and competencies as outlined in FM 6-22. Ask focused questions to identify if he relates these items to his role as a platoon sergeant.
- Explain to SFC Taylor that the leader's character, presence, and intellect are the basis for competent leadership and that development of the desired leader attributes requires that Army leaders adopt them through consistent self-awareness and lifelong learning.

3. Assist in Developing a Plan of Action

- Ask SFC Taylor to identify tasks that will facilitate the accomplishment of the agreed-upon performance objectives. Describe each by using the values, responsibilities, and competencies found on the NCOER and in FM 6-22.
- Discuss how each value, responsibility, and competency applies to the platoon sergeant position. Discuss specific examples of success and excellence. Ask SFC Taylor for suggestions to make the goals objective, specific, and measurable.
- Ensure that SFC Taylor leaves the counseling session with at least one example of a success or excellence bullet statement as well as sample bullet statements for each value and responsibility. Discuss SFC Taylor's promotion goals and ask him what he considers his strengths and weaknesses. Obtain copies of the last two master sergeant selection board results and match his goals and objectives.

4. Record and Close the Session

- Verify SFC Taylor understands the duty description and performance objectives.
- Stress the importance of teamwork and two-way communication.
- Ensure SFC Taylor understands that you expect him to assist in your development as a platoon leader—both of you have the role of teacher and coach.
- Remind SFC Taylor to perform a self-assessment during the next quarter.
- Set a tentative date during the next quarter for the follow-up counseling.

FM 7-0 & FM 7-1 (ATN): Summary of Changes

Chap 5

Ref: FM 7-0, Training for Full Spectrum Operations (Dec. '08); "Big Differences, New Ideas" FM 7-0 Information Paper, dated 16 Dec '08.

FM 7-0, Training for Full Spectrum Operations (Dec '08)

The 2008 version of Field Manual 7-0 is the 3rd edition of the Army's keystone training doctrine. Previous editions were published in 1988 as FM 25-100, Training the Force, and in 2002 as FM 7-0, Training the Force.

FM 7-0 is the guide for Army training and training management. It addresses the fundamental principles and tenets of training and the fundamentals of training modular, expeditionary Army forces to conduct full spectrum operations—simultaneous offensive, defensive, and stability or civil support operations—in an era of persistent conflict. Conducting effective training for full spectrum operations must be a top priority of senior leaders during both force generation and operational deployments.

This current rewrite of FM 7-0 focuses on the need to change the Army training mindset. The manual emphasizes a combat-seasoned force and the requirement to be able to conduct simultaneous offensive, defensive and stability or civil support operations anywhere on the spectrum of conflict. FM 7-0 incorporates the Army force generation process and introduces the concept of core mission essential tasks and the need to train on core full spectrum tasks until the unit is assigned a directed mission. Big differences/new ideas include:

- **First time our operations manual (FM 3-0) and training manual (FM 7-0) are completely synched.** The training management model was changed to mirror operations model of plan, prepare, and execute, with continuous assessment.

- **Change the Army mindset. . . no return to pre-9-11 focus on offense and defense in major combat operations.** The operational environment and requirements for the operating and generating forces have changed so significantly—we have a combat-seasoned force, we are in an era of persistent conflict. The Aim Point symbolically shows the necessary shift in training and education focus from general war to training on core tasks under conditions midway between general war and insurgency.

- **Leaders train as they will fight.** Even though we are a full-spectrum force—offense, defense, and stability or support ops, and even though we have entered a period of persistent conflict, our first priority is to fight and win our nation's wars. We can never lose that Warrior ethos.

- **What has not changed is that we're still a standards-based force; however, we must think, train, and educate differently to develop agile leaders and an expeditionary force.** We still train in accordance with tasks and standards; commanders define standards when they are not defined by the Army. Standards are constant but leaders change training conditions to develop Soldiers who can adapt to any environment and employ both lethal and non-lethal means with equal skill.

- **We can't train on all tasks . . . but must train on the most important tasks.** Commanders decide which tasks are most important using the battle command model of understand the environment, visualize the requirements, decide the tasks to be trained, and direct the training plan.

(Chg 1) FM 7-0 SMARTupdate

- **Training briefings are a two-step process . . . the dialogue and the training briefing/contract.** The commander proposes to the higher commander the tasks his/her unit will train during a pre-training briefing "dialogue." The tasks, conditions, resources required, and risks assumed then form the basis for the "contract" finalized between the two commanders during the training briefing.

- **Core Mission Essential Task List (CMETL) helps standardize Army capabilities by type unit AND provides the basis for full spectrum capabilities.** Units train on CMETL until they prepare for a directed mission by conducting Directed METL training--and only when they have sufficient dwell time to do so. Standardized by HQ DA, CMETL applies to brigade-sized units and above. Below brigade level, units will build and nest their METL based on the brigade's CMETL.

- **Developing agile, expeditionary leaders requires that the three training domains complement each other.** Training, education, and leader development are inextricably linked. The generating force must expand its focus beyond the institution to support the operating force as leaders and units prepare for deployments.

- **The Band of Excellence is gone . . . the ARFORGEN process increases readiness over time.** When sufficient dwell time exists, commanders will be able to train for full spectrum operations on an expeditionary cycle. Under ARFORGEN, commanders must have more flexibility in how they manage training.

- **Practice Mission Command in training . . . and exercise battle command routinely and frequently.** Commanders must exercise mission command in training so that subordinates are used to it and are ready to execute it. FM 7-0 emphasizes the importance of command and staff training occurring regularly to develop leaders skilled in the art and science of battle command.

FM 7-1 and the Army Training Network (ATN)

The Initial Operating Capability (IOC) of the Army Training Network (ATN) went online April 20, 2009 with the mission of becoming the one-stop shop and information source for Army training. **The ATN Web site, only available to users online through Army Knowledge Online (AKO) SSO log-in (https://atn.army.mil/),** has the most current training doctrine available. **Online "Training Management How-To" and "Training Solutions" in ATN will replace the hardcopy FM 7-1, Battle Focused Training.**

- **The ATN Training Solutions database** provides a resource to other units and Soldiers to discuss their training challenges and communicate how they overcame those challenges through resourcefulness and innovative leadership. These are formatted in the Plan/Prepare/Execute/Assess training model.

- **Training Management How To (TMHT)** will replace the applicable sections of FM 7-1, Battle Focused Training. The Initial Operating Capability (IOC) of ATN will include the content for CMETL, but as all sections are developed and posted to ATN, they will supersede that particular content of FM 7-1 until all of TMHT has been completed and posted. **When all the content of TMHT is complete sometime in 1st Q FY 10, FM 7-1 will be rescinded.**

- **ATN Products** are unit used and vetted training products for use and download. They do not represent Army doctrine, but represent those unit developed and used training tools that have proven successful.

- **The ATN Forum/Blog** was developed to provide an opportunity to collaborate and to share knowledge, expertise, and training management best practices.

I. Training for Full Spectrum Operations

Ref: FM 7-0, Training for Full Spectrum Operations (Dec. '08), chap. 1.

The primary mission of the Army is to fight and win the Nation's wars. Conducting offensive and defensive operations has long been the Army's core capability. However, the recent experience of operations in the Balkans, Iraq, and Afghanistan, coupled with today's operational environments, clearly indicates that the future will be an era of persistent conflict—one that will engage Army forces around the world to accomplish the Nation's objectives. This all points to the fact that the Army must adopt a new mindset that recognizes the requirement to successfully conduct operations across the spectrum of conflict, anytime, anywhere. FM 3-0 codified this forward-looking paradigm shift in the Army's operational concept:

Army forces combine offensive, defensive, and stability or civil support operations simultaneously as part of an interdependent joint force to seize, retain, and exploit the initiative, accepting prudent risk to create opportunities to achieve decisive results. They employ synchronized action—lethal and nonlethal—proportional to the mission and informed by a thorough understanding of all variables of the operational environment. Mission command that conveys intent and an appreciation of all aspects of the situation guides the adaptive use of Army forces.

I. The Strategic Landscape

The future will be one of persistent conflict. Today's operational environments are being shaped by multiple factors. These include science and technology, information technology, transportation technology, the acceleration of the global economic community, and the rise of a networked society. The international nature of commercial and academic efforts will also have dramatic effects. The complexity of today's operational environments guarantees that future operations will occur across the spectrum of conflict.

A. Future Operational Environments

An operational environment is a composite of the conditions, circumstances, and influences, which affect the employment of military forces and bear on the decisions of the commander (JP 3-0). Operational environments of the future will remain arenas in which bloodshed is the immediate result of hostilities between antagonists. Operational goals will be attained or lost not only by the use of lethal force but also by how quickly a state of stability can be established and maintained. Operational environments will remain dirty, frightening, and physically and emotionally draining. Death and destruction resulting from environmental conditions, as well as conflict itself, will create humanitarian crises. Due to the high lethality and long range of advanced weapons systems and the tendency of adversaries to operate among the population, the danger to combatants and noncombatants will be much greater than in past conflicts. State and non-state actors, can be expected to use the full range of options, including every diplomatic, informational, military, and economic measure at their disposal. This applies to all adversaries, regardless of their technological or military capability. In addition, operational environments will extend to areas historically immune from battle, including the homeland—the United States and its territories—and the territory of multinational partners, especially urban areas. Operational environments will probably include areas not defined by geography, such as cyberspace. Computer network attacks already cross borders and may soon be able to hit anywhere, anytime. With the exception of cyberspace, all operations will be conducted "among the people." Outcomes will be measured in terms of effects on populations.

Operational environments will remain extremely fluid. Coalitions, alliances, partnerships, and actors will change continually. Interagency and joint operations will be required to deal with this wide and intricate range of players. International news organizations, using new information and communications technologies, will no longer depend on states to gain access to the area of operations. These organizations will greatly influence how operations are viewed. They will have satellites or their own unmanned aerial reconnaissance platforms from which to monitor the scene. Secrecy will be difficult to maintain, making operations security more vital than ever. Finally, complex cultural, demographic, and physical factors will be present, adding to the fog of war. Such factors include humanitarian crises and ethnic and religious differences. In addition, complex and urban terrain will often become major centers of gravity and havens for potential threats. Tomorrow's operational environments will be interconnected, dynamic, and extremely volatile.

(Chg 1) FM 7-0
SMARTupdate

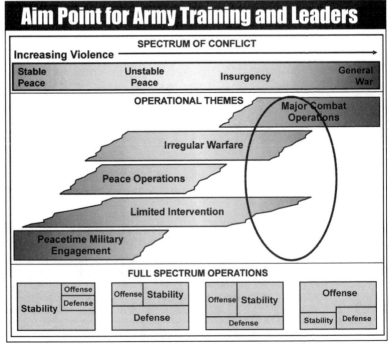

Ref: FM 7-0, Training for Full Spectrum Operations (Dec '08), fig. 1-1, p. 13.

The Aim Point
The challenges of today's operational environments require a change in the Army mindset. The oval on the diagram—called the aim point—indicates that the focus of Army training and leader development must shift leftward from the right side of the spectrum of conflict—from training under conditions of general war to conditions midway between general war and insurgency. Doing this enables Army forces to sustain the proficiency in irregular warfare and limited intervention developed over the last seven years of conflict while sustaining their capability for major combat operations.

B. Types of Threat & the Nature of Conflict

Ref: FM 7-0, Training for Full Spectrum Operations (Dec. '08), pp. 1-2 to 1-3.

States, nations, transnational actors, and non-state entities will continue to challenge and redefine the global distribution of power, concept of sovereignty, and nature of warfare. Threats are nation-states, organizations, people, groups, conditions, or natural phenomena able to damage or destroy life, vital resources, or institutions. Preparing for and managing these threats requires employing all instruments of national power—diplomatic, informational, military, and economic. Threats may be described through a range of four major categories or challenges: traditional, irregular, catastrophic, and disruptive. While helpful in describing threats the Army is likely to face, these categories do not define the nature of an adversary. In fact, adversaries may use any and all of these challenges in combination to achieve the desired effect against the United States.

Traditional threats emerge from states employing recognized military capabilities and forces in understood forms of military competition and conflict. In the past, the United States optimized its forces for this challenge. The United States currently possesses the world's preeminent conventional and nuclear forces, but this status is not guaranteed. Many nations maintain powerful conventional forces, and not all are friendly to the United States. Some of these potentially hostile powers possess weapons of mass destruction. Although these powers may not actively seek armed confrontation and may actively avoid U.S. military strength, their activities can provoke regional conflicts that threaten U.S. interests. Deterrence therefore remains the first aim of the joint force. Should deterrence fail, the United States strives to maintain capabilities to overmatch any combination of enemy conventional and unconventional forces.

1. Irregular Threats

Irregular threats are those posed by an opponent employing unconventional, asymmetric methods and means to counter traditional U.S. advantages. A weaker enemy often uses irregular warfare to exhaust the U.S. collective will through protracted conflict. Irregular warfare includes such means as terrorism, insurgency, and guerrilla warfare. Economic, political, informational, and cultural initiatives usually accompany, and may even be the chief means of, irregular attacks on U.S. influence.

2. Catastrophic Threats

Catastrophic threats involve the acquisition, possession, and use of nuclear, biological, chemical, and radiological weapons, also called weapons of mass destruction. Possession of these weapons gives an enemy the potential to inflict sudden and catastrophic effects. The proliferation of related technology has made this threat more likely than in the past.

3. Disruptive Threats

Disruptive threats involve an enemy using new technologies that reduce U.S. advantages in key operational domains. Disruptive threats involve developing and using breakthrough technologies to negate current U.S. advantages in key operational domains.

The Nature Of Future Conflict

By combining traditional, disruptive, catastrophic, and irregular capabilities, adversaries will seek to create advantageous conditions by quickly changing the nature of the conflict and moving to employ capabilities for which the United States is least prepared. The enemy will seek to interdict U.S. forces attempting to enter any crisis area. If U.S. forces successfully gain entry, the enemy will seek engagement in complex terrain and urban environments as a way of offsetting U.S. advantages. Methods used by adversaries include dispersing their forces into small mobile combat teams—combined only when required to strike a common objective—and becoming invisible by blending in with the local population. Threats can be expected to use the environment and rapidly adapt.

(Chg 1) FM 7-0 SMARTupdate

II. Effects of the Operational Environment

Ref: FM 7-0, Training for Full Spectrum Operations (Dec. '08), pp. 1-3 to 1-5.

Because the Army, the threats, and the Army's operational concept have changed, thinking about Army missions and capabilities must also change. The Army cannot train for the last war. Major combat operations include more than large-scale offensive and defensive operations; they also include stability operations.

All overseas Army operations combine simultaneous offensive, defensive, and stability operations. Operations within the United States and its territories simultaneously combine civil support, defense, and offense. Army forces must be not only capable of defeating the enemy's armed forces but also able to work in concert with the other instruments of national power—diplomatic, informational, and economic (the "whole of government")—to achieve national objectives. Army forces must be campaign capable as well. Once deployed, they may be required to operate for extended periods across the spectrum of conflict, from stable peace through general war, until strategic objectives are achieved. This campaign capability is the ability to sustain operations for as long as necessary to conclude operations successfully.

A. Basing Strategy And Organizations

The Army's basing strategy and formations have changed. Formerly, Army forces were forward-based and sustained with individual replacements; today Army forces are based primarily in the United States, with complete units deploying to and from operations. The Army has transformed itself into a modular, brigade-based, deployable force capable of expeditionary full spectrum operations. The Army National Guard and U.S. Army Reserve are converting from a strategic reserve to an operational force.

B. Full Spectrum Operations

The Army's new operational concept has changed Army operations significantly. All operations are now full spectrum operations. At present, the operational training domain is developing leaders with significant competencies in counterinsurgency operations. However, the Army's strategic depth requires leaders, Soldiers, and units with competencies in major combat and limited intervention operations as well. The other training domains must adjust to build and sustain these competencies.

Full spectrum operations require mentally agile leaders able to operate in any operational theme across the spectrum of conflict. Effective command and control focuses on commanders rather than staffs. Commanders, not staffs, drive effective decision-making. Commanders must be able to mass fires at decisive points and times and effects over time. Decentralized rather than centralized operations are the norm today and will likely remain so. All leaders, from the highest to the lowest levels, must understand both the art and the science of operations and battle command.

Leaders synchronize not only combined arms forces but also lethal and non-lethal effects. Training can no longer focus only on anticipated enemies. In any conflict, the population in the area of operations will be a key factor—especially in conditions of insurgency and unstable peace. Operations in this part of the spectrum of conflict occur among the people throughout a campaign; they are not just part of post-conflict operations. The military alone cannot solve all the problems faced in this environment. Unified action —involving joint and multinational forces, and interagency, nongovernmental, and intergovernmental organizations—now reaches to the tactical level. Leaders at each level must be prepared to operate in this environment. In addition, Soldiers will continue to depend on the support of Army civilians and contractors throughout a campaign.

Civil support operations will continue to involve Regular Army and Reserve Component Soldiers and civilians operating with nongovernmental, local, state, and federal agencies. Since the homeland is vulnerable to attacks and natural disasters, all components must be prepared to conduct civil support operations on short notice. Regular Army forces are normally involved in civil support when natural or manmade disasters and incidents within the United States and its territories exceed the capabilities of Reserve Component organizations and domestic civilian agencies.

C. Threats

In the past, the Army primarily trained to fight against other armies with conventional capabilities within clearly defined military and political boundaries. However, yesterday's Cold War enemies who planned to fight in predictable formations have been replaced by unpredictable, fleeting enemies who hide among the population. Today's enemies are adaptive, smart, and innovative. Their actions cannot be predicted with assurance. They will look for ways to attack friendly vulnerabilities. Rather than directly confront the Army's overwhelming superiority, enemies will attack with asymmetric means. In a single campaign, Army forces may fight multiple enemies with different agendas, rather than a single enemy unified by purpose or command. Army forces will not only have to deal with conventional armed forces but also interact with vastly different cultures and languages of civilian populations.

Today's information environment means that everything Soldiers do will be subject to viewing and listening by friends and enemies. The ability to get the Army's message out and compete in the information environment is often as important as physical actions on the battlefield. Commanders use information engagement to fight this battle. Information engagement influences perceptions and behavior by communicating information, building trust and confidence, and promoting support for Army operations.

D. Soldiers

Today's dangerous and complex operational environments require Soldiers who are men and women of character and intellect. Their character and competence represent the foundation of a values-based, trained, and ready Army. Soldiers train to perform tasks while operating alone or in groups. Soldiers and leaders develop the ability to exercise mature judgment and initiative under stress. The Army requires agile and adaptive leaders able to handle the challenges of full spectrum operations in an era of persistent conflict.

Commanders at all levels ensure their Soldiers operate in accordance with the law of war. The law of war [also called the law of armed conflict] is that part of international law that regulates the conduct of armed hostilities. It is the customary and treaty law applicable to the conduct of warfare on land and to relationships between belligerents and neutral states. The law of war includes treaties and international agreements to which the United States is a party as well as applicable customary international law.

E. Learning And Adapting

Contemporary operations challenge Army forces in many ways. The Army has always depended on its ability to learn and adapt. German Field Marshal Erwin Rommel observed that American Soldiers were initially inexperienced but learned and adapted quickly and well. Today's Army is more experienced than the one in North Africa during World War II; however, today's complex operational environments require organizations and Soldiers able to adapt equally quickly and well. Adaptable organizations learn constantly from experience (their own and others') and apply new knowledge to each situation. Agility and innovation are at a premium, as are creative and adaptive leaders. As knowledge increases, the Army continuously adapts its doctrine, organization, training, materiel, leadership and education, personnel, and facilities.

The Army as a whole must be versatile enough to operate successfully across the spectrum of conflict—from stable peace through unstable peace and insurgency to general war. Change and adaptation that once required years to implement must now be recognized, communicated, and enacted far more quickly.

The aim point concept is a major cultural change for Army leaders, Soldiers, and units. To be successful in future operations, the Army cannot look at operations today as temporary interruptions in preparing for major combat operations against a near-peer enemy. Nor can it afford to view operations dominated by the offense and defense and those dominated by stability as either/or propositions. Both usually occur simultaneously. Army forces must be well trained and able to deploy rapidly to conduct and win engagements and wars while remaining ready to conduct sustained stability operations.

Similarly, in operations dominated by stability they must remain prepared to conduct offensive and defensive operations. The predominate operation—offense, defense, or stability—is determined by the situation, objectives, or conditions to be achieved, desired end state, and level of violence. Commanders consider the simultaneous execution of these three elements of full spectrum operations in their mission analysis.

III. The Role Of Training

Effective training is the cornerstone of operational success. Through training, leaders, Soldiers, and units achieve the tactical and technical competence that builds confidence and agility. These characteristics allow Army forces to conduct successful operations across the spectrum of conflict. Army forces train using training doctrine that sustains their expeditionary and campaign capabilities. Focused training prepares leaders, Soldiers, and units to deploy, fight, and win. Achieving this competence requires specific, dedicated training on offensive, defensive, stability, and civil support tasks. The Army trains Soldiers and units daily in individual and collective tasks under challenging, realistic conditions. Training continues in deployed units to sustain skills and adapt to changes in the operational environment.

The United States' responsibilities are global; therefore, Army forces prepare to operate in any environment. Training management links training with missions. Commanders focus their training time and other resources on tasks linked to their doctrinal or directed mission. Because Army forces face diverse threats and mission requirements, senior commanders adjust their training priorities based on the likely operational environment. As units prepare for deployment, commanders adapt training priorities to address tasks required by actual or anticipated operations.

Army training includes a system of techniques and standards that allow Soldiers and units to determine, acquire, and practice necessary skills. Candid assessments, after action reviews, and applying lessons learned and best practices produce quality Soldiers and versatile units, ready for all aspects of an operational environment. The Army Training System prepares leaders, Soldiers, and units to employ Army capabilities adaptively and effectively in today's varied and challenging conditions.

Through training, the Army prepares Soldiers to win in land combat. Training builds teamwork and cohesion within units. It recognizes that Soldiers ultimately fight for one another and their units. Training instills discipline. It conditions Soldiers to operate within the law of war and rules of engagement. Training prepares unit leaders for the harsh reality of land combat. It emphasizes the fluid and disorderly conditions inherent in land operations.

Within these training situations, commanders emphasize mission command. To employ mission command successfully during operations, commanders and subordinate leaders must understand, foster, and frequently practice its principles during training.

Managing training for full spectrum operations presents challenges for leaders at all echelons. Training develops discipline, endurance, unit cohesion, and tolerance for uncertainty. It prepares Soldiers and units to address the ambiguities and complexities inherent in operations. During the Cold War, Army forces prepared to fight and win against a near-peer competitor. The Army's training focus was on offensive and defensive operations in major combat operations. As recently as 2001, the Army believed that forces trained to conduct the offense and defense in major combat operations could conduct stability and civil support operations just as effectively. However, the complexity of today's operational environments and commanders' legal and moral obligations to the population of an area of operations has shown that approach to be incorrect. Recent operational experience has demonstrated that forces trained exclusively for offensive and defensive tasks are not as proficient at stability tasks as those trained specifically for stability.

For maximum effectiveness, stability and civil support tasks require dedicated training, similar to training for offensive and defensive tasks. Similarly, forces involved in protracted stability or civil support operations require intensive training to regain proficiency in offensive and defensive tasks before engaging in large-scale combat operations. Therefore, a balanced approach to the types of tasks to be trained is essential to readiness for full spectrum operations.

Leaders, Soldiers, and units must be prepared to achieve military objectives throughout all phases of a campaign. Army forces must be trained to conduct full spectrum operations under the conditions of any operational environment, anywhere along the spectrum of conflict. The Army must train, organize, and develop capabilities for stability operations with the same intensity and focus that it does for combat operations.

The art of command takes on even greater significance in today's operational environments. Land operations occur among the people. While technology can enhance Army forces' effectiveness, land operations are basically a human endeavor involving human interactions. As a result, they are conducted in a complex realm dominated by fog, friction, and uncertainty. Command in this environment is an art, not a science. It requires leaders who can think creatively, understand their environment to a degree not required before, and can provide original solutions to ever changing problems posed by adaptable foes applying asymmetric capabilities.

IV. Meeting The Challenges Of Full Spectrum Operations

In an era of persistent conflict, uncertainty exists as to where Army forces will operate and what the mission will be. Therefore, commanders face two training challenges: preparing their units for the most likely missions, and developing the skills needed to adapt quickly and easily to operations anywhere on the spectrum of conflict.

To focus training and leader development in the operational training domain, Headquarters, Department of the Army, establishes core mission-essential task lists (core METLs, or CMETLs) for each brigade and higher echelon unit. CMETLs rarely change. They provide a mix of mission-essential tasks that cover offensive, defensive, stability, and civil support operations. Units train on collective and individual tasks derived from and appropriately supporting those broad CMETL tasks.

Units do not have the time or other resources required to train under the conditions of all operational environments along the spectrum of conflict. Therefore, Headquarters, Department of the Army, analyzes possible operational environments and determines the likely force package requirements for each operational theme at the points along the spectrum of conflict where Army forces are most likely to operate.

Based on this analysis and Headquarters, Department of the Army, guidance, Army command, Army Service component command, and direct reporting unit commanders focus their subordinate units' training on specific operational themes.

Commanders should leverage the experience of their combat-seasoned Soldiers. These veterans can help train other Soldiers and reduce the training time required for certain tasks. However, commanders should not assume that Soldiers and leaders who have served in combat are proficient in all tasks associated with a new position.

V. Implications of the "Aim Point"

Ref: FM 7-0, Training for Full Spectrum Operations (Dec. '08), pp. 1-8 to 1-9.

The aim point and standardized CMETL represent a change in mindset. They underlie a revision in how commanders prepare long- and short-range training plans. Previously, these plans focused solely on mission-essential tasks and how to train them. Now, developing these plans is a two-step process. The first step is a commander-to-commander dialog that discusses the following:

- Training conditions and corresponding resources required
- The proportion of effort to be allocated among offensive, defensive, stability, and civil support tasks
- The risks to readiness
- The core capabilities required of a unit as it adjusts its training focus to prepare for a directed mission

The second step is a training briefing during which the senior commander enters into a "contract" with subordinate commanders. The contract addresses the tasks to be trained, training conditions, risks associated with the training focus and conditions, and the resources required.

Army units must have the capability to train on stability tasks, such as "Providing essential services" and "Support to economic and infrastructure development," while sustaining proficiency in offensive and defensive operations. This training should include collecting accurate bottom-up intelligence and receiving and acting on top-down intelligence at the tactical level.

As much as possible, unit-training conditions realistically replicate the projected operational environment. For example, besides an opposing force, conditions should incorporate the cultures, languages, and key leaders in the projected area of operations. Training tasks should also address dealing with the news media, unified action partners, and special operations forces. In addition, training should incorporate the contributions of both lethal and non-lethal actions.

Operations require well-trained leaders, Soldiers, and units who are not only proficient in core war-fighting competencies but also mentally agile and able to adapt those competencies across the spectrum of conflict. Effective leaders and Soldiers are agile enough to readily seize fleeting opportunities. Their competencies can expand from those required for war-fighting to those supporting stability operations, for example, language skills, cross-cultural communication, enabling economic development and governance, and conflict resolution through negotiation and mediation. These leaders and Soldiers use their knowledge of culture and language to enable operations and leverage the instruments of national power to achieve objectives.

Complex operational environments have required the generating force's role to change from that of the pre-2001 institutional Army. Meeting the significant challenges of today's operational environments requires an integrated, coordinated team effort from both the operational Army and the generating force. The operational Army consists of those Army organizations whose primary purpose is to participate in full spectrum operations as part of the joint force. In contrast, the generating force consists of those Army organizations whose primary mission is to generate and sustain the operational Army's capabilities for employment by joint force commanders (FM 1-01). The generating force recruits, helps train, and equips Soldiers and units. It provides doctrine, mobile training teams, training support, and reach-back resources to help prepare leaders, Soldiers, and units for missions. The generating force supports training and education in institutions, at home stations, and in deployed units. The generating force remains ready to adjust course content to maintain a balance of capabilities for operations across each of the operational themes.

II. Principles of Training

Ref: FM 7-0, Training for Full Spectrum Operations (Dec. '08), chap. 2.

The seven principles of training provide a broad but basic foundation to guide how commanders and other leaders plan, prepare, execute, and assess effective training. Each principle contains an associated set of tenets that support and expand it.

The Army provides combatant commanders with agile individuals, units, and their leaders. These expeditionary forces are trained and ready to conduct (plan, prepare, execute, and assess) full spectrum operations in support of unified action anywhere along the spectrum of conflict. The Army accomplishes this by conducting tough, realistic, standards-based, performance-oriented training. Live, virtual, constructive, and gaming training enablers enhance this training. Units train while deployed, at home station, and at maneuver combat training centers (CTCs). Commanders lead and assess training to ensure the training is high quality and that individuals meet established standards. To meet the challenge of preparing for full spectrum operations, the Army takes advantage of the training capabilities found in the three training domains: institutional, operational, and self-development. Commanders apply seven principles to plan, prepare, execute, and assess effective training.

The Army's Seven Principles of Training

 I Commanders and other leaders are responsible for training

 II Noncommissioned officers train individuals, crews, and small teams

 III Train as you will fight

 IV Train to standard

 V Train to sustain

 VI Conduct multiechelon and concurrent training

 VII Train to develop agile leaders and organizations

(Chg 1) FM 7-0
SMARTupdate

Ref: FM 7-0, Training for Full Spectrum Operations (Dec '08), chap. 2.

I. Commanders and Other Leaders are Responsible for Training

Ref: FM 7-0, Training for Full Spectrum Operations (Dec. '08), pp. 2-1 to 2-4.

Commanders are ultimately responsible for the training, performance, and readiness of their Soldiers, Army civilians, and organizations. However, leaders across all echelons and throughout the operational Army and generating force are responsible for training their respective organizations. For example, a commander is responsible for training a unit, an operations officer for training the operations staff section, and a platoon leader and platoon sergeant for training a platoon. These leaders ensure their organizations are trained and mission-ready.

A. Commanders are the Unit's Primary Training Managers and Primary Trainers

The commander is the unit's primary training manager and primary trainer. Commanders develop their organization's mission-essential task list (METL), approve subordinate organizations' METLs, publish training and leader development guidance, and make resource decisions that allow subordinate leaders to train effectively. Senior noncommissioned officers (NCOs) at every level of command are vital to helping commanders meet their training responsibilities. Senior NCOs are often the most experienced trainers in the unit; they are therefore essential to a successful training program.

Company commanders personally manage their company's training. Commanders at battalion level and higher manage training through their operations officer, who develops the unit's training plans. However, to ensure effective unit training, those commanders remain involved in the training process. Effective training leads to well-trained units and ensures the welfare of Soldiers and civilians.

Commanders set the training direction by providing subordinates clear guidance without stifling initiative and innovation. Commanders ensure the unit is focused on the right tasks, conditions, and standards. To perform their responsibilities as the unit's primary training manager and primary trainer, commanders:

- Use mission command in training as well as operations
- Supervise the planning, preparation, execution, and assessment of training that results in proficient leaders, individuals, and organizations
- Ensure training supports the unit's needs
- Focus training on the unit's METL
- Provide and protect the required resources
- Incorporate safety and composite risk management (CRM) into all aspects of training
- Ensure training is conducted to standard
- Access subordinate leader and unit proficiency and provide feedback
- Develop and communicate a clear vision for training
- Ensure the training environment replicates the anticipated operational environment

B. Commanders Train Their Direct Subordinate Units and Guide and Evaluate Training Two Echelons Down

Commanders are responsible for training their direct subordinate units. They guide and evaluate two echelons down. For example, brigade commanders train battalions and evaluate companies; battalion commanders train companies and evaluate platoons. Commanders develop leaders at one and two levels below their own through personal interaction and by providing them clear guidance.

C. A Leader's Primary Objective Is to Train Subordinates and Organizations for Mission Success

Training subordinates, teams, and units for mission success involves training the unit to established standards under a variety of rapidly changing and stressful conditions. Leaders set intermediate objectives to prepare their units to reach this primary objective. They employ the Army's training management model to ensure mission accomplishment. Leaders focus training on the tasks most important to mission accomplishment. They avoid trying to do too much, since there is not enough time to do everything.

D. Leaders Motivate Their Subordinates Toward Excellence and Encourage Initiative And Innovation

Leaders create training conditions that prompt subordinates to be self-starters and creatively overcome challenges. Effective commanders practice mission command during training to create these opportunities. Mission command is the conduct of military operations through decentralized execution based on mission orders. Successful mission command demands that subordinate leaders at all echelons exercise disciplined initiative, acting aggressively and independently to accomplish the mission within the commander's intent.

E. Leaders Place High Priority On Training and Leader Development

A leader's primary focus is preparing subordinates and organizations to conduct full spectrum operations in a variety of operational environments. Preparation includes training for ongoing operations as well as likely contingencies. It means making the training tougher than the expected operation. Leaders at all levels make the most of every available training opportunity or event to build organizations and develop individuals. Good training develops good leaders, and good leaders provide good training.

F. Leaders Ensure Training Is Executed to Standard

The Army is a standards-based organization. Its leaders enforce established standards or establish and enforce standards where none exist. To ensure training meets standards, leaders stay involved during all training phases—planning, preparation, execution, and assessment. Leaders inspect training for quality and effectiveness. They ensure individuals and organizations meet training objectives and that training is supported by sufficient resources and qualified trainers. Leaders establish discipline in training by creating and maintaining a climate that drives individuals and organizations to meet the standards. A disciplined unit trains to standard, even when leaders are not present.

G. Leaders Continually Assess Individual and Organizational Proficiency

Leaders continually assess their own proficiency, that of subordinates, and that of their organizations. Leaders ensure training is relevant to individual and organizational needs so their subordinates are prepared to meet mission requirements. Leaders assist the commander by continually assessing not only individual performance and organizational proficiency but also training efficiency and effectiveness. Equally important, leaders provide feedback on performance to individuals and the organization through coaching, individual performance counseling, and after action reviews (AARs).

H. Leaders Enforce Safety And Manage Risks

Involved leaders minimize damage, injury, and loss of equipment and personnel. They do this by providing effective supervision, enforcing standards, and applying CRM. In some of the most dangerous operational environments and during the most complex missions, Army forces have experienced fewer losses than expected. This success is due to good leadership, comprehensive planning, effective supervision, and enforcing standards.

II. Noncommissioned Officers Train Individuals, Crews, and Small Teams

Ref: FM 7-0, Training for Full Spectrum Operations (Dec. '08), pp. 2-5 to 2-8.

NCOs are the primary trainers of enlisted Soldiers, crews, and small teams. Officers and NCOs have a special training relationship; their training responsibilities complement each other. This relationship spans all echelons and types of organizations. NCOs are usually an organization's most experienced trainers. Their input is crucial to a commander's overall training strategy and a vital ingredient of the "top-down/bottom-up" approach to training.

A. Training Is A Primary Duty Of NCOs; NCOs Turn Guidance Into Action

NCOs train, lead, and care for Soldiers and their equipment. They instill in Soldiers the Warrior Ethos and Army Values. NCOs take the broad guidance given by their leaders and identify the necessary tasks, standards, and resources. Then they execute the training in accordance with their leader's intent.

B. NCOs Identify Soldier, Crew, and Small-Team Tasks, And Help Identify Unit Collective Tasks That Support The Unit's Mission-Essential Tasks

To identify Soldier, crew, and small-team tasks, NCOs begin with individual Soldier tasks. Then they identify the individual, crew, and small-team tasks that link to or support the unit's mission-essential tasks. NCOs also help officers identify the collective tasks that support the unit's mission-essential tasks.

C. NCOs Provide and Enforce Standards-Based, Performance-Oriented, Mission-focused Training

Disciplined, mission-focused training ensures Soldier proficiency in the individual tasks that support an organization's mission-essential tasks. NCOs ensure key individual tasks are integrated into short-range and near-term training plans. NCOs plan, prepare, execute, and assess training. They help commanders and other leaders assess training by conducting internal AARs and participating in external AARs. NCOs provide candid feedback to commanders and other leaders on all aspects of training—especially individual, crew, and small team training.

D. NCOs Focus On Sustaining Strengths and Improving Weaknesses

NCOs quickly assimilate new Soldiers into the organization, continuously coach and mentor them, and hone their newly acquired skills. NCOs cross-train their Soldiers in critical skills and duties. Cross-training prepares Soldiers to accept positions of increased responsibility and take another Soldier's place if necessary. NCOs are dedicated to helping each Soldier grow and develop, both professionally and personally. This dedication is vital to developing future leaders. It is essential to ensuring the organization can successfully accomplish its mission, even when its leaders are absent.

E. NCOs Develop Junior NCOs and Help Officers Develop Junior Officers

NCOs train and coach Soldiers. Senior NCOs train junior NCOs for the next higher position well before they assume it. Senior NCOs help form high-performing officer-NCO teams and help clarify to junior officers the different roles of officers and NCOs in training. NCOs also help officers develop junior officer competence and professionalism and explain NCO expectations of officers.

IV. Train To Standard

Army training is performed to standard. Leaders prescribe tasks with their associated standards that ensure their organization is capable of accomplishing its doctrinal or directed mission. A standard is the minimum proficiency required to accomplish a task under a set of conditions. The goal in training is achieving mastery, not just proficiency. Leaders continually challenge individuals and organizations by varying training conditions to make achieving the standard more challenging.

A. Leaders Know and Enforce Standards

Enforcing standards provides individuals and organizations with a sound basis for training. Effective training is executed to Army standards, joint standards, or both. Standards include measures of performance that leaders use to evaluate the ability of individuals and organizations to accomplish tasks.

B. Leaders Define Success Where Standards Have Not Been Established

Individuals and organizations may be required to perform tasks based on emerging tactics, techniques, and procedures or new conditions. These tasks may not have established standards. Leaders adapt by redefining an existing task or establishing a standard to meet the situation. Leaders create achievable standards based on any or all of the following: commander's guidance; observations, insights, and lessons from similar operations; their professional judgment; and common sense. The next higher commander approves these standards. Where possible, commanders base new standards on doctrine, since doctrine provides the basis for a common vocabulary and evaluation criteria.

C. Leaders Train To Standard, Not To Time

Leaders allocate enough time to train tasks to standard. When necessary, they allocate time to retrain tasks under the same or different, preferably more difficult, conditions. Good leaders understand that they cannot train on everything; therefore, they focus on training the most important tasks. Leaders do not accept substandard performance in order to complete all tasks on the training schedule. Training a few tasks to standard is preferable to training more tasks below standard. Achieving the standard may require repeating tasks or restarting a training event. Leaders should allocate time for remedial training.

VI. Conduct Multi-echelon and Concurrent Training

Multi-Echelon Training

Multi-echelon training is a training technique that allows for the simultaneous training of more than one echelon on different or complementary tasks. It is the most efficient way to train, especially with limited resources. It requires synchronized planning and coordination by commanders and other leaders at each affected echelon. Multi-echelon training optimizes the use of time and resources. This is important in an environment characterized by frequent deployments and limited resources. Multi-echelon training can occur when an entire unit trains on a single task or when different echelons of a unit simultaneously train on different tasks.

Concurrent Training

Concurrent training occurs when a leader conducts training within another type of training. It complements the execution of primary training objectives by allowing leaders to make the most efficient use of available time. For example, an artillery battery commander supporting an infantry battalion during a non-firing maneuver exercise might conduct howitzer section training while the fire direction center maintains communications with fire support officers moving with the infantry.

(Chg 1) FM 7-0
SMARTupdate

III. Train As You Will Fight

Ref: FM 7-0, Training for Full Spectrum Operations (Dec. '08), pp. 2-5 to 2-8.

For twenty-first century full spectrum operations, "fight" includes lethal and non-lethal skills. "Train as you fight" means training under the conditions of the expected operational environment.

A. Train For Full Spectrum Operations and Quick Transitions Between Missions

Army organizations are required to conduct simultaneous offensive, defensive, and stability or civil support operations as well as support diplomatic, informational, and economic efforts. Effective training challenges leaders and organizations with rapidly changing conditions, requiring them to adapt to accomplish evolving missions. Commanders create training conditions that force subordinate leaders to quickly assess situations and develop innovative solutions. Doing this requires being able to train functionally diverse subordinate organizations. Leaders and subordinates put as much emphasis on rapid decision-making and execution as on deliberate planning and preparation.

B. Train For Proficiency In Combined Arms Operations and Unified Action

Combined arms proficiency is met through effectively integrating the war-fighting functions. It is fundamental to all Army operations. Individuals, units, and their leaders are trained to fight and win the Nation's wars; however, they also contribute to implementing the peace alongside and in support of the diplomatic, informational, and economic instruments of national power.

Unified action and joint interdependence require leaders aware of the institutional cultures of organizations making up or working with a joint force. Commanders and leaders should replicate unified action as much as possible during training. Live, virtual, constructive, and gaming training enablers can help replicate the conditions of an actual operational environment, including the contributions of unified action partners. Where possible, commanders establish pre-deployment training relationships that mirror the operational task organization. These habitual relationships help build a team prepared for unified action.

C. Train the Fundamentals First

Fundamentals, such as warrior tasks and battle drills, are a critical part of the crawl-walk-run concept. Warrior tasks are individual Soldier skills critical to Soldier survival. Battle drills are group skills designed to teach a unit to react and survive in common combat situations. Both focus individual training on performing basic tasks to a high degree of proficiency. Leaders assess whether or not their subordinates need to begin at the crawl stage. Training fundamentals first can ease training on more complex individual and collective tasks, such as those related to culture and foreign languages. It helps Soldiers become more agile and innovative. Soldiers well trained in basic tasks—such as physical fitness, lifesaving skills, marksmanship, and small-unit drills—are essential to units confidently and successfully completing collective tasks.

D. Make Training Performance-Oriented, Realistic, and Mission-Focused

Performance-oriented training involves physically performing tasks. It is an active, hands-on approach as opposed to a passive, listening one. Performance-oriented training focuses on results rather than process. It lets individuals and units train all tasks to standard. That training should be stressful physically and mentally to prepare individuals for conditions encountered during operations. Commanders and subordinate leaders plan realistic training. They integrate training support resources that replicate operational environment conditions as much as possible.

Training usually starts with a unit's core METL. METLs include core capability and general mission-essential tasks. Core capability mission-essential tasks are those the organization is designed to perform. General mission-essential tasks are those that all units, regardless of type, must be able to accomplish.

The Army has learned that developing proficiency in performing offensive and defensive tasks does not automatically develop proficiency in performing stability or civil support tasks. Similarly, an army that focuses only on stability or civil support tasks may have significant difficulties quickly transitioning to offensive and defensive operations.

E. Train For Challenging, Complex, Ambiguous, and Uncomfortable Situations

Leaders train their subordinates and organizations to deal with challenging, complex, ambiguous, and uncomfortable situations. Such conditions require agile individuals and their leaders to show initiative and creativity and to be comfortable with fog and friction. Under mission command, leaders require subordinates to exercise initiative by trying different solutions to challenging problems.

Effective training builds competent and confident units and leaders. It includes situations where varied and tough conditions test their discipline and resolve. Training under those conditions develop individuals with the ability to remain calm in chaotic uncertain conditions. Challenging training requires individuals to conduct continuous operations and different elements of full spectrum operations simultaneously. All Soldiers must develop the ability to assess quickly the level of force required. Training under realistic conditions requires Soldiers to use force commensurate with the situation. It also trains them to anticipate the second- and third-order effects of their actions.

F. Integrate Safety and Composite Risk Management Throughout Training

Risk management and safety are not risk aversion. Risk is inherent in Army training, since success in operations depends on tough, realistic, and challenging training. Managing risk applies to individual and collective training under any operational or training environment, regardless of the echelon, component, mission, or type of force. Composite risk management is the decision-making process for identifying and assessing hazards, developing and implementing risk mitigation actions to control risk across the full spectrum of Army missions, functions, operations, and activities (FM 5-19). CRM underpins the protection element of combat power. Leaders manage risks without degrading training realism. They identify hazards, mitigate risks, evaluate environmental considerations, and make decisions at the appropriate level. CRM provides knowledge leaders need to take prudent risks.

G. Determine and Use the Right Mix of Live, Virtual, Constructive, and Gaming Training Enablers

A combination of live, virtual, constructive, and gaming training enablers can help replicate an actual operational environment. Based on resources available—such as time, fuel, funds, and training areas—commanders determine the right mix of live, virtual, constructive, and gaming training enablers to effectively and efficiently train for a mission or rehearse an operation.

H. Train While Deployed

Training does not stop when a unit is deployed. Commanders should periodically review their directed METL to sustain or retrain certain tasks as needed. As time and resources allow, they should also train METL tasks to maintain proficiency during long deployments. Commanders consider the effects of the operational variables (political, military, economic, social, infrastructure, information, physical environment, and time on the area of operations before undertaking such training.

V. Train to Sustain

Ref: FM 7-0, Training for Full Spectrum Operations (Dec. '08), pp. 2-8 to 2-10.

Units must be capable of operating continuously while deployed. Maintenance is essential for continuous operations and is, therefore, an integral part of training. Maintenance is more than maintaining equipment; it includes maintaining and sustaining performance levels, personnel, equipment, and systems over extended periods. Leaders create training conditions that require units to do this.

A. Make Maintenance of Equipment, Individuals, and The Organization Part of Every Training Event

Commanders allocate time for individuals and units to maintain themselves and their equipment to standard during training events. This time includes scheduled maintenance periods (such as for preventive maintenance checks and services), assembly area operations, and physical training. Leaders train their subordinates to appreciate the importance of maintaining themselves and their equipment. Organizations perform maintenance during operations to the standards they practice in training. Maintenance training in this context includes not only taking care of equipment but also sustaining critical individual and collective skills. Maintenance training helps sustain mental and physical fitness, essential skills, and equipment readiness rates. Effective training prepares individuals and organizations to operate for long periods by including the maintenance tasks required to sustain operations.

B. Equipment Maintenance Is the Cornerstone of Sustainment

Functional, reliable, and maintained equipment is essential to mission success. All Soldiers are responsible for maintaining their equipment during training and operations. Leaders are responsible for ensuring they do so. Leaders ensure subordinates execute scheduled maintenance with the same intensity as other training events. These periods should have clear, focused, and measurable objectives. As with other types of training, leaders supervise, enforce standards, complete AARs, and hold subordinates accountable.

They lead by example to underscore that maintenance training is important to readiness. Effective maintenance training ensures organizational equipment is available when needed. It also reduces the effect of frequent deployments and high personnel tempo.

C. Soldiers and Civilians Maintain Entire Systems

Leaders train subordinates to maintain entire systems. For example, maintaining a fighting vehicle involves maintaining its components—weapons; radios; basic issue items; and chemical, biological, radiological, and nuclear equipment—as well as the vehicle itself. Units are systems that require sustainment in the form of rest, re-supply, rotation of shifts, and special training as required.

D. Leaders Train and Retrain Critical Tasks to Sustain Proficiency

Sustaining proficiency applies to maintaining skill proficiency, since physical health, memory, and skills deteriorate without regular use and periodic challenges. Limited training time requires leaders to pick the most important tasks to sustain or improve, for example, those tasks that are essential to mission accomplishment and perishable without frequent practice. Retraining tasks that individuals can perform to standard while not training tasks that individuals cannot perform wastes valuable training time. Commanders select the most important tasks when they prepare their METL. They consider AARs, trends, new equipment, and collaboration among leaders at all levels when they do this.

(Chg 1) FM 7-0
SMARTupdate

Commanders use the mix of live, virtual, constructive, and gaming training enablers that best sustains individual and collective skills.

E. Train To Sustain Core Individual and Collective Skills and Knowledge

Leaders balance the time spent training on METL tasks with time spent on such skills as physical and mental fitness, marksmanship, and navigation.

F. Sustain Leader Presence

A leader's physical presence determines how others perceive that leader. It is more than the leader just showing up; it involves the image that the leader projects. Presence is conveyed through actions, words, and the manner in which leaders carry themselves and make decisions. Setting the example for health, physical fitness, resilience, and calmness under pressure is the foundation of leader presence.

G. Train Staffs Routinely

The staff is an extension of the commander. It is a vital part of the commander's command and control system. Operations require staffs to operate continuously without losing proficiency. Staffs should train regularly and often, rather than in short bursts just before a major evaluation. An effective staff maintenance program progresses to a high level of proficiency. It includes:

- Operating over extended periods and distances
- Enforcing rest plans
- Maintaining tactical command and control information systems and other equipment
- Establishing security measures
- Cross-training

H. Leaders Develop a Sense of Stewardship In Subordinates

Resources include the following: individual and organizational equipment, installation property, training areas, ranges, facilities, time, the environment, and organizational funds. Protection of these assets is both a leader's and an individual's responsibility. Subordinates follow the example leaders set. Preserving readiness requires enforcing accountability for property and other resources across all echelons.

Well-disciplined individuals willingly take ownership of and properly care for their equipment. This sense of stewardship avoids costly and unnecessary expenditures on replacements. In addition, mission accomplishment requires individuals to be physically and mentally ready and have their equipment properly functioning and maintained. This readiness ensures their safety and security, as well as that of everyone else in the organization. Good stewardship is learned during tough training in which individuals learn to respect and trust themselves and their leaders. Good training also develops appreciation for the importance of well-maintained equipment and other resources.

I. Preventable Loss Is Unacceptable

Soldiers, Army civilians and their leaders are professionally obligated to protect the Nation's resources—human, financial, materiel, environmental, and informational. Preventable loss can be mitigated by integrating CRM throughout Army training.

VII. Train to Develop Agile Leaders and Organizations

The Army trains and educates its members to develop agile leaders and organizations able to operate successfully in any operational environment. The Army develops leaders who can direct fires in a firefight one minute and calmly help a family evacuate a destroyed home the next. The Army trains leaders who accept prudent risks to create opportunities to seize, retain, and exploit the initiative. This agility requires educated, highly trained, and well-disciplined individuals. They must also be physically tough, mentally agile, and well grounded in their core competencies and the Warrior Ethos. The Army needs people experienced and knowledgeable enough to successfully accomplish any mission along the spectrum of conflict and in any operational theme. Such individuals—expeditionary individuals and their leaders—can adapt to any situation and operate successfully in any operational environment.

A. Train Leaders in the Art and Science of Battle Command

Battle command is the art and science of understanding, visualizing, describing, directing, leading, and assessing forces to impose the commander's will on a hostile, thinking, and adaptive enemy. Battle command applies leadership to translate decisions into actions—by synchronizing forces and war fighting functions in time, space, and purpose—to accomplish missions. During the Cold War, the Army thought it knew what was necessary to succeed against a predictable enemy. Now the Army faces different challenges. These challenges result from multiple circumstances. Some have military causes; others result from actions by the population in the area of operations. These conditions require an unprecedented understanding of a wide variety of factors. Commanders think about these factors in terms of the operational variables (PMESII-PT) and mission variables (mission, enemy, terrain and weather, troops and support available, time available, civil considerations [METT-TC]). That understanding is essential to successful battle command.

Battle command is guided by professional judgment gained from several sources: experience, knowledge, education, intelligence, and intuition. Leaders improve their battle command skills through realistic, complex, and changing training scenarios. Training gives commanders greater understanding that enables them to make qualitatively better decisions than their opponents. Simultaneously, they focus their intuitive abilities on visualizing the current and future conditions of their operational environment.

Successful battle command involves timely, effective decisions based on combining judgment with information. It requires knowing when and what to decide. It also requires commanders to assess the quality of information and knowledge. Commanders identify important information requirements and focus subordinates and the staff on them.

Commanders anticipate the activities that follow decisions, knowing that once executed, the effects of those decisions are often irreversible. In exercising battle command, commanders combine analytical and intuitive approaches for decision-making. These skills are developed and honed through rigorous training and mentoring by senior commanders at every echelon.

B. Train Leaders Who Can Execute Mission Command

Commanders who train using mission command develop leaders who practice mission command and subordinates who are comfortable with and expect to operate using mission orders. (Mission orders is a technique for developing orders that emphasizes to subordinates the results to be attained, not how they are to achieve them. It provides maximum freedom of action in determining how to best accomplish assigned missions [FM 3-0].) If mission command is not practiced in training, leaders will not use it in operations.

Mission command requires an environment of trust and mutual understanding. Training under mission command increases trust and allows the unit to achieve unity of effort by focusing on the commander's intent. Subordinates develop initiative and the ability to develop creative solutions to problems—in short, they become more agile. Effective mission command requires leaders who can develop clear intent statements—brief statements that provide a clear purpose and end state. As with battle command, commanders and other leaders at every level employ mission command in training and operations.

C. Develop an Expeditionary Mindset in Soldiers and Army Civilians

Organizations are only as agile as their people are, especially their leaders. Expeditionary individuals and their leaders are knowledgeable and experienced enough to conduct full spectrum operations in any operational theme anywhere along the spectrum of conflict—and they know it. Persistent conflict is producing a force of seasoned Soldiers with multiple operational experiences. Home station training and rotations at the maneuver CTCs are incorporating offensive, defensive, and stability operations into major combat operations and irregular warfare scenarios—and in others as needed. However, eveloping an expeditionary mindset requires complementing operational experiences with self-development through reading and simulations. It also requires institutional training that provides broadening and introspective experiences.

Effective institutional training allows Soldiers and Army civilians to reflect on their strengths and weaknesses and take the steps necessary to develop and enhance their skills and knowledge. Reading AARs and lessons learned by individuals and units in operations augments personal knowledge and experiences. Expeditionary leaders are versatile in their knowledge, skills, behaviors, and competencies. These leaders master the skills and competencies associated with other branches in order to train their modular units. Institutional experiences, home station training, CTC exercises, and self-development all contribute to producing expeditionary leaders and units.

D. Educate Leaders to Think

Expeditionary leaders are trained to think critically and originally. These leaders know how to conduct operations. Just as important, they know how to develop novel, original solutions to complex tactical situations in actual operational environments. Effective training cultivates a leader's ability to develop workable tactical concepts, quickly choose among alternatives, and modify their actions as the operational environment changes. These skills involve a mix of education and experience, reinforced through training, exercises, and day-to-day operations. Expeditionary leaders understand that no single solution to a problem exists; what worked yesterday may not work today. They can apply their skills and knowledge to solve recurring problems—and new ones as they arise. Leaders also develop their subordinate leaders' skills by creating a training environment that challenges subordinates to think beyond familiar drills and common solutions. Leaders teach subordinates that operations do not always occur under the same conditions, in sequence, or with logical transitions.

E. Train Leaders and Organizations to Adapt to Changing Mission Roles and Responsibilities

Training adaptable leaders and organizations requires creativity and imagination. Commanders and other leaders prepare themselves, their subordinates, and their units for unfamiliar situations, to include employing both lethal and non-lethal means. Leaders develop flexible subordinates—subordinates who do not freeze in unfamiliar situations. Leaders train subordinates to perform at both their current and the next level of responsibility. That training prepares individuals to assume the next higher position quickly when needed. Live, virtual, constructive, and gaming training enablers let leaders inexpensively train and retrain tasks under varying conditions.

To make units agile, commanders and senior NCOs help subordinates develop their intuition. Leaders coach subordinates through various situations comprising varying conditions and degrees of force. That coaching helps subordinates recognize similar situations and intuitively know how to handle them without being limited by a single "approved solution." Leaders help subordinates recognize alternative—even nonstandard —solutions to complex challenges rather than relying on past solutions that may not fit the situation.

Battle drills are important combat skills; they teach Soldiers how to react instinctively in life-and death situations, where aggressiveness may be more important than finesse or where immediate action is more important than deliberate decision making. However, well-trained Soldiers can quickly identify situations where battle drills do not fit, think their way through them, and act to resolve the situation.

F. Create a "Freedom To Learn" Environment

Leaders foster an organizational climate that allows subordinate leaders to think their way through unanticipated events and react to unfamiliar situations. Freedom to learn does not mean accepting substandard performance. It means establishing a standard that rewards creativity, innovation, and initiative—and a command climate that allows honest mistakes. Leaders focus on what was completed and how individuals responded to the situation. If results are unsatisfactory, subordinates learn from mistakes through feedback. They analyze why they failed to achieve the desired results, discover how to adapt, and then try again. Leaders also solicit recommendations from subordinates being trained.

Subordinates who think they are not allowed to fail or try innovative means to accomplish tasks avoid taking risks and attempting imaginative solutions. The best lessons are often learned through failure. However, repeated failures of the same task can indicate an inability to learn or the need to reassess the training technique, training, or both. Today's dynamic operational environments require individuals and their leaders to learn while operating. This important skill requires agile leaders who can learn from their mistakes under pressure and adapt successfully to a new but similar situation. Learning while operating is not the same as having the freedom to learn; it is the product of it. A training environment in which individuals have the freedom to make mistakes produces individuals better able to learn and adapt during operations.

G. Give Subordinates Feedback

The Army's primary feedback technique is the AAR. Leaders use AARs to provide feedback based on observations and assessments of performance during training and operations. AARs are essential for developing agile leaders and subordinates. Feedback helps all individuals learn from training. It allows them to reflect on what they did and how they can improve future performance. AARs are not critiques; they are a means of self-discovery led by a facilitator. AARs help leaders and subordinates understand how and why actions unfolded as they did and what should be done next time to avoid the same mistakes or repeat successes. Leaders can use AARs to gauge training effectiveness and whether changes are needed in future training. Well-planned and well-executed AARs form the building blocks of learning organizations.

III. The Army Training System

Ref: FM 7-0, Training for Full Spectrum Operations (Dec. '08), chap. 3.

This section discusses the Army Training System, which prepares Soldiers, Army civilians, organizations, and their leaders to conduct full spectrum operations.

I. Foundations Of Army Training

The foundations of Army training are discipline, sound principles and tenets, and a responsive training support system.

A. Discipline

The essential foundation of any good training program is discipline. Good commanders and leaders instill discipline in training to ensure mission success. Discipline in training can be summed up this way:

- Disciplined individuals do the right thing when no one is looking, even under chaotic or uncertain conditions. Discipline demands habitual and reasoned obedience, even when leaders are absent.
- Disciplined individuals perform to standard, regardless of conditions. They have repeatedly practiced tasks to standard, sustained training standards, and trained under conditions closely replicating expected operational environments.
- Discipline is an individual, leader, and organizational responsibility. It is essential to mission success. Well-trained, disciplined individuals and organizations increase the likelihood of success
- Discipline in training relates to the Army Values. Success in all three training domains demands it

B. Principles

The purpose of Army training is to provide combatant commanders with trained and ready Army forces. Training builds individual confidence and competence while providing individuals with essential skills and knowledge. Individuals and organizations need skills and knowledge to operate as part of expeditionary Army forces conducting full spectrum operations in any operational environment. The principles of training apply to all Army training, regardless of topic, component, location, or duration. The Army applies these principles to planning, preparing, executing, and assessing individual and organizational training in three distinct but linked training domains: institutional, operational, and self development.

C. Training Support

Developing leaders and preparing Soldiers, Army civilians, staffs, and units for full spectrum operations requires a team effort. The generating force and operational Army share this responsibility. Fulfilling it requires close coordination, integration, and synchronization. While each training domain has specific responsibilities, some intentional overlap ensures all tasks needed for full spectrum operations are trained.

The ability to conduct quality training relies on a training infrastructure designed to prepare subordinates and leaders for the challenges of an operational environment. The Army's training support system provides training support products, services, and facilities necessary to replicate a relevant training environment.

II. Training and Education

Ref: FM 7-0, Training for Full Spectrum Operations (Dec. '08), pp. 3-2 and 3-4 to 3-5.

The Army Training System comprises training and education. Training is not solely the domain of the generating force; similarly, education continues in the operational Army. Training and education occur in all three training domains. Training prepares individuals for certainty. Education prepares individuals for uncertainty. Education enables agility, judgment, and creativity. Training enables action.

Ref: FM 7-0, Training for Full Spectrum Operations (Dec '08), fig. 3-2, p. 35.

Training develops tactical and technical, individual and collective skills through instruction and repetitive practice. Training uses a crawl-walk-run approach that systematically builds on the successful performance of each task. The stage at which a Soldier or unit enters training depends on the leader's assessment of the current readiness level; not everyone needs to begin at the crawl stage. Mastery comes with practice under varying conditions and by meeting the standards for the task trained.

Army training prepares individuals and organizations by developing the skills, functions, and teamwork necessary to accomplish a task or mission successfully. Training is generally associated with "what to do." Well-trained organizations and individuals react instinctively, even in unknown situations. Training also helps develop leaders and organizations able to adapt to change under unfamiliar circumstances. Soldiers and teams who execute a battle drill to standard in a new situation under the stress of combat exemplify the result of good training. Repetitive training on a task under varying conditions develops intuition on how to approach the task under new or unfamiliar conditions.

Education, in contrast, provides intellectual constructs and principles. It allows individuals to apply trained skills beyond a standard situation to gain a desired result. It helps develop individuals and leaders who can think, apply knowledge, and solve problems under uncertain or ambiguous conditions. Education is associated with "how to think." It provides individuals with lifelong abilities that enable higher cognitive thought processes. Education prepares individuals for service by teaching knowledge, skills, and behaviors applicable to multiple duty positions in peace or war. Educated Soldiers and Army civilians have the foundation needed to adapt to new and unfamiliar situations.

Foundations of Leader Development

The Army is committed to training, educating, and developing all its leaders—officers, warrant officers, noncommissioned officers, and Army civilians—to lead organizations in the complex and challenging operational environments of the twenty-first century. Training and education develop agile leaders and prepare them for current and future assignments of increasing responsibility. Army leaders require character, presence, and intellectual capacity:

- Leaders of character practice the Army Values, empathize with those around them, and exemplify the Warrior Ethos

- Leaders with presence display military bearing; are physically fit, composed, confident; and are resilient under stress

- Leaders with intellectual capacity possess mental agility, make sound decisions, are innovative, employ tact in interpersonal relations, and know their profession

The Army training and leader development model helps develop trained and ready units led by competent and confident leaders. Leader development is a deliberate, continuous, sequential, and progressive process. It develops Soldiers and Army civilians into competent and confident leaders who act decisively, accomplish missions, and care for subordinates and their families. It is grounded in the Army Values. The aptitude for command, staff leadership, and special duties (such as teaching, foreign internal defense team leadership, attaché duties, and joint staff assignments) all contribute to leader development and affect future assignments and promotions.

Leader development occurs through the lifelong synthesis of knowledge, skills, and experiences gained through the three training domains. Each domain provides distinct experiences and has specific, measurable actions that develop leaders.

Competent and confident leaders are essential to successfully training units, and ultimately to employing those units in operations. Uniformed leaders are inherently Soldiers first; they remain technically and tactically proficient in basic Soldier skills. Civilian leaders master the skills and knowledge required of their position. They hone their leadership abilities to provide organizations with both leadership and management skills. All leaders seek to be agile and able to observe, understand, and react to the operational environment. These leaders exercise mission command and apply relevant knowledge, skills, and experiences acquired through training and education to accomplish missions.

Commanders and other leaders play key roles in the three training domains by developing subordinate leaders with the following characteristics:

- Are tactically and technically competent, confident, and agile
- Can successfully employ their units across the spectrum of conflict
- Possess the knowledge and skills needed to train and employ modular force units and operate as a part of a unified action
- Are culturally astute
- Can prepare mission orders that meet their commander's intent
- Are courageous, seize opportunities, and effectively manage risk
- Take care of their people

III. Training Domains

The three training domains complement each other, providing a synergistic system of training and education. The integration of the domains is critical to training Soldiers, Army civilians, and organizations. That integration is especially vital to developing expeditionary Army forces that can successfully conduct full spectrum operations on short notice anywhere along the spectrum of conflict. Conducting full spectrum operations requires competent, confident Soldiers experienced and knowledgeable in a multitude of areas. Skills not developed in one domain are made up in the others. For example, Soldiers who have not deployed on disaster relief operations need to read and understand observations, insights, and lessons from these operations. Leaders assess subordinates' competencies to determine capability gaps.

A. Institutional Training Domain

The institutional training domain is the Army's institutional training and education system, which primarily includes training base centers and schools that provide initial training and subsequent professional military education for Soldiers, military leaders, and Army civilians. It is a major component of the generating force. The institutional domain provides initial military training, professional military education, and civilian education. Comprised of military and civilian schools and courses, this domain provides the foundational skills and knowledge required for operational assignments and promotions.

Army centers and schools teach specialty skills, warrior tasks, battle drills, and individual skills. These are enhanced and broadened through operational assignments and self- development. It also provides functional training and support to the operational training domain. Leaders and individuals master the basics of their profession in institutional training. This allows units to focus on collective training, while also sustaining and enhancing individual skills and knowledge. The institutional training domain supports Soldiers and Army civilians throughout their careers. It is a key enabler for unit readiness.

The institutional training domain provides a framework that develops critical thinkers. These leaders can visualize the challenges of full spectrum operations and understand complex systems. They are mentally agile and understand the fundamentals of their profession and branch. Branch schools provide a basic understanding of how their branch and the other branches interact. Institutions of higher learning, such as senior service colleges and civilian graduate schools, take leaders out of their "comfort zone," helping them become mentally agile.

1. Support to the Field

Training for full spectrum operations requires closely linking the institutional training domain with the operational training domain. The institutional training domain does more than train and educate; it is where Army doctrine is developed and taught. Doctrine establishes the framework for all the Army does. It provides the basis for establishing standards for tasks and missions. The institutional domain is an extensive resource that exists to support the operational domain.

The institutional training domain, as requested and as available, provides training products to help commanders and other leaders train their units. These products include the following: combined arms training strategies, training support packages, mobile training teams, on-site courses, distance training, and distributed learning courses.

Mobile training teams are a particularly valuable resource. They can provide subject matter expertise; help commanders train Soldiers, teams and units; and can develop Soldiers by bringing courses to them. Individuals and units reach back to the generating force for subject matter expertise and for self-development training and education.

IV. Training and Education Lifecylce of Soldiers and Civilians

Ref: FM 7-0, Training for Full Spectrum Operations (Dec. '08), pp. 3-3 to 3-4.

Soldiers and Army civilians begin training the day they enter the Army. They continue training until the day they retire or separate. Individuals train to build the skills and knowledge essential to a trained, expeditionary Army. Training prepares individuals, units, staffs, and their leaders to conduct full spectrum operations along the spectrum of conflict. This lifelong learning occurs in all three training domains—institutional, operational, and self-development—and involves self-assessment.

A. Institutional

The Soldier is, first of all, a warrior. Soldier training begins in the generating force. In schools and training centers, Soldiers train on individual tasks that ultimately support their projected unit's core capability mission-essential tasks. Soldiers are also exposed to the skills of other branches while in schools and training centers. Finally, Soldiers train on warrior tasks—critical tasks that all Soldiers must perform in full spectrum operations. Armed with basic skills from the institution, Soldiers are assigned to a unit. There they integrate into a team and begin training in the operational training domain. In contrast, most Army civilians enter the Army with the skills and knowledge required for their position.

B. Operational

Operational assignments build on the foundation of individual skills learned in schools. Unit leaders introduce new skills required by a Soldier's specialty. In addition, Soldiers master collective tasks that support the unit's mission-essential tasks. In units, individuals train to standard on individual and collective tasks—first with their unit and then as an integrated component of a combined arms team, which may participate in unified action. Major training events, combat training center (CTC) exercises, and operational deployments provide additional experiences necessary for building fully trained units.

Army civilians usually gain operational experience in the generating force; however, civilians support both the operational Army and the generating force. They fill positions that make it possible to man, equip, resource, and train operational Army units. Army civilians provide the skills and continuity essential to the functioning of Army organizations and programs.

C. Self-Development

Self-development is just as important as other individual training. It allows individuals to expand their knowledge and experience to supplement training in the institutional or operational training domains. Self-development can enhance skills needed for a current position or help prepare an individual for future positions. It can mean the difference between failure and success. Individuals are responsible for their own professional growth and for seeking out self-development opportunities. As professionals, Soldiers and Army civilians discipline themselves to pursue training and education on and off duty. Self-development can take many forms.

D. Lifelong Training And Education

Soldiers and Army civilians cycle between the institutional and operational domains for training and education throughout their careers. They supplement training, education, and experience with structured, guided, and individualized self-development programs. Individuals return to schools and centers at certain points to gain new skills and knowledge needed for the next duty assignment and to prepare them for higher levels of responsibility. They return to units, sometimes at the next higher grade, assume new responsibilities, and apply the knowledge and experience from schools to operations.

2. Initial Military Training

Initial military training provides the basic knowledge, skills, and behaviors individuals need to become Soldiers, succeed as members of Army units, contribute to mission accomplishment, and survive and win on the battlefield. Initial military training is given to all new Soldiers. It motivates Soldiers to become dedicated and productive and qualifies them in warrior tasks and knowledge. It instills an appreciation for the Army's place in a democratic society, inspires the Warrior Ethos, and introduces the Army Values.

Newly commissioned officer training focuses on developing competent, confident small-unit leaders trained in tactics, techniques, procedures, and field craft. Newly appointed warrant officer training focuses on developing competent and confident leaders technically proficient in systems associated with individual functional specialties. Enlisted Soldier training focuses on qualifications in the designated military occupational specialty tasks and standards defined by the branch proponent. When Soldiers arrive in their first unit, leaders continue the socialization and professional development process.

3. Professional Military Education and the Civilian Education System

Professional military education and the Civilian Education System help develop Army leaders. Training and education for officers, warrant officers, noncommissioned officers, and Army civilians is continuous and career-long. These programs integrate structured programs of instruction—both resident (at a school or center) and nonresident (distance training, distributed learning, or mobile training teams).

Formal training and education are broadening experiences. They provide time to learn and to teach others. Student leaders can use this time to reflect and introspectively assess the status of their knowledge, skills, and abilities—and how to improve them. Professional military education and the Civilian Education System are progressive and sequential.

4. Functional Training

Functional training qualifies Soldiers, Army civilians, and their leaders for assignment to positions requiring specific skills and knowledge. Functional training supplements the basic skills and knowledge gained through initial military training, professional military education and the Civilian Education System. Functional courses accomplish one or more of the following:

- Meet the training requirements for particular organizations (for example, airborne or contracting officer training)
- Meet the training requirements of a particular individual's assignment or functional responsibility (such as language or sniper training)
- Address force modernization training requirements and meet theater- or operation-specific training requirements (such as detainee operations or high-altitude, rotary-wing flight training)

B. Operational Training Domain

Soldier, civilian, and leader training and development continue in the operational training domain. The operational training domain consists of the training activities organizations undertake while at home station, at maneuver combat training centers, during joint exercises, at mobilization centers, and while operationally deployed.

1. Commander and Leader Responsibilities

Commanders are responsible for unit readiness. Subordinate leaders help commanders achieve mission readiness by ensuring all training and leader development contribute to proficiency in the unit's mission-essential tasks and meet the Army standard.

2. Unit Training

Unit training reinforces foundations established in the institutional training domain and introduces additional skills needed to support collective training. Units continue individual training to improve and sustain individual task proficiency while training on collective tasks. Collective training requires interaction among individuals or organizations to perform tasks, actions, and activities that contribute to achieving mission-essential task proficiency. Collective training includes performing collective, individual, and leader tasks associated with each training objective, action, or activity. Unit training occurs at home station, maneuver CTCs, and mobilization training centers. It also takes place in joint training exercises and while operationally deployed. Unit training develops and sustains an organization's readiness by achieving and sustaining proficiency in performing mission-essential tasks.

3. Major Training Events

Unit training is executed through training events. These events include situational training exercises, external evaluations, command post exercises, and deployment exercises. They create opportunities to train organizations and develop agile leaders. Major training events help individuals, units, and their leaders improve and sustain their tactical and technical skills. Some units have not undergone a Battle Command Training Program or maneuver CTC experience recently. Commanders of these units use live, virtual, constructive, and gaming training enablers to provide combined arms and unified action training experiences. Major training events let commanders assess their unit's mission-essential task proficiency. These events also allow leaders to solve unfamiliar problems and hone their decision making skills. Major training events provide opportunities for obtaining observations, insights, and lessons on units' use of tactics, techniques, and procedures.

4. Operational Missions

Operational missions reinforce what individuals and organizations learn in the institutional and operational training domains. Deployments let individuals, staffs, and units develop confidence in the skills they developed during training. Individuals, staffs, and units also improve performance based on observations, insights, and lessons gained during operations. Training continues during a deployment—whenever and wherever a commander can fit it in.

C. Self-Development Training Domain

Learning is continuous for professionals. Training and education in the institutional and operational training domains cannot meet every individual's needs in terms of knowledge, insights, intuition, experience, imagination, and judgment. Professionals need to pursue improvement in the self-development training domain as well. The self-development training domain includes planned, goal-oriented learning that reinforces and expands the depth and breadth of an individual's knowledge base, self-awareness, and situational awareness; complements institutional and operational learning; enhances professional competence; and meets personal objectives. Self-development enhances previously acquired knowledge, skills, behaviors, and experiences. Self-development focuses on maximizing individual strengths, minimizing weaknesses, and achieving individual development goals. Individuals establish self-development goals and identify ways to achieve them in their self-development plan.

Professionals at all levels continually study Army and joint doctrine, observations, insights, lessons, and best practices. They learn from military history and other disciplines as well. Soldiers start their self-development plans during initial military training. Army civilians begin their self-development plans when they are hired. Self-development plans provide commanders and other leaders a means to improve Soldiers' and Army civilians' tactical and technical skills. A self-development plan follows all individuals from position to position throughout their careers.

V. Combat Training Center Program

Ref: FM 7-0, Training for Full Spectrum Operations (Dec. '08), pp. 3-8 to 3-9.

CTCs support training and leader development in both the operational and institutional training domains; they are not a separate training domain but serve as a bridge between the domains. The three maneuver CTCs (the National Training Center, Joint Readiness Training Center, and Joint Multinational Readiness Center) and the Battle Command Training Program comprise the Army's CTC program. The CTC program is not a place; it is a training concept that supports an expeditionary Army. The CTCs help commanders develop ready units and prepare agile leaders to conduct full spectrum operations in uncertain situations at any point along the spectrum of conflict. The CTCs are a critical element of transforming the Army. Doctrinally based, they help units and their leaders master doctrine. They drive the transformation of training for an expeditionary army. As they help the Army transform, the CTCs continue to transform themselves by focusing on the following imperatives:

- The CTC experience must be demanding—both physically and intellectually
- The opposing forces and training environment must help drive the development of innovative leaders and organizations
- Units must be prepared to fight upon arrival at a CTC—just as they would in operations
- Full spectrum operations—offensive, defensive, and stability or civil support—conducted within the operational themes of major combat operations and irregular warfare—will be the norm during CTC exercises
- Scenarios must challenge the intellect of leaders and test their skills in a unified action environment
- The CTCs must leverage live, virtual, and constructive training enablers to integrate unified action partners and broaden the training experience
- Observer-controller/trainers must have a solid breadth and depth of experience
- Feedback must focus on output and not on process
- Feedback must be timely so leaders can make corrections
- Observer-controller/trainers must know and enforce standards. Restarting or repeating a mission develops leaders and units more than continuing to the next mission when the current mission was not executed to standard.
- CTCs must reflect threat trends and future capabilities
- CTCs provide assistance to units at home station within existing resources and scheduling priorities
- CTCs exist to help commanders increase unit readiness to deploy as they progress through each Army force generation (ARFORGEN) phase.

V. Mission-Essential Task Lists (METL)

Ref: FM 7-0, Training for Full Spectrum Operations (Dec. '08), chap. 4.

Because sufficient resources, especially time, are not available, units cannot train to standard on every task needed for all operations across the spectrum of conflict. Therefore, commanders focus training on the most important tasks—those that help units prepare to conduct operations.

A mission-essential task is a collective task a unit must be able to perform successfully to accomplish its doctrinal or directed mission. All mission-essential tasks are equally important. Since organizations must be capable of performing all elements of full spectrum operations, sometimes simultaneously, they cannot afford to train exclusively on one element at the expense of the others. Similarly, they cannot feasibly be proficient in all tasks at all points on the spectrum of conflict. Therefore, commanders use their METL to focus organizational training.

Mission-Essential Task Lists (METLs)

 Joint mission-essential task list (Joint METL or JMETL)

 Core mission-essential task list (Core METL or CMETL)

 Directed mission-essential task list (Directed METL or DMETL)

Ref: FM 7-0, Training for Full Spectrum Operations (Dec '08), chap. 4.

(Chg 1) FM 7-0 SMARTupdate

There are three types of mission-essential task list:

- Joint mission-essential task list (joint METL or JMETL), which is derived from the Universal Joint Task List
- Core mission-essential task list (core METL or CMETL), which is standardized and based on doctrine and the organization's mission according to its authorization document
- Directed mission-essential task list (directed METL or DMETL), which is developed by the commander upon receipt of a directed mission

Units train on only one METL at a time.

Mission Focus

Mission focus is the process used to derive training requirements from a unit's core capabilities as documented in its authorization document (a table of organization and equipment [TOE] or table of distribution and allowance [TDA]) or from a directed mission. A directed mission is a mission the unit is formally assigned to execute or prepare to execute. Commanders normally assign a directed mission in an execute order, operation order, or operation plan.

Commanders ensure their unit members train as they will fight by using mission focus to guide the planning, preparation, execution, and assessment of their training program. Mission focus is achieved primarily through performing a mission analysis and focusing training on tasks essential for mission accomplishment. Mission focus is critical throughout the entire training process. Mission focus enables commanders and staffs at all echelons to develop structured training programs that focus on mission-essential training activities and address tasks specified for all Army units in AR 350-1.

Commanders use mission focus to allocate resources for training based on mission requirements. An organization cannot attain proficiency on every mission-essential task because of time or other resource constraints. Commanders build a successful training program by consciously focusing on those tasks most critical to mission accomplishment. They identify those tasks on the unit METL.

Commanders and staffs assess the unit's state of training in terms of the METL. They determine each task's training priority. Commanders consider two factors when assigning training priorities: their assessment of the unit's proficiency in each task, and the risk to future operations entailed by accepting a lower level of proficiency on that task. Commanders assign training priorities in coordination with the higher commander.

The METL provides the foundation for the unit's training strategy and, subsequently, its training plans. Commanders develop training strategies to attain proficiency in mission essential tasks. All mission-essential tasks are essential to mission readiness; therefore, mission-essential tasks are not prioritized. However, commanders focus efforts and resources on those tasks assessed as needing the most training.

Battle Command and Training Management

Commanders exercise a modified form of battle command to manage training. They determine:

- Tasks requiring training
- Priority of training effort
- How to replicate the conditions of the operational theme or projected operational environment
- Risk involved in not training certain tasks to standard

Understanding the expected conditions is essential to deciding which tasks to train, the conditions to replicate, and which risks are prudent. Conditions can be either those described by an operational theme or those likely to be encountered in a directed mission. Visualizing the required state of readiness and how to achieve it leads to developing a training strategy that describes the ends, ways, and means of attaining mission readiness. Finally, the commander describes that strategy in a training plan and directs its accomplishment. By participating in and overseeing training, commanders can assess the state of readiness and the value of the training.

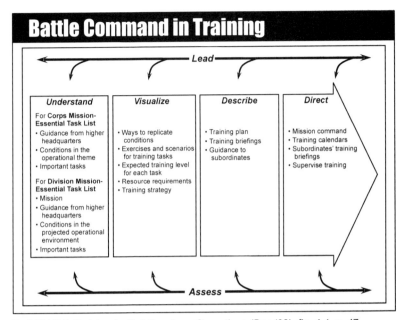

Battle Command in Training

Lead

Understand	Visualize	Describe	Direct
For **Corps Mission-Essential Task List** • Guidance from higher headquarters • Conditions in the operational theme • Important tasks For **Division Mission-Essential Task List** • Mission • Guidance from higher headquarters • Conditions in the projected operational environment • Important tasks	• Ways to replicate conditions • Exercises and scenarios for training tasks • Expected training level for each task • Resource requirements • Training strategy	• Training plan • Training briefings • Guidance to subordinates	• Mission command • Training calendars • Subordinates' training briefings • Supervise training

Assess

Ref: FM 7-0, Training for Full Spectrum Operations (Dec '08), fig. 4-1, p. 47.

I. Joint Mission-Essential Task List

A JMETL is a list of tasks that a joint force must be able to perform to accomplish a mission. JMETL tasks are described using the common language of the Universal Joint Task List. Joint force commanders select them to accomplish an assigned or anticipated mission. A JMETL includes conditions and standards as well as the tasks themselves. It requires identifying command-linked and supporting tasks.

Army organizations often provide forces to joint force commanders. A theater army, corps, or division headquarters may be designated as joint force headquarters. This assignment requires the designated Army headquarters to develop a JMETL. The combatant commander or joint force commander who established the joint task force approves its JMETL. Commanders of Army forces assigned or attached to a joint force ensure their unit's DMETL nests with the joint force's JMETL.

CJCSI 3500.01E and CJCSM 3500.03B provide an overview of the Joint Training System.

II. Core Mission-Essential Task List

A unit's core mission-essential task list is a list of a unit's corps capability mission-essential tasks and general mission-essential tasks. Units train on CMETL tasks until the unit commander and next higher commander mutually decide to focus on training for a directed mission. Then units transition to a DMETL. A CMETL normally focuses unit training in the reset phase of ARFORGEN; however, it can focus training in other ARFORGEN phases if the unit does not receive a directed mission. Units conduct CMETL training under the conditions found in a single operational theme and at an appropriate point on the spectrum of conflict (for example, midway between insurgency and general war) based on higher headquarters' guidance.

Core METL (CMETL) Components

Ref: FM 7-0, Training for Full Spectrum Operations (Dec. '08), pp. 4-8 to 4-10.

CMETLs include two types of tasks:

- A core capability mission-essential task is a mission-essential task approved by Headquarters, Department of the Army, that is specific to a type of unit resourced according to its authorization document and doctrine
- A general mission-essential task is a mission-essential task approved by Headquarters, Department of the Army, that all units, regardless of type, must be able to accomplish. CMETLs are supported by task groups, supporting collective tasks, and supporting individual tasks.

Notional Core METL and Supporting Tasks

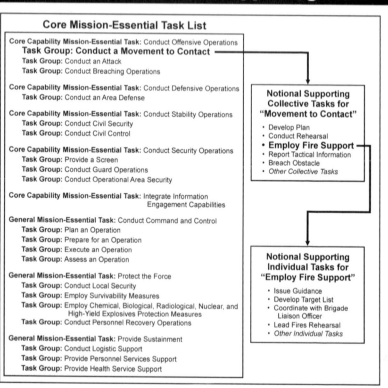

Ref: FM 7-0, Training for Full Spectrum Operations (Dec '08), fig. 4-2, p. 49.

1. Task Groups and Supporting Collective Tasks

A task group is a set of collective tasks necessary to accomplish a specific part of a mission essential task. For example, task groups for the mission-essential task "Conduct offensive operations," might be "Conduct an attack" and "Conduct a movement to contact." To accomplish a task group, a unit must be able to conduct the related supporting collective tasks.

Supporting collective tasks are the tasks that make up a task group. The unit's CATS usually lists supporting collective tasks. Commanders assign training priorities to appropriate task groups based on their assessment of the unit's proficiency in each task group and the importance of the task group to potential missions. Then they identify specific supporting collective tasks to train. Identifying these important supporting collective tasks allows the commander to establish the tasks that:

- Integrate the war fighting functions
- Receive the highest priority for resources such as ammunition, training areas, facilities (including live, virtual, constructive, and gaming training enablers), materiel, and funds
- Receive emphasis during evaluations
- Support the higher organization's METL

2. Supporting Individual Tasks

Developing an effective training strategy requires cross walking collective, leader, and individual tasks with each mission-essential task or task group. This crosswalk may involve subordinate commanders, staffs, command sergeants major, first sergeants, and other key officers, NCOs, and Army civilians. Senior NCOs understand the unit's METL; therefore, they are the best qualified to integrate individual tasks into mission-essential tasks during training.

After supporting collective tasks have been identified, the command sergeant major or first sergeant, with other key NCOs, develops a supporting individual task list for each collective task. Soldier training publications and CATSs are sources of appropriate individual tasks.

Some non-mission-specific requirements are critical to the health, welfare, individual readiness, and cohesiveness of a well-trained organization. Commanders select non-mission-specific requirements on which the organization needs to train. The command sergeant major or first sergeant usually helps the commander with this.

3. Identifying Tasks, Setting Prioirities, and Accepting Risk

Headquarters, Department of the Army, standardizes CMETL tasks and supporting task groups for echelons above battalion. However, commanders at all levels determine the collective and individual tasks to train, the training priority of each task, and the risk associated with not training other collective tasks.

The intellectual process associated with METL development has not changed from the traditional process; however, now their CMETL provides commanders with a framework for training their units to perform all elements of full spectrum operations: offense, defense, stability, and civil support.

The supporting collective task lists for each task group can be extensive. Commanders react correctly by saying they cannot train on all the tasks listed. Instead of trying to train on too many tasks, commanders should consult with their higher commander and consider the conditions associated with the assigned operational theme. Lower commanders then focus training on the tasks most important to accomplishing the mission in that operational theme. The higher commander underwrites the subordinates' acceptance of the risk of not training on the other tasks. Tasks not trained are usually those peripheral to the mission or those the commander has assessed that the unit can perform without significant additional training. The higher and subordinate commanders' experiences affect their judgment of what to train and what not to train. Commanders can use the battle command framework to help focus their training efforts and develop training plans.

The assignment of an operational theme for CMETL training helps commanders identify the most important tasks. Given enough time, it may be possible to train sequentially on CMETL tasks under two different operational themes; however, training for more than one operational theme simultaneously is likely to be counterproductive.

Standardization

In today's modular, expeditionary Army, commanders and leaders expect certain capabilities of organizations assigned to their force package. Standardized CMETLs and focused training conditions at brigade and above help meet these expectations in two ways: they enhance the Army's ability to rapidly assemble force packages, and they minimize the additional training needed for the most probable directed missions. Maintaining a CMETL training focus provides the Nation the strategic depth required for unforeseen contingencies. Headquarters, Department of the Army, adjusts training conditions periodically as it reassesses likely operational environments. Commanders cannot, and do not need to, train on all CMETL related collective and individual tasks. Instead, they train on those tasks they deem most important. Commanders accept prudent risks on the others.

Proponents develop standard CMETLs for brigade-sized and higher level units based on unit authorization document mission statements, core capabilities, and doctrine. Headquarters, Department of the Army, approves—and updates, as needed—these CMETLs after Armywide staffing. CMETLs for corps, divisions, BCTs, functional brigades, and multifunctional support brigades are synchronized to ensure appropriate supporting-to-supported alignment of mission-essential tasks. Proponents ensure the appropriate CMETL is the basis for a unit's combined arms training strategy (CATS).

Most brigade and higher level commanders can find their CMETL in their organization's CATS. Battalion and company commanders develop and align their CMETLs to support their higher organization's CMETL. Platoons and below plan and execute collective and individual tasks that support the company's CMETL. Staffs identify and train on task groups and supporting collective and individual tasks that support the headquarters company's CMETL—they do not have a "staff METL." Commanders of units for which a CMETL is not published develop a CMETL based on the unit's authorization document and doctrine. The next higher commander with ADCON approves this CMETL.

The CMETL for Reserve Component units is the same as that of Regular Army units with the same authorization document. State homeland security tasks for Army National Guard units are treated as a directed mission and require creating a DMETL. The Army National Guard command with ADCON approves the DMETL for Army National Guard units assigned a civil support mission.

III. Directed Mission-Essential Task List

A directed mission-essential task list is a list of the mission-essential tasks a unit must perform to accomplish a directed mission. When a unit is assigned a mission, the commander develops a DMETL by adjusting the unit's CMETL based on mission analysis and the higher commander's DMETL. Once the DMETL is established, it focuses the unit's training program until mission completion. Theater-assigned and theater-committed support units perform the same functions whether deployed or not deployed. Therefore, these types of units, as well as units in support of specific operation plans, train based on a DMETL.

Developing a Directed Mission-Essential Task List

The DMETL development technique helps commanders identify tasks in which an organization must be proficient to accomplish its directed mission. This technique can also be used by units to develop a CMETL, if none exists for the unit. The technique is a guide, not a fixed process. It melds the directed mission and the training and leader development guidance with other inputs filtered by commanders and subordinate leaders to help commanders determine directed mission-essential tasks. Commanders personally analyze the directed mission and involve subordinate commanders, staffs, and their command sergeant major or first sergeant in DMETL development. Subordinates help identify tasks essential to mission accomplishment. Their participation aids in developing a common understanding of the organization's critical mission requirements. This understanding allows DMETLs of subordinate organizations to support the higher headquarters' or supported organization's DMETL.

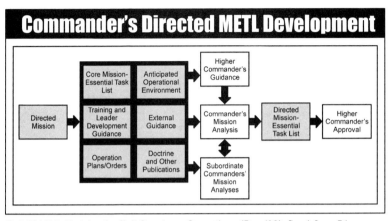

Commander's Directed METL Development

Ref: FM 7-0, Training for Full Spectrum Operations (Dec '08), fig. 4-3, p. 51.

Applying the DMETL development technique:

- Focuses the organization's training on essential tasks
- Provides a forum for professional discussion and leader development among senior, subordinate, and adjacent (peer) commanders and staffs concerning the links between mission and training
- Enables subordinate commanders, staffs, and key NCOs to crosswalk collective, leader, and individual tasks to the mission
- Leads to commitment of the organization's leaders to the organization's training plan

Directed Mission-Essential Task List Approval

DMETL approval resides with the next higher commander unless otherwise specified. Commanders of units projected to be assigned to, attached to, or under operational control of a deploying or deployed force coordinate with that force's commander during DMETL development. The higher commander with ADCON approves the DMETL and ensures that the unit's DMETL supports the deploying or deployed force's DMETL. This may involve consulting with the receiving force commander. When Reserve Component units are mobilized, DMETL approval shifts to First Army or the appropriate Army Service component command.

Directed Mission-Essential Task List (DMETL) Development Fundamentals

Ref: FM 7-0, Training for Full Spectrum Operations (Dec. '08), pp. 4-11 to 4-13.

The following fundamentals apply to DMETL development:
- A DMETL is derived from the commander's analysis of a directed mission
- Directed mission-essential tasks apply to the entire unit. A DMETL does not include tasks assigned solely to subordinate organizations
- Each organization's DMETL supports and complements the DMETL of the higher headquarters or the headquarters to which it provides support
- Resource availability does not affect DMETL development. The DMETL is an unconstrained statement of tasks required to accomplish the unit's mission.
- Where directed mission-essential tasks involve emerging doctrine or nonstandard tasks, commanders establish tasks, conditions, and standards based on their professional judgment, guidance, and observations, insights, and lessons from similar operations

Higher commanders approve standards for these tasks as part of DMETL approval.

During DMETL development, commanders consider how they intend to integrate the war fighting functions through plans and orders to conduct combined arms operations. Commanders employ the war fighting functions to ensure that tasks necessary to build, sustain, and apply combat power are collectively directed toward accomplishing the mission. A war fighting function is a group of tasks and systems (people, organizations, information and processes) united by a common purpose that commanders use to accomplish missions and training objectives (FM 3-0). The war fighting functions are:
- Movement and maneuver
- Intelligence
- Fires
- Sustainment
- Command and control
- Protection

Commander's Mission Analysis

The starting point for DMETL development is the organization's directed mission. In some cases, higher commanders may want to identify an operational theme for the projected operation—major combat operations, irregular warfare, peace operations, limited intervention, or peacetime military engagement—to help focus Soldiers and leaders and create a mindset. (Normally they do this in their training and leader development guidance.) This provides the means to coordinate, link, and integrate a focused DMETL and appropriate supporting collective and individual tasks throughout the organization.

When time is limited, commanders may specify DMETL tasks for subordinate units. Commanders may need to be more prescriptive in their training and leader development guidance as well. When specifying DMETL tasks, commanders acknowledge a commensurate level of risk involved. Risk also occurs when there is not enough time to analyze all aspects of the mission. Those conditions may result in subordinate commanders and staffs failing to include a task on which the unit must train to prepare completely.

Commanders consider several factors during their mission analysis and subsequent DMETL development. These include the following:

- The unit's CMETL
- Plans and orders
- The anticipated operational environment
- External guidance
- Doctrine and other publications

1. Unit CMETL

A CMETL can serve as a starting point for DMETL development, since some of the unit's core capabilities may be the capabilities needed to accomplish the directed mission. These core capabilities are derived from the unit's mission as documented in doctrine and paragraph 1 of the unit's authorization document —the fundamental reasons for the unit's existence.

2. Plans and Orders

Operation plans and orders provide missions and related information that are important in determining required tasks for training. Input for training plans may include:

- Deployment order
- Execution of a contingency plan

3. Anticipated Operational Environment

An operational environment is described in terms of the eight operational variables: political, military, economic, social, information, infrastructure, physical environment, and time (PMESII-PT). Each affects how Army forces conduct (plan, prepare, execute, and assess) military operations. Commanders tailor forces, employ diverse capabilities, and support different missions to succeed in today's complex operational environments. The operational variables form the basis for determining the conditions under which a unit will not only operate but also under which it will train. These conditions, when combined with the standards for the DMETL tasks, help commanders assess unit readiness for a mission.

4. External Guidance

External guidance serves as an additional source of tasks that relate to a unit's directed mission. Sources of external guidance include:

- Commander's training and leader development guidance
- Higher headquarters' DMETL or the DMETL of the deployed or deploying supported force
- Higher headquarters' or the receiving force's directives
- Mobilization plans (for Reserve Component units)
- Force integration plans

5. Doctrine and Other Publications

Doctrine and other sources can provide additional information relating to a directed mission. These include:

- FM 7-15, The Army Universal Task List
- JCSM 3500.04E, The Universal Joint Task List
- AR 350-1, Army Training and Leader Development
- CATSs and proponent-developed collective tasks and drills
- Proponent-developed CMETLs approved by Headquarters, Department of the Army

Transitioning From A Core METL To A Directed METL

At the time agreed to by the unit commander and the higher commander, the unit's training focus transitions from CMETL tasks and assumed conditions of an operational theme to DMETL tasks and conditions that portray the anticipated operational environment. Since a directed mission may be assigned during any ARFORGEN phase, commanders prepare to quickly adapt their training and training support systems from a CMETL to a DMETL focus. Organizations undergoing ARFORGEN are notified of an upcoming mission or deployment early enough for commanders to adjust their METL and training focus. A unit begins training on DMETL tasks upon achieving the CMETL proficiency agreed to by the unit commander and the next higher commander. Exceptions include units with insufficient time between operational deployments to train on CMETL tasks, and units assigned a mission significantly different from their doctrinal mission, capabilities, and equipment. Such units may begin training on DMETL tasks immediately upon learning of a new mission.

Ref: FM 7-0, Training for Full Spectrum Operations (Dec '08), fig. 4-4, p. 53.

Army Training Management

Ref: FM 7-0, Training for Full Spectrum Operations (Dec. '08), chap. 4.

This section describes Army training management—the process used by Army leaders to identify training requirements and subsequently plan, prepare, execute, and assess training. Army training management provides a systematic way of managing time and resources and of meeting training objectives through purposeful training activities.

The Army Training Management Model

Ref: FM 7-0, Training for Full Spectrum Operations (Dec '08), fig. 4-5, p. 54.

The foundation of Army training is the Army training management model. This model mirrors the operations process described in FM 3-0. There are two primary differences between the two: First, while battle command drives the operations process, the METL drives training management. And second, the training management model includes bottom-up feedback to support commanders' assessments.

Planning is addressed on pp. 6-2 to 6-16. Preparation is addressed on pp. 7-13 to 7-16. Execution is addressed on pp. 7-1 to 7-12. Assessment is addressed on pp. 8-1 to 8-10.

Top-Down/Bottom-Up Approach To Training

The top-down/bottom-up approach to training is a team effort that applies mission command to training. This approach requires senior leaders to provide training focus, direction, and resources. Subordinate leaders develop objectives and requirements specific to their organization's needs and provide feedback on training proficiency. They also identify specific organizational training needs and execute training to standard according to the training schedule or event training plan. Guidance, based on mission and priorities, flows from the top down and results in subordinate unit identification of specific collective and individual tasks that support the higher headquarters' mission essential tasks. Input from the bottom up is essential because it identifies training needed to achieve task proficiency.

I. Plan

Conducting training to standard begins with planning. Units develop training plans that enable them to attain proficiency in the mission-essential tasks needed to conduct full spectrum operations under conditions in likely operational environments. Commanders determine a training strategy for the unit and prepare training plans. Developing these plans involves identifying and scheduling training events, allocating time and resources, and coordinating installation support. Commanders perform long-range, short-range, and near-term planning. They present a training briefing to their higher commander to obtain approval of their long- and short-range plans. Commanders also request approval of the commander-selected collective tasks that support the METL during this briefing.

Mission Focus and METL

Planning extends the mission-focus process that links the METL with the subsequent preparation, execution, and assessment of training. Centralized, coordinated planning develops mutually supporting, METL-based training at all unit echelons. Planning involves continuous coordination from long-range planning, through short-range and near-term planning, and ultimately leads to training execution.

See pp. 5-31 to 5-40 for further discussion.

Long-range, Short-range, and Near-term Planning

Long-range, short-range, and near-term planning all follow the same process. Commanders at all levels assess training, provide guidance, and publish training plans. The only difference among echelons is the complexity of assessment, scope, scale, and form of the training and leader development guidance. Planning begins with two principal inputs: the METL and training assessment.

See pp. 6-11 to 6-16 for further discussion.

Training Assessments

Training assessments provide focus and direction to planning by identifying training tasks that are new, where performance needs improvement, or where performance needs to be sustained. Training assessments provide commanders with a starting point for describing their training strategy. The training assessment compares the organization's current level of training proficiency with the desired level of proficiency based on Army standards. This results in training requirements that are necessary to achieve and sustain mission-essential task proficiency. The commander, assisted by key leaders, develops a training strategy that meets each training requirement.

See pp. 8-1 to 8-10 for further discussion.

Army Force Generation (ARFORGEN)

Ref: FM 7-0, Training for Full Spectrum Operations (Dec. '08), pp. 4-1 to 4-3.

The Army supports national policy by organizing, training, equipping, and providing forces to the combatant commands. The force size and capabilities mix are driven by the National Military Strategy, the Joint Strategic Capabilities Plan and combatant commanders' requirements. The Army prepares and provides campaign capable, expeditionary forces through ARFORGEN. ARFORGEN applies to Regular Army and Reserve Component (Army National Guard and U.S. Army Reserve) units. It is a process that progressively builds unit readiness over time during predictable periods of availability to provide trained, ready, and cohesive units prepared for operational deployments. ARFORGEN takes each unit through a three-phased readiness cycle: reset, train/ready, and available.

The Army's shift to modular organizations and the need to conduct full spectrum operations as part of unified action have changed the way the Army views training and readiness in units. Army formations are no longer based on large, fixed divisions. Brigade-sized, functional organizations—brigade combat teams (BCTs), modular support brigades, and functional brigades—have replaced the larger, hierarchical ones.

Units are tailored through ARFORGEN to create force packages to meet specific mission requirements. Force packages often are composed of units from multiple commands and installations. Thus, modular brigades often deploy and work for headquarters other than the one exercising administrative control (ADCON) over them. Senior commanders are responsible for the training and readiness of these units until they are assigned or attached to a force package.

Both the generating force and the operational Army participate in and respond to ARFORGEN. The generating force supports operational Army training. Operational Army commanders develop plans for training mission-essential tasks. Commanders prioritize resource allocation based on the following factors: time available, training time required, resource availability, and the directed mission. The generating force adjusts level of support to meet operational Army requirements.

1. Reset Phase

Units enter the reset phase when they redeploy from long-term operations or complete their planned deployment window in the available force pool. Units conduct individual and collective training on tasks that support their core or directed mission-essential task lists. Because of personnel retention and historically strong affiliation with local units, Reserve Component units may see less personnel turbulence upon redeployment than Regular Army units.

2. Train/Ready Phase

Units move to the train/ready phase when they are prepared to conduct higher level collective training and prepare for deployment. Units with a directed mission progress as rapidly as possible to achieve directed mission capability. Prior to receiving a directed mission, units focus on developing their core capabilities. In addition to preparing for operational requirements, Reserve Component units train for homeland security and homeland defense missions. Army National Guard units train to meet state-established requirements as well. Combatant command requirements accelerate the process as needed and influence when units are manned, equipped, and trained.

3. Available Phase

Forces and headquarters deploying to an ongoing operation or available for immediate alert and deployment to a contingency are in the available phase. At the end of the available phase, units return to the reset phase, and the cycle begins again.

A. Training Objectives

After mission-essential tasks are selected, commanders identify training objectives for each task. A training objective is a statement that describes the desired outcome of a training activity in the unit. It consists of the task, conditions, and standard:

- **Task**. A clearly defined and measurable activity accomplished by individuals and organizations.
- **Conditions**. Those variables of an operational environment or situation in which a unit, system, or individual is expected to operate and may affect performance.
- **Standard**. A quantitative or qualitative measure and criterion for specifying the levels of performance of a task. A measure provides the basis for describing varying levels of task performance.

A criterion is the minimum acceptable level of performance associated with a particular measure of task performance.

The conditions and standards for the majority of a unit's collective training tasks are identified in applicable training and evaluation outlines. A training and evaluation outline is a summary document that provides information on collective training objectives, related individual training objectives, resource requirements, and applicable evaluation procedures for a type of organization. CATSs contain training and evaluation outlines. These can be accessed through DTMS. The following resources can assist cdrs and staffs in developing collective and individual training objectives:

- Combined arms training strategies
- Soldier training publications
- DA Pamphlet 350-38, Standards in Training Commission
- Deployment or mobilization plans
- FM 7-15, The Army Universal Task List
- The Universal Joint Task List Portal

B. Training Strategy

A training strategy describes the ways and means the commander intends to use to achieve and sustain training proficiency on mission-essential tasks. The strategy is based on the commander's assessment and discussions with the higher commander. Training strategies include the following:

- Tasks to be trained
- Training audience
- Training objectives
- Order in which the tasks are to be trained, given limited time and other resources
- Frequency at which tasks are trained
- Types of events used to create conditions for training tasks
- Conditions under which the tasks are to be trained
- Resources required to execute the training strategy
- Alternative ways of training tasks

C. Combined Arms Training Strategies (CATS)

CATSs are publications that provide commanders with a template for task-based, event-driven organizational training. They can be adapted to the unit's requirements based on the commander's assessment. There are two types of CATS's: those that are unique to a unit type (unit CATS), and those that that address a functional capability common to multiple units (a functional CATS).

Fundamentals of Planning for Training

Ref: FM 7-0, Training for Full Spectrum Operations (Dec. '08), pp. 4-15 to 4-17.

Adhering to the following fundamentals contributes to well-developed training plans:

1. Maintain a Consistent Mission Focus

Each headquarters involves its subordinate headquarters when developing training plans. Based on the higher headquarters' plans, subordinate commanders prepare plans with a consistent mission focus.

2. Coordinate with Habitually Task-Organized Supporting Organizations

Commanders of BCTs and battalion task forces plan for coordinated combined arms training that includes their habitually supporting organizations. Commanders of other units deploying with BCTs actively participate in developing their supported unit's training plans and develop complementary training plans.

3. Focus on the Correct Time Frame

Long-range training plans in the Regular Army and mobilized Reserve Component units extend out at least one year. They may cover an entire ARFORGEN cycle. Reserve Component long-range plans consider a minimum of two years or an entire ARFORGEN cycle. Short-range training plans in the Regular Army and mobilized Reserve Component units normally focus on an upcoming quarter; however, their focus may be dictated by a particular ARFORGEN cycle. Reserve Component short-range training plans typically use a one-year time frame. Near-term planning for the Regular Army and mobilized Reserve Component units starts six to eight weeks before the execution of training; Reserve Component near-term planning starts approximately four months prior. Time frames are flexible and determined between appropriate commanders.

4. Focus on Organizational Building Blocks

Organizational building blocks include the following: individual and small-unit skills, leader development, battle rosters, and staff training.

5. Focus on Unit's Mission-Essential & Supporting Tasks

Effective training plans focus on raising or sustaining unit proficiency on mission-essential tasks.

6. Incorporate Composite Risk Management into All Plans

CRM involves identifying, assessing, and controlling risks arising from operational factors and making decisions that balance risk costs with mission training benefits.

See pp. for further discussion of CRM.

7. Lock-In Training Plans

Unplanned or unanticipated changes disrupt training and frustrate subordinates. Planning allows organizations to anticipate and incorporate change in a coordinated manner. Stability and predictability can result from locking in training plans. This stability is crucial to training Reserve Component units, where a disruption or delay in training has a significant impact.

8. Make the Most Efficient Use of Resources

Time and other training resources are always limited. When allocating them, commanders give priority to the training that contributes most to achieving and sustaining operational proficiency levels.

D. Training Resources

Ref: FM 7-0, Training for Full Spectrum Operations (Dec. '08), pp. 4-20 to 4-22.

Commanders use their assessments of mission-essential and critical collective tasks to set training resource priorities. Resources include, for example, time, facilities, ammunition, funds, and fuel. When possible, commanders confirm resources before publishing long- and short-range training plans. Otherwise, resource shortfalls may require deleting low-priority training requirements, substituting less-costly training alternatives, or reallocating resources to execute METL training not resourced.

Commanders give resource priority to events that support training on mission-essential tasks. All tasks may not require equal training time or other resources. Commanders allocate training resources to sustain the METL proficiency based on their assessments of past performance and current proficiency in performing mission-essential tasks.

When available resources limit the size or number of live training events (such as field training and live fire exercises), commanders can substitute a mix of virtual and constructive simulation exercises. Using these simulations helps commanders maintain training proficiency while staying within resource constraints. Commanders determine how these substitutions will affect attaining desired proficiency levels and provide this information to the next higher commander. The higher commander either provides additional resources or approves the constrained resource plan.

Higher commanders estimate resources required to support their training strategies by assessing subordinate units' fiscal resource projections. Higher commanders complete similar analyses to estimate ammunition, facilities, and other resource requirements. Based on these analyses, higher commanders allocate resources to subordinates. Higher and subordinate commanders discuss this resource allocation during the dialog preceding the training briefing. Subordinate commanders include the events and associated resources allocated to them in the long-range training plan. Installation Management Command manages all ranges, training areas, and TADSS. Therefore, unit commanders work closely with installation and garrison commanders concerning training resource requirements.

1. Live, Virtual, and Constructive Training

The Army relies on a creative mix of live, virtual, constructive, and gaming training enablers to provide realistic training. Live, virtual, and constructive training is a broad taxonomy that covers the degree to which a training event uses simulations. Units perform, for example, field training exercises, live fire exercises, deployment exercises, and battle drills under live conditions that replicate an actual operational environment as closely as possible. This is especially true at the battalion level and below. Virtual, constructive, and gaming training enablers are used to supplement, enhance, and complement live training. They can help raise the entry level of proficiency for live training and reduce time needed to prepare training. They can also provide a variety of training environments, allowing multiple scenarios to be replicated under different conditions. Based on training objectives and available resources—such as time, ammunition, simulations, and range availability—commanders determine the right mix and frequency of live, virtual, and constructive training to ensure organizations use allocated resources efficiently.

Live Training

Live training is training executed in field conditions using tactical equipment. It involves real people operating real systems. Live training may be enhanced by TADSS and tactical engagement simulation to simulate combat conditions.

Virtual Training

Virtual training is training executed using computer-generated battlefields in simulators with the approximate characteristics of tactical weapon systems and vehicles. Virtual training is used to exercise motor control, decision-making, and communication skills. Sometimes called "human-in-the-loop training," it involves real people operating simulated systems. People being trained practice the skills needed to operate actual equipment, for example, flying an aircraft.

Constructive Training

Constructive training uses computer models and simulations to exercise command and staff functions. It involves simulated people operating simulated systems. Constructive training can be conducted by units from platoon through echelons above corps. A command post exercise is an example of constructive training.

Gaming

Gaming is the use of technology employing commercial or government off-the-shelf, multi-genre games in a realistic, semi-immersive environment to support education and training. The military uses gaming technologies to create capabilities to help train individuals and organizations. Gaming can enable individual, collective, and multi-echelon training. Gaming can operate in a stand-alone environment or be integrated with live, virtual, or constructive enablers. It can also be used for individual education. Employed in a realistic, semi-immersive environment, gaming can simulate operations and capabilities.

Using Live, Virtual, Constructive, and Gaming Enablers

Using a mix of live, virtual, constructive, and gaming training enablers enhances an organization's ability to train effectively and efficiently. These enablers let commanders simulate participation of large units, scarce resources, or high-cost equipment in training events. Using these enablers reduces the resources required (including maneuver space) to conduct training. For example, properly using these enablers lets commanders perform command and control tasks in a combat vehicle based on messages from higher headquarters, adjacent units, and subordinates without those elements participating in the training.

Brigade-sized and larger units rely more on constructive training events to attain and sustain their proficiency. Battalion-sized and smaller units attain and sustain proficiency and develop warrior tasks primarily using live training.

2. The Army Training Support System (TADSS)

The Army's training support system provides resources to support commanders' training strategies on request. The training support system provides—

- Products—instrumentation and TADSS
- Services—training support operations and manpower
- Facilities—ranges, simulation centers, and training support centers

Leaders use these products, services, and facilities to provide a training environment that replicates projected operational environments. The training support system provides tools to execute Soldier, leader, staff, and collective training at any location. The system also enables school programs of instruction and training strategies, such as CATSs and weapons training strategies. In addition, the system provides the operations staff for ranges, command and control training capabilities, training support centers, and training area management. These resources help leaders focus on the training rather than the training support requirements.

The Army is adapting installation training support system capabilities to enable CMETL and DMETL training. Range modernization supports new weapons systems, integrates command and control information systems, and allows units to conduct training using a variety of scenarios. Urban operations facilities and combined arms collective training facilities support training for urban operations. Battle command training centers support many types of training, among them, operator and leader training on command and control information systems, staff section training, command post exercises, and mission rehearsal exercises.

E. Training Events

Commanders link training strategies to training plans by designing and scheduling training events. Training events are building blocks that support an integrated set of training requirements related to the METL. During long-range planning, commanders and staffs broadly assess the number, type, and duration of training events required to complete METL training. Included in long-range training plans, these events form the resource allocation framework. They also provide early planning guidance to subordinate commanders and staffs. In the subsequent development of short-range training plans, senior commanders describe training events in terms of METL-based training objectives, scenarios, resources, and coordinating instructions. Typical training events include joint training exercises, situational training exercises, live-fire exercises, and combat training center (CTC) exercises.

II. Training Briefings

Commanders present a training briefing to their higher commander to obtain approval of their long-and short-range training plans.

Creating a training briefing has two steps: first a dialog, and then the formal training briefing. The importance of this two-step collaboration cannot be overstated.

Step 1: Dialogue With Next Higher Commander

Prior to the training briefing, a unit commander and the next higher commander conduct a dialog. The dialog focuses on either CMETL or DMETL training. The dialog's purpose is to determine the specific task groups and supporting collective tasks to be trained. This dialog helps commanders agree on the following:

- Commander's assessment of unit readiness in light of, the operational theme (for CMETL training), or the operational theme and projected operational environment (for DMETL training).
- The conditions under which the unit is to train
- Key challenges to readiness
- Any nonstandard or unavailable resources required to replicate those conditions
- Risks involved with accepting a lower training level on selected tasks

In the case of CMETL training, the dialog helps commanders estimate how long it will take to achieve CMETL proficiency before the unit begins training on its DMETL. The dialog saves both commanders' time during the training briefing. It also ensures that the training unit's plan is synchronized with the higher commander's vision and Department of the Army's focus.

Step 2: The Training Briefing

The second step, the training briefing, results in an approved training plan and a resource contract between commanders. The higher commander determines the timing of the dialog and briefing. However, both should be held early enough to ensure that resources can be locked in for the training unit.

Traing Briefing Subjects

A training briefing focuses on two subjects: how the unit commander intends to achieve proficiency in the CMETL or DMETL tasks identified during the dialog, and the resources required to do so. While each unit's CMETL usually remains constant, the operational theme determines the training conditions, and the assessment determines the supporting collective tasks to be trained. Those training conditions and the unit's experience with the mission-essential tasks determine the priority of effort devoted to the supporting task groups and collective and individual tasks. For example, if the unit is to train under irregular warfare conditions, the commander may decide to focus more on collective tasks supporting the core mission-essential task

III. Time Management

Ref: FM 7-0, Training for Full Spectrum Operations (Dec. '08), p. 4-22.

Installation commanders use time management cycles—such as red-green-amber and training mission-support—to manage time requirements and resources. The purpose of establishing a time management cycle is to give subordinate commanders predictability when developing their training plans. These cycles establish the type of activity that receives priority during specific periods. Time management cycles identify and protect training periods and resources that support training so subordinate units can concentrate on METL training during those times. This predictability helps commanders meet and sustain technical and tactical competence, maintain training proficiency, and support the installation.

"Green-Amber-Red" Time Management System

Green Cycle

- Training focus primarily on collective tasks with individual and leader tasks integrated during multiechelon training
- Maximum soldier attendance at prime time, mission essential training
- Coincides with availability of major resources and key training facilities or devices
- Administrative and support requirements that keep personnel from participating in training eliminated to the maximum extent possible
- Leaves and passes limited to the minimum essential

Amber Cycle

- Small unit, crew, leader and individual soldier training emphasized
- Provides time for soldier attendance at education and training courses
- Some sub-organizations may be able to schedule collective training
- Scheduling of periodic maintenance services
- Selected personnel diverted to support requirements when all available personnel in organizations in red period are completely committed to support requirements

Red Cycle

- Maximize self development
- Diverts the minimum essential number of personnel to perform administrative and support rqmts
- Sub-organizations take advantage of all training opportunities to conduct individual, leader, and crew training
- Support missions/details accomplished with unit integrity to exercise the chain of command and provide individual training opportunities for first line supervisors, as time permits. Unit taskings can be used to reduce the number of permanent special duty personnel within installations and communities.
- Leaves and passes maximized. When appropriate, block leave may be scheduled.
- Routine medical, dental, and administrative appointments coordinated and scheduled with installation support facilities

Ref: FM 7-0 (Oct '03), fig. 4-6, p. 4-11. (This chart is not replicated in the '08 FM 7-0).

Time management periods are depicted on long-range planning calendars. Typically, cycles last anywhere from four to eight weeks. A common cycle consists of three periods, one focused on collective training, one on individual training, and one on installation support. However, specific cycles and their lengths vary among installations according to the local situation and requirements, such as ARFORGEN phases, unit deployment dates, and installation size and type.

No one solution for time management exists, since so many factors affect managing time and prioritizing resources. A system that works at one installation may not work at another. Different circumstances require different solutions. Allocation of available training time is a significant resource consideration in Reserve Component planning for training.

(Chg 1) FM 7-0
SMARTupdate

"Conduct stability operations" than those supporting offensive or defensive operations. When a unit receives a directed mission, the two commanders determine the unit's DMETL and when the unit will transition from CMETL to DMETL training. The two commanders repeat the above process to develop an approved training plan and contract to achieve DMETL proficiency.

Training Briefing Topics

Training briefings produce "contracts," verbal or otherwise, between the higher commander and supporting and subordinate commanders. The contract is an agreement on the following:

- Tasks to be trained
- Training conditions
- Resources required to create those conditions
- Risks associated with where the commanders are focusing training
- When the unit will transition from CMETL to DMETL training (for CMETL training briefings)

In agreeing to the negotiated training plan, the higher commander agrees to provide the required resources, including time, and to minimize subordinate unit exposure to unscheduled taskings. The subordinate commander agrees to execute the approved training plan and conduct training to standard. This shared responsibility helps maintain priorities, achieve unity of effort, and synchronize actions to achieve quality training and efficient resourcing.

Division commanders receive a training briefing from all assigned or attached brigades for which they have responsibility and from the battalions subordinate to those brigades. Brigade commanders and command sergeants major personally present the overview of the brigade training plan; battalion commanders and command sergeants major brief battalion training plans. All habitually associated commanders participate in preparing and presenting training briefings. Brigade commanders follow a similar process internally with their battalions and separate companies.

Installation Management Command representatives should attend all training briefings. Coordination between commanders and the installation representatives is required to ensure installation training resources are available and properly allocated.

The training briefing is a highlight of a commander's leader development program. The briefing gives commanders an opportunity to coach and teach subordinates. In addition to discussing their philosophies and strategies for conducting training and full spectrum operations, commanders may also address doctrine, force integration, and leader development. This interaction enables subordinate commanders and senior NCOs to better understand how their training relates to the mission-focused training programs of their higher commanders and peers.

Training Briefing Format

The higher commander specifies the format and content of training briefings. However, the briefing guidance should be flexible enough to allow subordinates latitude to highlight their initiatives and priorities. The command sergeant major normally provides an analysis of the unit's individual training proficiency and discusses planned individual training and education.

Readiness Issues

Units should not discuss readiness issues during training briefings unless the issues are training related. Statistical, logistic, manning, or other management data are more appropriate to readiness review forums. They distract participants from the overall focus of the training briefing.

IV. Training Plans

A training plan translates the commander's training and leader development guidance and training strategy into a series of interconnected requirements and events to achieve the commander's training objectives. Planning documents include the frequency and duration of each training event and the resources required. Required resources and events drive planning considerations. The three types of training plans are long-range, short-range, and near-term.

Long, Short, and Near-Term Planning

Long-Range	Short-Range	Near-Term
Disseminate mission-essential task list and supporting collective tasks	Refine and expand on the appropriate portions of the long-range plan	Refine and expand on the short-range plan by holding training meetings
Conduct commander's assessment	Cross-reference each training event with specific training objectives	Publish event training plans or operation orders as needed
Establish training objectives for each mission-essential task	Identify and allocate short-lead-time resources, such as local training facilities	Determine best sequence for training
Schedule projected major training events		Provide specific guidance for trainers
Identify long-lead-time resources and allocate major resources, such as major training area rotations	Coordinate the short-range calendar with all support agencies	Allocate training support system products and services, including training aids, devices, simulators, simulations, and similar resources
Identify available training support system products and services; identify new requirements	Publish the short-range training and leader development guidance and planning calendar	Publish detailed training schedules
Coordinate long-range calendars with supporting agencies to eliminate training distracters	Provide input to unit training meetings	Provide the basis for executing and evaluating training
Publish long-range training and leader development guidance and planning calendar		
Provide a basis for the command operating budget		
Provide long-range training input to higher headquarters		

Ref: FM 7-0, Training for Full Spectrum Operations (Dec '08), table 4-1, p. 69.

(Chg 1) FM 7-0 SMARTupdate

A. Long-Range Planning

The long-range training plan starts the process of implementing the commander's training strategy. Long-range plans identify the major training events for the unit along with the resources required to execute the training events. A long-range plan normally covers 12 months for Regular Army and mobilized Reserve Component units. It covers two years to an entire ARFORGEN cycle for other Reserve Component units. However, commanders can adjust the time frame covered to meet their needs.

A long-range training plan consists of training and leader development guidance and the long range-planning calendar. Senior commanders publish training and leader development guidance early enough to give their units enough time to plan, both during operations and in peacetime. Guidance from senior command echelons is critical to developing and integrating subordinate Regular Army and Reserve Component long-range training plans. Therefore, long lead times, consistent with the ARFORGEN cycles, are normal. Each headquarters follows an established timeline so subordinates have time to prepare their plans. Higher headquarters should give subordinate units more planning time than they keep for themselves.

Long-Range Training and Leader Development Guidance

Ref: FM 7-0, Training for Full Spectrum Operations (Dec. '08), pp. 4-29 to 4-30

Training and leader development guidance includes the commander's training assessment. Commanders down to company level can develop this guidance. Commanders ensure their guidance aligns with their higher commander's guidance. Commanders prepare their subordinate leaders for the mission at hand and develop them for their next duty position. Unit training and leader development guidance is based on the Chief of Staff, Army's, training and leader development guidance.

Commanders refer to the higher commander's guidance when developing their own training and leader development guidance. The higher commander's training and leader development guidance forms the basis for the dialog that determines the mix of tasks to train, how much time to spend on training various tasks, and other resources needed.

Subordinate commanders use their training and leader development guidance as a ready reference to perform training throughout the long-range time frame. Commanders determine the period the guidance covers based on the mission and situation. The time frame can span an entire ARFORGEN cycle or part of it. Alternatively, commanders can establish a time frame of a calendar year or more, again depending on mission and situation. Units of both the generating force and operational Army publish training and leader development guidance.

Training and leader development guidance topics

- Commander's training philosophy
- Commander's concept for training
- METL and supporting collective tasks to be trained
- Guidance for conducting major training events
- Resources for training
- Guidance for leader development
- Training conditions
- Command priorities
- Leader development program
- Combined arms training
- Unified action training, as applicable
- Long-range planning calendar
- Major training events and exercises
- Organizational inspection program
- Battle staff training
- Individual training
- Self-development training
- Standardization
- Training evaluation and feedback
- New equipment training and other force integration considerations
- Resource allocation
- Time management cycles
- Composite risk management

Long-Range Planning Calendar

The long-range planning calendar depicts the schedule of events described in the training and leader development guidance. Major training events and deployments scheduled beyond the plan's time frame also appear on the long-range planning calendar. Upon approval by the higher commander (normally during a training briefing), long-range planning calendars are locked in. This provides planning stability for subordinate units. Only the approving commander can change a long-range planning calendar. The approving commander agrees to allocate and protect the required resources, including time.

Reserve Component units require extended planning guidance. Therefore, Regular Army and Reserve Component planners forecast major events that require Reserve Component participation up to five years into the future. They include such major events as annual training periods and overseas training deployments. Both Regular Army and Reserve Component long-range planning calendars contain this information.

During long-range planning, commanders organize training time to support METL training and mitigate training distracters. (Time management cycles are one technique for doing this.) In addition to individual requirements, such as leave and medical appointments, units may have temporary duty and other support functions at the installation level.

Preparing the Long-Range Calendar

Ref: FM 7-1 Battle Focused Training, pp. 4-47 to 4-49.

The following four steps are suggested for preparing the long-range planning calendar. Applying these four steps is an iterative process—the steps are adjusted to synchronize plans and coordinate activities as resources are refined.

1. Post Required Training Events on the Calendar

The first step is to post required training events on the calendar. These are requirements that are directed by higher headquarters. These events provide excellent training opportunities for the battalion commander and subordinate leaders. The dates of these events should be annotated. Commanders and leaders should use blocked window periods if exact exercise dates are tentative or unknown at the time of publication. RC units must post AT and IDT dates first.

2. Schedule Other Requirements

The second step is to identify and schedule other requirements that impact on training. Commanders reduce training distracters by properly identifying required events early in the planning process.

3. Schedule Unit-Controlled Exercises & Other Training

The third step is to schedule unit-controlled exercises and other training. Commanders schedule the events based on the unit's training strategy. These unit-controlled exercises are designed to improve or sustain the unit's METL proficiency and support higher headquarters'- directed training requirements. For example, the battalion commander could schedule a TEWT, a CPX, an FCX, and STXs prior to a brigade FTX.

The long-range planning calendar is staffed with outside agencies that can impact on training. It is coordinated with subordinate and higher commanders, installation commanders, and supporting CS and CSS units. (Similarly, short-range and near-term training plans are coordinated with these same staff agencies.)

4. Post the Time-Management System

The fourth step is to post the time management system, which highlights prime time training periods available to the unit and support periods. Commanders then focus their resource and exercise planning to take advantage of prime time training, and look for other opportunities for small unit, crew, and individual training during support periods.

B. Short-Range Planning

Ref: FM 7-0, Training for Full Spectrum Operations (Dec. '08), pp. 4-30 to 4-32.

Short-range training plans consist of the short-range training and leader development guidance and a planning calendar. These plans refine the guidance contained in the long-range training and leader development guidance and planning calendar. They allocate resources to subordinate units and provide a common basis for near-term planning. When designing training events, planners allocate enough time to conduct the training to standard and time for retraining, if necessary.

Short-Range Training and Leader Development Guidance

Short-range training and leader development guidance enables commanders and key leaders to further prioritize and refine guidance contained in the long-range guidance. Commanders should publish the short-range guidance early enough for subordinate commanders to develop their short-range training plans. This guidance should be synchronized with the appropriate ARFORGEN phases and should be provided to subordinate commands and installations before training starts. After receiving guidance from their higher headquarters, subordinate units down to company level publish their short-range training guidance.

Example of Regular Army Training Cycle

Action	Publication Date	Time Frame
Division, or similar level command, publishes training and leader development guidance	3 months prior to start of training	3 months
Brigade publishes training and leader development guidance	2 months prior to start of training	3 months
Battalion, squadron, and separate company publish training and leader development guidance	6 weeks prior to start of training*	3 months
Conduct training briefing	At discretion of commanders; prior to start of training	3 + months

*To allow sufficient time for near-term planning at company level before the start of the training; must be synchronized with the Army force generation cycle, when appropriate.

Ref: FM 7-0, Training for Full Spectrum Operations (Dec '08), table. 4-3, p. 71.

Reserve Component commanders develop training and leader development guidance the same way as Regular Army commanders do except that Reserve Component timelines are normally longer than those of the Regular Army. Often Reserve Component unit commanders publish their short-range training and leader development guidance as annual training guidance. Additionally, Reserve Component unit commanders develop a plan for post-mobilization training. Commanders update this plan concurrently with the short-range training plan.

Example of Army Reserve Training Cycle

Action	Date	Time Frame
Division, or similar level command, publishes training and leader development guidance	6 to 8 months prior to start of fiscal year	1 + years
Brigade and separate battalion publish training and leader development guidance	4 to 6 months prior to start of fiscal year	1 + years
Battalion, squadron, and separate company publish training and leader development guidance	3 to 4 months prior to start of fiscal year	1 + years
Conduct training briefing	At discretion of commanders; prior to start of training	1+ years

Ref: FM 7-0, Training for Full Spectrum Operations (Dec '08), table. 4-4, p. 71.

Short-Range Planning Calendar

The short-range planning calendar refines the long-range planning calendar and provides the timelines necessary for small-unit leaders to prepare training schedules and event training plans.

In preparing a short-range calendar, leaders add details to further refine the major training events contained on the long-range planning calendar. Some examples of these details include:

- The principal daily activities of major training events
- Home station training scheduled to prepare for major training events, evaluations, and deployments
- Mandatory training that supports the METL, such as command inspections as part of the organizational inspection program, Army physical fitness tests, weapons qualification, and preventive maintenance checks and services
- Significant non-training events or activities, such as national holidays and installation support missions

The short-range training calendar is coordinated with appropriate Installation Management Command and supporting agencies. This coordination creates a common training and support focus for supported and supporting units.

C. Near-Term Planning

Ref: FM 7-0, Training for Full Spectrum Operations (Dec. '08), pp. 4-30 to 4-32.

Near-term planning is performed at battalion level and lower. It includes conducting training meetings and preparing training schedules and event training plans. Near-term planning is done to:

- Schedule and execute training events specified in the short-range training plan
- Provide specific guidance to trainers
- Make final coordination for allocating training resources
- Complete final coordination with other organizations scheduled to participate in training as part of the task organization
- Prepare detailed training schedules

Near-term planning normally covers the six to eight weeks before the training for Regular Army units and four months before the training for Reserve Component units. In coordination with the higher headquarters, commanders determine which timeline works best for them and their subordinate units. Formal near-term planning culminates when the organization publishes its training schedule.

Training Meetings

The single most important company meeting is the training meeting. Training meetings create the bottom-up flow of information regarding the specific training needs of the small-unit, staff, and individual Soldier. Training meetings address only training.

Normally platoons, companies, and battalions hold weekly training meetings. At company and platoon level, meetings directly concern the specifics of training preparation, execution, and pre-execution checks. At battalion level, training meetings primarily cover training management issues.

Training Schedules

Near-term planning results in a detailed training schedule. Senior commanders establish policies to minimize changes to training schedules. At a minimum, training schedules:

- Specify when training starts and where it takes place
- Allocate adequate time to train all tasks to standard, including time to repeat training when standards are not met
- Specify individual, leader, and collective tasks on which to train
- Provide multi-echelon and concurrent training topics to make maximum use of available training time
- Specify who prepares, executes, and evaluates the training
- Provide administrative information concerning uniform, weapons, equipment, references, and safety precautions

Command training schedule responsibilities consist of the following:

- Company commanders approve and sign their company's draft training schedule
- Battalion commanders approve and sign the schedule and provide necessary administrative and logistic support. Training is considered locked in when the battalion commander signs the training schedule.
- The brigade commander reviews each training schedule published in the brigade
- The brigade's higher headquarters reviews selected training schedules and the list of unit-wide training highlights

Senior commanders provide feedback to subordinates on training schedule quality. Those commanders visit training to ensure that training objectives are met and tasks are trained to standard.

I. Training Meetings

Ref: FM 7-1 Battle Focused Training, chap. 4, pp. 4-75 to 4-78.

Training meetings are non-negotiable-they are key to near-term planning. Training meetings create the bottom-up flow of information regarding specific training proficiency needs of the small unit, staff, and individual soldier. Training meetings are planned and appear on the training schedule.

Training Meetings

The purpose of the training meeting is to-
1. Identify leader and unit training tasks
2. Review preparation for upcoming training to include, for example-
   • Leader and unit preparatory training
   • Rehearsals for trainers, evaluators, and OCs
   • OPFOR training and preparation
   • Training site preparation
   • TADSS issue and maintenance
3. Provide a forum for leaders, trainers, and evaluators to give feedback on the training executed during the past week
4. Provide commanders with a continuous source of "bottom-up" input for periodic training assessments

Ref: FM 7-1, p. 4-75.

At training meetings, each echelon reviews recently conducted training. They also refine and plan training for the next 6 to 8 weeks.

Training meetings provide guidance to ensure the quality of training. Well-structured, organized, and recurring training meetings impact directly on the unit's mission. Training meetings should last no more than 1 hour and nothing should be discussed but training (leaders should not discuss readiness status issues, nor treat the meeting as a command and staff meeting, etc.).

Training meetings provide the forum to plan and coordinate training that is mission-focused and demanding. Training meetings are conducted weekly for AC, and monthly for RC at battalion and company level.

I. Battalion Training Meetings

Note: For guidance on company-level training meetings, see p. 6-20.

At training meetings, each echelon reviews recently conducted training. They also refine and plan training for the next 6 to 8 weeks.

Suggested Battalion Training Meeting Participants
- Commander
- Command sergeant major
- Executive officer
- Company commanders and 1SGs
- Specialty platoon leaders (scouts, mortar, support and medical)
- Coordinating staff (S1, S2, S3, S4, S5 and S6)
- Special staff (Chemo, BMO, physician's assistant (PA) and chaplain (UMT))
- Direct support (DS) CS and CSS unit representatives (FSO, ALO, engineer, ADA, MI and BSB SPO)

When appropriate, RC commanders may want to include participants from the AC associate organization. RC commanders should take necessary actions to ensure that companies attend battalion-level training meetings when geographic dispersion is a challenge. Essential training information can be exchanged using video tele-conference (VTC), email, or other means, but there is no substitute for face-to-face discussions during training meetings.

Suggested Agenda

At training meetings, each echelon reviews recently conducted training. They also refine and plan training for the next 6 to 8 weeks. At battalion level, the following agenda may be used:
1. Review QTG or YTG
2. Review recently conducted training (briefed by company commanders), to include-
   - Assess training conducted since the last meeting
   - Review reasons for training planned, but not conducted
   - Update the current status of training proficiency
3. Brief near-term training to-
   - Discuss any new guidance received from higher commanders
   - Publish training scheduled for the next 4 to 6 weeks (next 4 months for RC)
   - Review and complete pre-execution checks (document training distractors from higher headquarters)
   - Issue commander's guidance for training scheduled 6 to 8 weeks out (4 months out for RC)
   - Review preparations for multiechelon training
4. Review the short-range plan
5. Review projected resources

Ref: FM 7-1, p. 4-75.

Training Meetings

Ref: FM 7-1 Battle Focused Training, fig. 4-48, p. 4-77.

- **Are non-negotiable at battalion and company level**
- **Focus on:**
  - **Battalion level:** training management issues for the next 6 to 8 weeks
  - **Company, battery, troop level**: specifics of executing scheduled training to standard
  - **Platoon and squad level**: Identify essential platoon/squad/crew collective, leader, and individual soldier task(s) training requirements.
  - Input those identified platoon/squad/crew, leader, and individual soldier training requirements
  - Brief and review published training schedules with the platoon/squad/crew

- **Are conducted by commanders; CSMs and 1SGs assist commanders**
  - Post unit training schedules
  - Are routinely scheduled on the same week day and same time
  - Follow a published agenda and do not exceed allotted time
  - Are conducted weekly for AC and monthly for RC at battalion and company level

- **CSMs and 1SGs ensure that individual soldier training supports collective unit training**
- **Are a vehicle for leader development**
- **Are a forum to:**
  - Ensure that training is METL-related
  - Solicit evaluation feedback
  - Solicit training requirement input from platoon leaders and platoon sergeants
  - Assess current status of training proficiency
  - Identify key soldier changes and resource requirements
  - Review commander's current training guidance, short-range plan, and projected resources
  - Provide guidance on pre-execution checks
  - Ensure that risk management is integrated into preexecution checks
  - Monitor pre-execution checks
  - Resolve problems identified during pre-execution checks updates
  - Identify and coordinate multiechelon training opportunities
  - Share training tactics, techniques, and procedures (TTP)
  - Allocate resources and approve ongoing near-term training

- **Result in a coordinated and locked-in training schedule**

Training Plans, Mtgs & Schedules

II. Company Training Meetings

Ref: FM 7-1 Battle Focused Training, app. B.

Training is the Army's number one priority. Company training meetings are key to near-term planning and are non-negotiable. Accordingly they appear on the weekly training calendar. Training meetings create the bottom-up flow of information regarding specific training proficiency needs of the unit and individual soldiers. Training meetings are conducted by leaders to review past training, identify and plan necessary retraining, plan and prepare future training, and exchange timely training information between leaders

Feedback is an important aspect of training meetings and is used to refine the training plan. This feedback takes many forms, for example, personal observation, after action reviews (AARs), and informal evaluations. The training meeting is a primary forum for discussing training assessments.

A. Objective

Company training meetings review completed training, deconflict training issues, plan and prepare future training, and exchange timely training information between participants. Training meetings are not a forum for discussing administrative operations and activities. Training is the sole topic. The training meeting focuses on three key tasks-

- Assessing completed training to determine the effectiveness of individual, leader, and collective training conducted since the last training meeting.
- Coordinating near-term training to confirm specific instructions and details to conduct the training.
- Planning for short-range training to develop future training plans that refine the short-range training plan

B. Participants

Leader participation is essential for a successful company training meeting.

- Company commander
- Executive officer
- First sergeant
- Platoon leaders
- Platoon sergeants
- Master gunner/Chief of firing battery/Shop supervisor
- Maintenance team chief
- Supply sergeant
- NBC NCO
- Others as required
  - Food service NCO
  - Direct support, unit representatives (FSO, ALO, Engineer, ADA, MI and BSB)

C. Responsibilities

Participants in company training meetings have the following responsibilities:

- The company commander is responsible for the efficient conduct of the training meeting.
- The XO coordinates training for all the soldiers in sections or attachments without platoon leaders or platoon sergeants.
- The 1SG assists the commander with individual soldier training assessments, provides guidance and advice on training plans, and reviews pre-execution checks discussed during the training meeting.
- Platoon leaders brief the collective task proficiency of their platoon, provide the commander and other members of the company with feedback on details of near-term training, and recommend collective training tasks for short-range training.
- Platoon sergeants brief individual soldier tasks, brief specific essential pre-execution checks for near-term training, and recommend individual soldier tasks for short-range training.
- Key NCOs, such as master gunners, attend training meetings and advise the commander on specialized training. For example, the master gunner works with the 1SG to track individual and crew-served weapon qualification, and helps leaders with gunnery training assessments.
- Maintenance team chiefs coordinate the maintenance efforts of the company and work with the commander and XO to ensure that timely support is provided. The maintenance team chief provides input on the status of maintenance training in the company, recommends maintenance-related training, and informs the commander of scheduled services and inspections.
- Supply sergeants advise the commander on supply-related issues, inspections, and inventories. Supply sergeants also work with the XO and 1SG to coordinate necessary support from outside sources.
- Attached leaders attend training meetings to coordinate their training efforts with those of the company. To "train as you fight," commanders fully integrate the training of all habitually-associated units.
- RC companies may have AC associate personnel attend the training meetings. These personnel bring valuable experience and the latest training techniques from AC units.

D. Training Meeting Time and Place

The company meeting follows the battalion training meeting by no more than two days. Company training meetings generally are conducted on the same day and time each week.

Selecting a time to conduct training meetings depends on several factors. The main considerations include-

- Enabling leaders to attend
- Minimizing training disruptions
- Allowing subordinate leaders time to prepare
- Local policy

Selecting a time for RC companies to conduct training meetings is more challenging. There are three alternatives-

- Conduct the meeting during a regularly scheduled drill session
- Conduct the meeting during an additional training assembly (ATA)
- Conduct the training meeting during a "for points only" or non-paid assembly

Company Training Meeting Agenda

Ref: FM 7-1 Battle Focused Training, app. B.

There are three phases to company training meetings. They are assessment of the training completed, preparation for near-term training, and planning for short-range training. The agenda maintains a focus for all to see, understand, and follow.

Time Requirements

Company training meetings should not exceed one hour. Occasional situations may require meetings to last more than one hour, but these are the exception. The key is for the commander to achieve the meeting objectives as quickly and efficiently as possible.

A. Assessment of Completed Training

Commanders begin the meeting by discussing the training completed. The bottom-up input by the platoon leaders and platoon sergeants is critical to the assessment of the collective, leader, and individual training proficiency of the unit.

Assessment of Completed Training

Platoon Assessment	Training Shortfalls	METL Update
■ Collective, Leader and Soldier Training ■ "T", "P", "U" Snapshot	■ Training Planned but Not Conducted ■ Reason for Not Executing ■ Retraining Plan	■ Training Assessment Guide Sheet ■ Platoon Input ■ Personal Observation

Ref: FM 7-1, fig. B-3, p. B-5.

Assessment of completed training may reveal training that is incomplete or not conducted to the Army standard. Retraining should be conducted at the first opportunity-ideally, during the conduct of training. However, when this cannot happen, it may be necessary to adjust subsequent training planning to retrain on those tasks that were not performed to standard.

In reviewing retraining requirements, company leaders consider a number of factors-

* The number of soldiers or elements involved.
* If the retraining is sequential to other planned training-does the retraining need to be accomplished before completing a future task?
* Resource availability (ranges, instructors, logistics, etc.).
* Original planning for the task and modification as necessary.
* When and where to reschedule the training at the first available opportunity.

1. Platoon Assessments

Platoon leaders and platoon sergeants assess collective and soldier proficiency since the last training meeting. This assessment is a "T", "P", "U" snapshot of all training conducted by the platoon. The sources of the platoon assessment may be formal or informal.

As each platoon completes the training assessment, training shortfalls are addressed. A training shortfall occurs when training has been planned, but is not conducted. Platoon leaders must explain to the commander why the training was not executed, and show the plan to reschedule the missed training.

2. METL Update

After all platoons complete their training assessments and discuss any training shortfalls, the commander updates the company METL assessment.

B. Preparation for Near-Term Training

The next step in the company training meeting process is to apply new training requirements, and to conduct pre-execution checks for the planned training.

Preparation for Near-Term Training

Command Guidance

- New or Unscheduled Requirements
- Only Training-Related Issues

Pre-Execution Check Review

- Informal Planning
- Detailed Coordination
- AC Commanders - 4 to 6 Weeks out
- RC Commanders - Next 3 months
- Focus is on Details
- Risk Assessment

Ref: FM 7-1, fig. B-4, p.B-6.

A critical part of the training meeting is the discussion of pre-execution checks. Pre-execution checks include the informal planning and detailed coordination conducted during preparation for training. The primary trainer indicated on the training schedule briefs pre-execution checks.

C. Planning For Short-Range Training

The commander must check the battalion long-range training calendar. Events indicated on the battalion calendar or found in the CTG are put on the company training schedule first. After these events are posted, the commander begins planning company training to train tasks necessary to support battalion training events. He plans training on company identified tasks and begins to develop pre-execution checks to fix responsibilities for the training.

1. Platoon Leader/Platoon Sergeant Input

Based on their training assessments, platoon leaders and platoon sergeants develop plans to improve training proficiency. These plans are prepared and briefed to the commander during the training meeting.

2. Training Schedule Development

Commanders receive input from all platoons and other elements of the company before formulating the draft training schedule. Because of support limitations or other conflicts, the commander may have to disapprove a training event that a platoon requested, or move it to another week (AC) or month (RC). Once all conflicts are resolved, the commander develops a rough draft of the next training schedule.

III. Platoon Training Meetings

Platoon Training Meetings

At platoon training meetings, the following agenda may be used, focusing on the details of training tasks required:

1. Review recently conducted training (briefed by squad or section leaders) to-
   - Assess training conducted since the last meeting (collective and soldier tasks).
   - Review reasons for training planned, but not conducted.
   - Determine the current status of training proficiency.
2. Brief near-term training to-
   - Apply new guidelines from higher commanders, especially new or unscheduled requirements.
   - Review pre-execution checks for training scheduled for the next 4 to 6 weeks (next 3 months for RC).
3. Identify essential soldier, leader, and collective training needs to be sent up the chain of command through the next higher-level training meeting.
4. Ensure that information passed out at company training meetings reaches every soldier through their platoon chain of command

Ref: FM 7-1, p. 4-76.

Platoon training meetings are organized very similar to company training meetings, only less formal in nature. They are held every week (every month for RC during inactive duty training) and generally last about 30 minutes. Only key leaders attend; each squad- or section-level unit is represented by a single NCO. Keeping the number of leaders to an essential minimum allows for a more candid and efficient exchange of information. A typical list of attendees for a platoon meeting are listed below.

- Platoon leader
- Platoon sergeant
- Squad leaders/section leaders

Some platoons do not neatly fit the mold of infantry or armor platoons. For these platoons the platoon leader and PSG together decide who should attend the meeting, keeping in mind that the objective is to have each section represented by one NCO. For example, a maintenance platoon without a platoon leader may have a list of attendees that resembles the list shown below.

- Platoon sergeant
- Recovery section sergeant
- Services section sergeant
- Maintenance team chief
- PLL section sergeant

Whatever the composition of the list of participants, the platoon sergeant ensures that all NCOs are prepared for the meeting. This means everyone being on time and properly equipped. At a minimum, NCOs need to bring the following to a platoon meeting:

- Leader book
- Paper and pencil/pen
- Training schedules
- Calendar

What to Bring to the Training Meeting

Ref: TC 25-30, pp. 3-4 to 3-9.

The key to success is leaders having everything at their fingertips so that they can effectively participate in the meeting process.

Commander
- Company battle rosters
- Training meeting work sheet
- Mission essential task list with current assessment
- Most current Command Tng Guidance
- Long- and short-range calendars
- Company training schedules
  — Past week/month
  — Approved future schedules
- Applicable manuals
- Applicable OPORDs, MOIs, and training support requests

Executive Officer
- Maintenance schedule
- Inspection schedule
- Current DA Form 2406
- Supply inventory schedule
- Headquarters and headquarters company (HHC) training schedules
- Status of resources requested for training

First Sergeant
- Leader book
- Company battle rosters
- Company duty rosters
- Battalion duty schedules
- Taskings
- Appointment schedules
- Schools schedules
- Inspection schedules
- Miscellaneous information (APFT, height/weight data)

Plt Leader/Plt Sergeant
- Leader book
- Platoon assessment work sheets
- Training schedules
- Preexecution checklists
- Training and evaluation outlines (TEO) for future training
- Platoon battle rosters
- Future training work sheets

Master Gunner
- Leader book
- Training schedules
- Battle rosters

- Individual/crew weapon qualification records
- Unit Conduct-of-Fire Trainer (UCOFT) training results
- Gunnery training plans

Battle Staff NCO
- Training schedules
- Maintenance schedule
- Staff inspection schedule
- Maintenance Team Chief
- Leader book
- Battle roster
- Training schedules
- Maintenance schedule
- Inspection schedule
- Current DA Form 2406

Supply Sergeant
- Leader book
- Training schedules
- Supply inventory schedules (10 percent inventories)
- Inspection schedules

Training NCO
- Training schedule
- Battle roster
- SDT schedules
- Schools information

NBC NCO
- Leader book
- Training schedules
- NBC equipment services schedule
- Inspection schedule

Slice Leaders/Attachments
- Leader books
- Training schedules (own unit & company)
- Applicable SOPs
- Command training guidance
- Long- and short-range training calendars

Food Service NCO
- Leader book
- Training/inspection schedule
- Mess equipment service schedule

Training Meeting Work Sheets

Purpose
The purpose of the training meeting work sheet is to help the commander maintain focus during the training meeting. The commander partially fills out the work sheet prior to the training meeting with notes and general plans for future training. During the meeting the work sheet is used to record training notes and assessment results.

Format
The recommended format for the training meeting work sheet a simple two-column form. Each column is then broken down into week-long blocks. The left side of the work sheet is reserved for the commander's notes and "reminders" of issues to address during the meeting. The right side of the work sheet is filled out during the meeting and is used to help complete future training schedules.

NOTE: The training meeting work sheet is an informal training management tool used by the company commander. It should not be inspected.

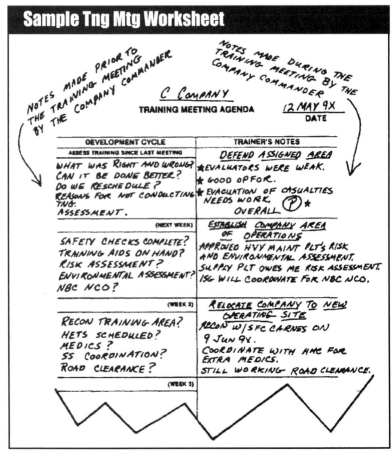

Sample Tng Mtg Worksheet

NOTES MADE PRIOR TO THE TRAINING MEETING BY THE COMPANY COMMANDER

NOTES MADE DURING THE TRAINING MEETING BY THE COMPANY COMMANDER

C COMPANY
TRAINING MEETING AGENDA   **12 MAY 9X**
                              DATE

DEVELOPMENT CYCLE	TRAINER'S NOTES
ASSESS TRAINING SINCE LAST MEETING	DEFEND ASSIGNED AREA
WHAT WAS RIGHT AND WRONG? CAN IT BE DONE BETTER? DO WE RESCHEDULE? REASONS FOR NOT CONDUCTING TNG. ASSESSMENT.	★EVALUATORS WERE WEAK. ★ GOOD OPFOR. ★ EVACUATION OF CASUALTIES NEEDS WORK. ⑦ ★ OVERALL
(NEXT WEEK)	ESTABLISH COMPANY AREA OF OPERATIONS
SAFETY CHECKS COMPLETE? TRAINING AIDS ON HAND? RISK ASSESSMENT? ENVIRONMENTAL ASSESSMENT? NBC NCO?	APPROVED HVY MAINT PLT'S RISK AND ENVIRONMENTAL ASSESSMENT. SUPPLY PLT OWES ME RISK ASSESSMENT. 1SG WILL COORDINATE FOR NBC NCO.
(WEEK 2)	RELOCATE COMPANY TO NEW OPERATING SITE
RECON TRAINING AREA? HETS SCHEDULED? MEDICS? SS COORDINATION? ROAD CLEARANCE?	RECON W/ SFC CARNES ON 9 JUN 9X. COORDINATE WITH HHC FOR EXTRA MEDICS. STILL WORKING ROAD CLEARANCE.
(WEEK 3)	

Ref: TC 25-30, fig. 3-3. p. 3-4.

Training Plans, Mtgs & Schedules

II. Training Schedules

Ref: FM 7-1 Battle Focused Training, chap. 4, pp. 4-78 to 4-81.

Near-term planning results in detailed training schedules. The training schedule is the unit's primary management tool to ensure that training is conducted in a timely manner by qualified trainers, with the necessary resources, to the Army standard.

At a minimum, the training schedule should-

- Allocate adequate time for training preparation
- Specify when training starts and where it takes
- Allocate adequate time for scheduled training and retraining as required
- Specify the individual, leader, and collective tasks to be trained
- Provide concurrent training topics that efficiently use available training time
- Specify who conducts the training and who evaluates the training
- Provide administrative information concerning uniform, weapons, equipment, and references

The training planning process links the unit METL with the execution of battle focused training. Planning for training is a continuous, integrated process done in parallel at all organizational levels for long-range, short-range, and near-term planning. The planning process culminates with the publication of training schedules and leads to training execution.

Draft Training Schedules and Pre-Execution Checks
Draft training schedules and pre-execution checks must be initiated at least 6 to 8 weeks (4 months for RC) prior to the training. This ensures that resources are coordinated and external support is requested. For AC, training schedules are published 4 to 6 weeks prior to execution; for RC, 3 months prior.

Company and Battalion Commander Approval
The company commander signs the training schedule, which identifies the specific unit training needs that have been planned. The battalion commander then signs the training schedule, thereby giving it final approval. The battalion commander's signature finalizes the training "contract," and verifies that necessary resources will be provided. Once the battalion commander approves and the signs the training schedule, it is locked in and constitutes an official order. Only the approving authority can authorize changes to the training schedule. For example, the battalion commander is authorized to approve changes to an approved and signed company, battery, or troop training schedule. Higher headquarters must protect subordinate units from unprogrammed events, activities, and other distracters.

Subordinate Leader Responsibilities
Leaders must ensure that daily training is conducted to standard and adheres to the training schedule. CSMs, 1SGs, and other NCO leaders are key to ensuring that training is conducted to standard. Commanders establish procedures to minimize changes to the training schedules.

Training Schedule Development
Ref: FM 7-1 Battle Focused Training, fig. 4-52, p. 4-80.

Training schedule development at company level focuses on the specifics of training to be conducted for the next 6 to 8 weeks. The training schedule provides detailed information necessary for executing training to the Army standard. Near-term planning culminates when the unit executes the training on the training schedule.

Training schedules should:

- Specify when training starts and where it takes place
- Allocate adequate time for scheduled training and retraining as required to correct anticipated deficiencies
- Specify individual, leader, and collective tasks to be trained
- Provide concurrent training topics that will efficiently use available training time
- Specify who conducts the training and who evaluates the training
- Provide administrative information concerning uniform, weapons, equipment, references, and safety precautions

A. Commander Responsibilities
Ref: FM 7-1, Battle-Focused Training, fig. 4-51, p. 4-79.

The company commander signs the training schedule, which identifies the specific unit training needs that have been planned. The battalion commander then signs the training schedule, thereby giving it final approval. The battalion commander's signature finalizes the training "contract," and verifies that necessary resources will be provided. Once the battalion commander approves and the signs the training schedule, it is locked in and constitutes an official order. Only the approving authority can authorize changes to the training schedule. For example, the battalion commander is authorized to approve changes to an approved and signed company, battery, or troop training schedule. Higher headquarters must protect subordinate units from unprogrammed events, activities, and other distracters.

Division Commanders
- Review selected training highlights
- Visit and assess selected highlighted training events

Brigade commanders
- Review published training schedules
- Visit and assess selected training

Battlalion Commanders
- Battalion commanders approve training schedules. Their signature validates the company plan and provides required resources. Approved and signed training schedules lock in training and constitute an official order.

Company Commanders
- Company commanders sign training schedules and submit them to the battalion commander for final approval.

All Commanders
- All commanders establish procedures to minimize training schedule changes.

B. Steps to Training Schedule Development

Training schedule development is the primary focus of training meetings at battalion level. Outlined below are suggested steps to develop an AC training schedule:

Weeks T-8 to T-6
- Assess training and identify specific collective, leader, and individual soldier tasks that require additional training
- Platoon leaders and sergeants, squad leaders and team leaders provide input on tasks that require additional training
- Approve draft training schedules
- Request Class I, III, IV, and V supplies, TADSS, training areas, ranges
- Provide pre-execution checks guidance; begin pre-execution checks

Week T-5
- Company cdr finalizes and signs training schedules; bn cdr approves/signs
- NCOs provide commander with individual soldier training objectives
- Confirm support requests; lock in resources
- Identify trainer, evaluator, OC, and OPFOR rehearsal requirements
- Resolve scheduling conflicts

Week T-4
- Post training schedules in the company area
- Identify and brief trainers, evaluators, OCs, and OPFOR on responsibilities
- Conduct initial trainer, evaluator, OC, and OPFOR backbriefs

Week T-3
- Begin rehearsals for trainers, evaluators, OCs, and OPFOR
- Recon training areas, ranges, firing points, etc; resolve schedule conflicts
- Conduct IPR for trainers, evaluators, OCs, and OPFOR

Week T-2
- Continue trainer, evaluator, OC, and OPFOR rehearsals and preparation
- Conduct final IPR

Week T-1
- Draw and test engagement simulation equipment and other training aids
- Complete pre-execution checks. This includes trainer, evaluator, OC, and OPFOR rehearsals, and training site preparation
- Brief soldiers on details of training

T Week
- Conduct training
- Conduct AARs (and retraining as necessary)

Week T+1
- Conduct recovery. This includes those actions to complete accountability actions for organizational and individual equipment and after-operations PMCS
- Conduct final AAR for the training event
- Solicit training evaluation feedback
- Solicit training requirement input from platoon leaders and platoon sergeants
- Assess current status of training proficiency

Effective Training

Ref: FM 7-0 Training the Force, chap. 5, pp. 5-5 to 5-6.

Effective training builds proficiency, teamwork, confidence, and cohesiveness. Effective training is competitive. Although individuals and organizations may sometimes compete against one another, they should always compete to achieve the prescribed standard.

Training and Evaluation Outline (T&EO)
Effective collective, leader, and individual training are guided by the use of T&EOs. The T&EO provides summary information concerning collective training objectives as well as individual and leader training tasks that support the collective training objectives.

Individual Training
The individual soldier is the heart of any unit's ability to conduct its mission. The ability to perform individual/leader skills to standard is founded in the institutional training base, but it is honed and maintained by effective, periodic repetition of tasks.

Leader Training
Leaders spend virtually all available training time supervising the training of subordinates. Often, they do not increase their own understanding of how to fight as combat or support leaders. Therefore, senior commanders view leader training as a continuous process that encompasses more than periodic officer and NCO professional development classes. Senior commanders establish a positive training environment that encourages subordinates to become adaptive leaders capable of independent thinking on the move, and of timely decision making based on broad, effects-based intent guidance, mission orders, and a shared vision of the battlefield.

Battle Rosters
Battle rosters are maintained at battalion level and below to track key training information on selected mission essential systems. They track such pertinent training data as crew stability and manning levels, and qualification status. A key aspect of battle rosters is the designation of qualified back-up operators or crewmembers assigned in other positions in the organization. During the execution of training, battle rostered crewmembers train with their designated crews at available opportunities. Commanders must discipline the battle roster system.

Battle Staff Training
Battle staff training develops and sustains planning, coordination, execution, and other staff functions related to wartime mission requirements. Commanders train battle staffs primarily through a mix of constructive and virtual simulations. Battle staffs train to integrate and coordinate the BOS internally within their own headquarters, horizontally with other staffs at the same organizational level, and vertically with higher and subordinate organizational staffs.

JIM (Joint, Interagency, Mulitinational) Training
Joint training is conducted using approved joint doctrine and TTPs, and must be consistent with assigned joint missions and priorities. When assigned as a JFC, Army commanders establish joint training objectives and plans, execute and evaluate joint training, and assess training proficiency. Multinational training optimizes contributions of member forces by matching their missions with their capabilities, and uses available training assistance programs.

III. Composite Risk Management (CRM)

FM 5-19 Composite Risk Management.

CRM is a decisionmaking process used to mitigate risks associated with all hazards that have the potential to injure or kill personnel, damage or destroy equipment, or otherwise impact mission effectiveness. In the past, the Army separated risk into two categories, tactical risk and accident risk. While these two areas of concern remain, the primary premise of CRM is that it does not matter where or how the loss occurs, the result is the same—decreased combat power or mission effectiveness.

Composite Risk Management

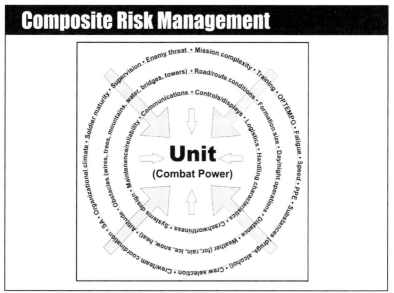

Ref: FM 5-19, fig. 1-1, p. 1-1.

The guiding principles of CRM are as follows:

- **Integrate CRM into all phases of missions and operations.** Effective CRM requires that the process be integrated into all phases of mission or operational planning, preparation, execution, and recovery.
- **Make risk decisions at the appropriate level.** CRM is only effective when the information is passed to the appropriate level of command for decision.
- **Accept no unnecessary risk.** Accept no level of risk unless the potential gain or benefit outweighs the potential loss. CRM is a decisionmaking tool to assist the commander, leader, or individual in identifying, assessing, and controlling risks in order to make informed decisions that balance risk costs (losses) against mission benefits (potential gains).
- **Apply the process cyclically and continuously.** CRM is a continuous process applied across the full spectrum of Army training and operations, individual and collective day-to-day activities and events, and base operations functions to continuously identify and assess hazards, develop and implement controls, and evaluate outcomes.
- **Do not be risk averse.** Identify and control the hazards; complete the mission.

I. Application to the Training Process

Ref: FM 5-19 Composite Risk Management, chap. 5.

As part of the Army's training development process, the systems approach to training management (SAT) is a systematic approach to making training and educational decisions. The SAT process is used in Total Army School System Training Battalions and all subordinate organizations responsible for managing or performing training or related functions. This includes evaluating the training as well as the personnel, products, and institutions conducting the training. CRM is a vital component of the training-development process.

The major concern of all commanders is to ensure their Soldiers and units are trained to perform their mission to standard and survive. To ensure mission-focused training, Soldiers, staffs, and units must perform under realistic and stressful conditions. CRM balances benefits against potential losses. It provides commanders and leaders with the tools to accomplish realistic training while preserving the scarce resources of personnel, time, and equipment. When used properly, CRM is a training enabler.

A. Application to the SAT Process

The SAT is a systematic, spiral approach to making collective, individual, and selfdevelopment training decisions for the Army. It determines—

- Whether or not training is needed
- What is to be trained
- Who gets the training
- How, how well, and where the training is presented
- The training support and resources required to produce, distribute, implement, and evaluate those products

The process involves five training related phases: analysis, design, development, implementation, and evaluation.

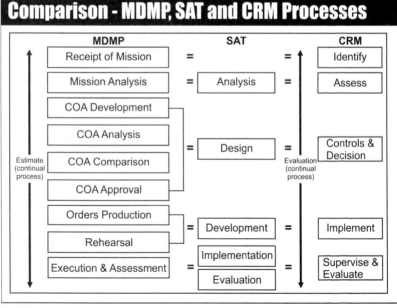

Comparison - MDMP, SAT and CRM Processes

MDMP	SAT	CRM
Receipt of Mission	= =	Identify
Mission Analysis	= Analysis =	Assess
COA Development		
COA Analysis	= Design =	Controls & Decision
COA Comparison		
COA Approval		
Orders Production	= Development =	Implement
Rehearsal		
Execution & Assessment	= Implementation =	Supervise & Evaluate
	Evaluation	

Estimate (continual process) — Evaluation (continual process)

Ref: FM 5-9, fig. 5-1, p. 5-19.

Evaluation is continuous throughout the SAT process with feedback for corrective actions. It permeates all phases. It is the cement that ensures training and training products are effective in producing trained units and Soldiers. Products are evaluated either formally (product validation) or informally to determine currency, efficiency, and effectiveness. The entire process must operate within a given set of resources. The CRM process runs simultaneously and continuously to ensure training remains within the specified level of risk allowed for each event.

B. Integration into Realistic Training

Commanders and leaders are required to make informed risk decisions. This ensures that training is conducted realistically and in a manner that protects the well-being of the Soldiers being trained. This enables Soldiers, leaders, and units to survive and win over the full range of military operations.

Training developers and trainers provide safe training to achieve force protection by designing, developing, and implementing realistic, viable training that—

- Does not unnecessarily jeopardize lives and equipment
- Eliminates or minimizes the risks involved in relation to the training benefits
- Includes controls to eliminate/reduce the risk or hazard
- Conserves and preserves resources
- Complies with federal, state, and local laws, regulations, and restrictions
- Integrates safety, risk management, and force protection considerations into training and training materials where appropriate

Proponent training developers will ensure all training products—

- Include appropriate safety, risk, and protection statements, cautions, notes, and warnings
- Identify training risk and assigns a risk level to every proponent lesson
- Are validated by the Branch Safety Manager for CRM integration
- Include controls necessary to minimize or eliminate hazards during training
- Address CRM and the CRM process as it applies operationally to the training subject

The training development process fixes responsibility, institutionalizes operational safety, and leads to decisionmaking at the command level appropriate to the identified level of risk. Using CRM in the training-development process ensures the following:

- Safe training
- Fewer injuries and deaths
- Reduced incidents of lost time
- Lower costs (facility, training, and equipment repairs)

CRM is never complete. It is a continuing cycle that requires everyone be constantly alert to training risks and to take immediate action to eliminate them or reduce their severity. Safety, risk management, and accident prevention are a commander's, manager's, and individual's responsibility. Proponent training developers, trainers, and subordinate personnel should use the generic risk management information contained in training support products to review and update hazards and controls to adjust for current conditions.

Composite Risk Management (CRM)

Ref: 2007 Army Posture Statement, addendum B

The Army recognizes that Soldiers and civilians are vital Army assets whether engaging the enemy, resetting at home station, or visiting family in their hometown. Composite Risk Management (CRM) is the Army's primary risk management process for identifying and controlling risks across the full spectrum of Army missions, functions, operations, and activities.

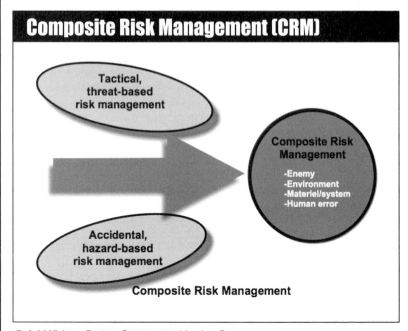

Composite Risk Management

Ref: 2007 Army Posture Statement, addendum B.

CRM supplements a focus on the main operation with consideration of other risks to give a complete picture of exposure. There is no separation of tactical or accidental, deployed or garrison, field or work area, on duty or off duty risks—it is risk management 24/7. The enemy, materiel, the environment, and human factors—during a mission or outside of it—all interact. Commanders, leaders, and individual Soldiers and civilians apply CRM through the identification of all hazards then determining and applying appropriate control measures to mitigate those hazards.

While readiness and force preservation remain a commander and leader responsibility, we continue our efforts to create a culture in which everyone, down to the individual, applies CRM. CRM is an enabler of our success and the vehicle we are using to transform our mindset in how we address and mitigate risk.

CRM links risk management to readiness and shifts our approach from accident-centric to people-centric. The lynchpin of successful CRM is engaged leaders at all echelons—engaged leaders who are actively involved with their formations' activities on and off duty and who work tirelessly to preserve our combat power.

II. Application to Other Functional Areas

Ref: FM 5-19 Composite Risk Management, chap. 6, pp. 6-1 to 6-2.

The death of a Soldier in combat or due to an accident can have a devastating effect on a unit's morale and effectiveness. The effects of criminal acts, suicide, sexual assault, and reckless behavior can also cripple an organization's morale and destroy its combat effectiveness.

The principles of CRM become indispensable in addressing issues that impact Soldiers both on and off the battlefield. Effective CRM is on-going and cyclic. The risk management process is integrated into the development of all SOPs and the development process for all policies that address issues of behavior, health, and criminal activity.

By applying the principles of risk management when identifying hazards associated with suicide, sexual assault, and POV accident prevention, commanders can take the initiative to identify and mitigate risks associated with these hazardous behaviors and situations before they impact on our units.

A. Sexual Assault Prevention

The prevention of sexual assault is a command and an individual responsibility. Sexual assault destroys teamwork, undermines the good order and discipline of the military, destroys unit morale, and impacts personal combat readiness. Effective CRM identifies the potential hazards, conditions, or situations that may lead to criminal behavior. Early identification of these conditions and active intervention reduces the likelihood of Soldiers attempting sexual assault or becoming a victim of a sexual assault. The principles of risk management can play a pivotal role by assisting the commander with tools to enhance policy awareness and training. By conducting command climate assessments, complaints processing awareness briefings, and overall assistance concerning the prevention of sexual harassment, commanders can mitigate the risks associated with sexual harassment.

B. Suicide Prevention

Each year the Army needlessly loses Soldiers to suicide. Suicide continues to be a problem that demands every leader's attention. The causes of suicide are difficult to understand, but by applying the principles of risk management, leaders and Soldiers alike can better identify "at risk" Soldiers. They then can take appropriate actions to prevent the tragedy of suicide. The role of Army leadership in suicide prevention cannot be overemphasized. Military leaders monitor and protect those under their command. A military leader can more effectively promote and sustain protective factors in a military setting than in a civilian one. Quality leaders endorse, advocate, authorize, and even mandate suicide prevention as a priority. It is important for all commanders and leaders to recognize that mental wellness is part of the triad of overall individual fitness (along with physical and spiritual fitness).

C. POV Accident Prevention

POV accidents continue to be the leading cause of accidental death for Soldiers. Every Soldier has an individual responsibility to prevent accidents. Commanders and leaders must also be vigilant in the identification of high-risk behavior. CRM assists commanders and leaders in recognizing those hazards, behaviors, and/or situations that may lead to tragedy. The Director of Army Safety has prepared a POV risk management toolbox for commanders and leaders. This toolbox provides a comprehensive set of tools and controls that have proven successful in preventing POV accidents throughout the army. The toolbox and other automated CRM POV tools are available at https://crc.army.mil/home.

III. Composite Risk Management Steps

Ref: FM 5-19, chap. 1, pp. 1-2 to 1-15.

1. Identify hazards

A hazard is a condition with the potential to cause injury, illness, or death of personnel; damage to or loss of equipment or property; or mission degradation. A hazard may also be a situation or event that can result in degradation of capabilities or mission failure. Hazards exist in all environments—combat operations, stability operations, base support operations, training, garrison activities, and off-duty activities. The factors of mission, enemy, terrain and weather, troops and support available, time available, and civil considerations (METT-TC) serve as a standard format for identification of hazards, on-duty or off-duty.

2. Assess hazards to determine risk

This process is systematic in nature and uses charts, codes and numbers to present a methodology to assess probability and severity to obtain a standardized level of risk. Hazards are assessed and risk is assigned in terms of probability and severity of adverse impact of an event/occurrence. There are three substeps in this step:

- **Assess the probability of the event or occurrence.**
- **Estimate the expected result or severity of an event or occurrence.**
- **Determine the specified level of risk** for a given probability and severity using the standard risk assessment matrix. *See FM 5-19, fig 1-4, p. 1-8.*

3. Develop controls and make risk decisions

The process of developing and applying controls and reassessing risk continues until an acceptable level of risk is achieved or until all risks are reduced to a level where benefits outweigh the potential cost.

- **Develop controls**. For each hazard, develop one or more controls that will eliminate or reduce the risk of the hazard. Specify who, what, where, when, and how for each control.
- **Find control measures**. For each hazard, as controls are developed, revise the evaluation of the level of risk remaining (residual risk), assuming the controls for it are implemented.
- **Reassess risk**. With controls applied, risk must be reassessed to determine the residual risk associated with each hazard and the overall residual risk for the mission.
- **Make risk decisions**. Overall residual risk must be determined by considering the residual risks for all of the identified hazards. The residual risk for each hazard may be different, depending on the assessed probability and severity of the hazardous incident. Overall residual risk is determined based on the greatest residual risk of all the identified hazards. The overall residual risk of the mission will be equal to or higher than the highest identified residual risk.

4. Implement controls

Leaders and staffs ensure that controls are integrated into SOPs, written and verbal orders, mission briefings, and staff estimates. The critical check for this step is to ensure that controls are converted into clear and simple execution orders.

5. Supervise and evaluate

- **Supervise**.Supervision is a form of control measure. Supervision ensures subordinates understand how, when, and where controls are implemented. It also ensures that controls are implemented, monitored, and remain in place.
- **Evaluate**. The evaluation process occurs during all phases of the operation, and as part of the AAR & assessment following completion of the operation/activity.

Training Plans, Mtgs & Schedules

VI. Leader's Books

Ref: TC 25-30, app. B.

Leaders are responsible for providing training assessments to the chain of command on their soldiers and units. Commanders use these assessments to make training decisions. The purpose of the leader book is to give leaders a tool that efficiently tracks soldier and unit training status.

The leader book is a tool maintained by leaders at all levels for recording and tracking soldier proficiency on mission-oriented tasks. The exact composition of leader books varies depending on the mission and type of unit. Specific uses are to–

- Track and evaluate soldiers' training status and proficiency on essential soldier tasks
- Provide administrative input to the chain of command on the proficiency of the unit; for example platoon, section, squad, team, or crew
- Conduct soldier performance counseling

Daily Evaluations and Soldier Counseling
Leaders books are an integral part of everyday training. Leaders habitually carry their leader books with them during the training day. Shortly after training is evaluated leaders update the appropriate section of their leader book. By keeping up with the current status of the training of their soldiers, ldrs can give timely and accurate assessments.

Company and Platoon Training Meetings
Leader books are "part of the uniform" for both company and platoon training meetings. Accurate leader books add credibility to training assessments, and form the basis for requesting training.

NOTE. Leader books should not be formally inspected, however, their periodic review by the chain of command is appropriate. Leaders should not lose sight of the purpose of leader books-that of being a self-designed tool to assist leaders in tracking the training proficiency of their soldiers. They come in many shapes and forms; there is no approved solution or format.

A. Soldier Administrative Data

Administrative soldier data sheets contain everything leaders need to know about their soldiers. The form can be SATS generated or one developed by the leader. Recommended information for soldier data sheets includes the following:

- Name, rank, age, and duty position
- Current weapon qualification
- APFT score/date
- Height/weight data
- Family data
- Special medical data

Knowing this type of information allows leaders to better provide training which meets their soldiers' personal needs.

B. Co METL/Plt Suporting Collective Task List

Leaders need to maintain copies of both company METL and platoon supporting collective task lists in their leader books. Having these lists and current assessments helps leaders to select the appropriate individual, and collective tasks that require training emphasis.

This form can be in any format that the leader chooses. A recommended technique is to list the task, the current assessment, and also a "why" for the assessment.

Common Task Test Proficiency
Common Task Test (CTT) proficiency is critical information for all leaders. GO/NO GO data should be recorded for each soldier, along with the date. Knowing this allows ldrs to select appropriate opportunity training. Since company HQs maintain individual soldiers' DA Forms 5164, leaders must develop their own system for tracking CTT proficiency.

Essential Soldier Task Poficiency
Leaders select and track the proficiency of MOS-specific tasks which support the company METL/platoon supporting collective task list. By knowing the exact status of these essential tasks leaders can quickly identify weaknesses and plan and conduct training to improve proficiency.

Unit Collective Task Proficiency
Leaders need to know the proficiency of their units to perform the collective tasks and drills that support the platoon supporting collective task list. Leaders derive section/squad/crew collective tasks from the applicable MTPs. Units without a published MTP must determine for themselves   which collective tasks and drills support the platoon supporting collective tasks. In many cases the section/squad/crew collective task list will be identical to the platoon list.

SATS does not provide a collective task proficiency tracking form. Recommended information for collective task proficiency forms includes-
- Collective tasks
- Assessment blocks (T-P-U or GO/NO GO)
- Date training last executed
- Reason for assessment/strategy to improve

C. Soldier Counseling Forms and Status

Soldier counseling is an essential element of a leader's duties. The leader book is a natural focal point for performance counseling. The extent that counseling can be tracked with the leader book is the leader's decision.

Training Execution
& Training Exercises

Ref: FM 7-0, Training for Full Spectrum Operations (Dec '08), pp. 4-35 to 4-37 and FM 7-1, Battle Focused Training (Sept '03), chap 5 and chap 6.

Training execution occurs at all echelons, from a unified action training exercise to a first-line leader conducting individual training. Ideally, leaders execute training using the crawl-walk-run approach—as appropriate and tailored to the individual's, team's, or unit's needs and capabilities—to build confidence over time and emphasize fundamentals and standards. Effective training execution, regardless of the specific collective, leader, and individual tasks being executed, requires adequate preparation, effective presentation and practice, and thorough evaluation. After training is executed, leaders ensure individuals recover from training and review successes and challenges to apply observations, insights, and lessons to future training and operations.

Training Execution

I. Prepare for Training	II. Conduct of Training	III. Recovery from Training
▪ Select tasks ▪ Plan the training ▪ Train the trainer ▪ Recon the site ▪ Condut risk assessment ▪ Issue training plan ▪ Rehearse ▪ Conduct pre-execution checks	▪ Conduct pre-execution checks ▪ Supervise, evaluate hazard controls ▪ Implement hazard controls ▪ Execute training ▪ Conduct AAR ▪ Retrain at first opportunity	▪ Conduct after operations maintenance checks and services ▪ Equipment accountability ▪ Turn-in support items ▪ Close out training sites ▪ Conduct AARs ▪ Individual soldier recovery ▪ Conduct final inspections ▪ Conduct risk management

Ref: FM 7-1, Battle Focused Training (Sept '03), fig. 5-1, p. 5-2.

I. Leader Roles in Training Management

Ref: FM 7-0, Training for Full Spectrum Operations (Dec '08), pp. 4-4 to 4-5.

Officers, NCOs, and Army civilians have complementary roles and responsibilities to plan, prepare, execute, and assess training and to ensure training is conducted professionally and to standard.

A. Officers

Commanders and other officers are involved in all aspects of training, from planning and preparation to execution and assessment. Planning for training is centralized and coordinated to align training priorities and provide a consistent training focus throughout all unit echelons. In contrast, the execution of training is decentralized. Decentralization promotes bottom-up communication of mission-related strengths and weaknesses of each individual and organization. Decentralized execution promotes subordinates' initiative in training their organizations. However, senior leaders remain responsible for supervising training, developing leaders, and providing feedback.

Commanders do more than plan and oversee training; they also prepare and execute both individual and collective training, as appropriate. Officers personally observe and assess training to instill discipline and ensure units are meeting Army standards. The unit senior NCO plays a significant role in helping the commander supervise the unit's training program. Senior NCOs observe and assess the quality of training and adherence to standards down to the organization's lowest levels. Commanders check the adequacy of external training support during training visits and require prompt and effective corrections to resolve support deficiencies. Commanders make coordination of training support for subordinate units a priority for unit staffs. Senior NCOs at every level perform these same actions.

By personally visiting training in progress, commanders and senior NCOs communicate the paramount importance of training and leader development to subordinate organizations and leaders. They receive feedback from subordinate Soldiers and leaders during training visits. Feedback allows commanders and senior NCOs to identify and resolve systemic problems in areas such as the following: planning, leadership, leader development, management, and support. Based on their observations and other feedback, commanders provide guidance and direct changes to improve training and increase readiness. The most beneficial training visits by senior leaders occur unannounced or on short notice. Such visits prevent excessive preparation—a training distraction—by subordinate organizations.

Warrant officers must be technically and tactically focused and able to perform the primary duties of technical leader, advisor, and commander. Through progressive levels of expertise in assignments, training, and education, warrant officers perform these duties during all operations and at all levels of command. While their primary duties are those of a technical and tactical leader, warrant officers also provide training and leader development guidance, assistance, and supervision. Warrant officers provide leader development, mentorship, and counsel to other warrant officers, officers, NCOs, and Army civilians. Warrant officers lead and train functional sections, teams, or crews. Finally, they serve as critical advisors to commanders in conducting organizational training.

B. Noncommissioned Officers

NCOs are responsible for the care and individual training of Soldiers. Command sergeants major, first sergeants, and other key NCOs select and train specific individual and small-unit tasks. They also help identify unit collective tasks. All these tasks support the organization's mission-essential tasks. Commanders approve the tasks selected and then supervise and evaluate training along with the organization's officers and NCOs.

NCOs focus on the skills and knowledge Soldiers need to develop their fundamental competencies. Mastery of tasks occurs through repetition. This foundation—which includes such skills as marksmanship, protection, military occupational specialty skills, and physical fitness—is essential to unit readiness. NCOs integrate newly assigned enlisted Soldiers into organizations and develop them professionally throughout their assignment. First-line leaders train Soldiers to conduct individual tasks in their squads, crews, teams, and equivalent small organizations. First-line leaders and senior NCOs emphasize standards-based, performance-oriented training to ensure Soldiers achieve the Army standard. NCOs cross-train their subordinates to reduce the effects of unit losses and develop future leaders. Command sergeants major, first sergeants, and other senior NCOs coach junior NCOs and junior officers to help them master a wide range of individual tasks.

Commanders allocate time during collective training for NCOs to conduct individual training. The time allocated allows for repetition of tasks. NCOs train individuals to standard and understand how individual task training relates to mission-essential tasks and supporting collective tasks. Commanders select individual, crew, and small-team tasks to be trained based on recommendations from NCOs. NCOs base recommendations on their evaluation of training deficiencies. NCOs recommend tasks for training at training meetings. When the commander approves tasks for training, the tasks are incorporated into the unit's training plans and subsequent training schedules. NCOs plan and prepare the approved training, execute after action reviews (AARs) during training, and provide feedback on individual Soldier performance during training meetings. For efficiency, Soldiers assigned a low-density military occupational specialty may be trained together by a senior NCO.

C. Army Civilians

The Army Civilian Corps provides stability and continuity for the Army. Army civilians generally serve in organizations longer than their military counterparts. They provide specialized skills and knowledge in day-to-day Army operations. Normally, Army civilians are assigned to the generating force; however, they are integral to manning, equipping, resourcing, and training both the generating force and operational Army. Army civilians both support and lead Army operations. Army civilian leaders plan, prepare, execute, and assess training of their subordinates and organizations. They follow the principles of training and the use of tools of this chapter to focus the training of their organizations.

II. Crawl-Walk-Run Training

Ref: FM 7-0, Training for Full Spectrum Operations (Dec '08), pp. 4-36 to 4-37 and FM 7-1, Battle Focused Training (Sept '03), pp. 5-4 to 5-10.

The crawl-walk-run technique is an objective, incremental, standards-based approach to training. Tasks are initially trained at a very basic level (crawl), then become increasingly difficult (walk), and finally approach the level of realism expected in combat (run). Training starts at the basic level, beginning with the crawl stage. However, leaders first assess individual and unit training levels. Some individuals and organizations may be ready for the walk, or even the run stage, depending on their experience.

Crawl-Walk-Run

Crawl	Walk	Run
Soldiers	**Soldiers**	**Soldiers**
■ Train each task step ■ Train task steps in sequence ■ Train complete task until done correctly	■ Train to training objective standard ■ Train with more realism ■ Learn transfer skills that link other tasks ■ Work as crews or small units	■ Train collectively to achieve and sustain proficiency ■ Train under conditions that simulate actual combat ■ Develop effective team relationships
Leaders/Trainer	**Leaders/Trainer**	**Leaders/Trainer**
■ Talk through and demonstrate each task ■ Supervise step-by-step practice ■ Coach frequently ■ Control the environment	■ Walk through task using more realism ■ Increase complexity ■ Demonstrate authorized field expedients ■ Participate as leader of crew or small units ■ Observe, coach, and review	■ Add realism and complexity ■ Combine tasks ■ Review Soldier and collective performance ■ Practice leader tasks ■ Work with Soldiers as a team ■ Coach and teach subordinate leaders

Ref: FM 7-1, fig. 5-2, p. 5-5.

Crawl stage events are simple to perform and require minimal support. The crawl stage focuses on the basics of the task and proceeds as slowly as needed for individuals and the organization to understand task requirements. Walk stage training becomes incrementally more difficult. It requires more resources from the unit and home station and increases the level of realism and the pace. At the run stage, the level of difficulty for training intensifies. Run-stage training requires the resources needed to create the conditions expected in the projected operational environment. Progression from crawl to run for a particular task may occur during a one-day training exercise or may require a succession of training periods.

In crawl-walk-run training, tasks and standards remain the same; however, the conditions under which they are trained change. Live, virtual, constructive, and gaming training enablers help provide the variable conditions for supporting a crawl-walk-run training strategy. Ways to change conditions include the following:

- Increasing the difficulty of conditions under which tasks are being performed
- Increasing the tempo of the training
- Increasing the number of tasks being trained
- Increasing or decreasing the number of personnel involved

Trainers use the crawl-walk-run approach to determine the amount of detail to include in practice. If individuals or organizations are receiving initial training on a task, trainers emphasize basic conditions. If individuals are receiving sustainment training, trainers raise the level of detail and realism until conditions replicate an actual operational environment as closely as possible. Trainers challenge those with considerable experience to perform multiple training tasks under stressful conditions.

Trainers conduct training using the combination of demonstrations, conferences, discussions, and practice appropriate to the experience of those being trained. They inform individuals of the training objectives (tasks, conditions, and standards) and applicable evaluation procedures. Trainers immediately follow presentations with practice to convert information into usable individual and collective skills.

III. Characteristics of Effective Training

Ref: FM 7-0, Training for Full Spectrum Operations (Dec '08), pp. 4-35 to 4-36.

Properly presented and executed training is realistic, safe, standards-based, well-structured, efficient, effective, and challenging.

1. Realistic

Realistic training requires organizations to train the way they intend to operate in all dimensions of the projected operational environment. Realistic training includes all available elements of combined arms teams and, as appropriate, organizations or individuals normally involved in unified action. It optimizes the use of TADSS to replicate the stresses, sounds, and conditions of actual operations.

2. Safe

Safe training is the predictable result of performing to established tactical and technical standards. Through CRM, leaders at all echelons ensure safety requirements are integral, not add-on, considerations to all aspects of planning, preparing for, executing, and assessing training.

3. Standards-Based

Standards-based training complies with joint and Army doctrine and is technically correct. Adherence to standards should not stifle innovation and prudent risk taking. Field manuals, CATSs, and other training publications provide information to facilitate training, coach subordinate trainers, and evaluate training results. Training and evaluation outlines (contained in CATSs) provide information concerning collective training objectives. These outlines also include individual and leader training tasks that support collective training objectives.

4. Well-Structured

Well-structured training contains a mixture of initial, sustainment, and improvement training events. It also consists of a mix of individual and leader tasks incorporated into collective tasks. It organizes and sequences training events to allow units to meet their training objectives.

5. Efficient

Efficient training makes the best use of training resources. Efficiently executed training makes the best use of everyone's time.

6. Effective

Effective training builds proficiency, teamwork, confidence, and cohesiveness. Effective training allows commanders and their organizations to achieve their training objectives.

7. Challenging

Challenging training is competitive. Although individuals and organizations may sometimes compete against one another, they should always compete to achieve the prescribed standard. Once the standard has been achieved, trainers alter the conditions to make the task more challenging. If the standard is not achieved, trainers take corrective actions and repeat the training. They do this until the standard is met. Training is done to standard, not to available time.

V. Presentation of Training

Trainers execute training using three basic methods of presentation. They are-

- Demonstration (the preferred method)
- Conference
- Lecture (the least preferred method)

These methods may be used in any combination to present training. The trainer's selection of a specific method depends on the complexity of the task(s) and proficiency of the soldiers (or unit) being trained.

A. Demonstration

Demonstration is the preferred method of presentation used at company level and below. Demonstrations accelerate the learning process. The impact of a brief visual demonstration showing the correct method of execution of a given task to standard cannot be overstated. Seeing a task performed correctly provides greater understanding than any amount of explanation. Demonstrations stimulate soldier interest by providing realism that other techniques do not offer. Demonstrations-

- Save time by showing soldiers the correct way to perform a task
- Use the leader as the primary trainer whenever possible
- Present information in a manner that properly motivates
- Conclude when soldiers understand the task

Trainers conduct demonstrations with very simple, basic tools such as map boards, dry-erase boards, and sand tables, or with more advanced tools such as simulations and simulators. The sand tables and terrain models can be used to conduct rock drills to demonstrate tasks before and after executing them on the ground during squad and platoon training. Sand tables and terrain models can also be used during STX and LFX rehearsals and AARs. Some basic guidance for effective use of sand tables, terrain models, and rock drills includes-

- Keep the model simple. Cardboard cutouts, pieces of wood, or rocks may represent equipment and units
- Keep the training informal. Soldier participation is essential because soldiers learn from one another
- Present information that soldiers and leaders need to perform the task. Trainers should check for soldier understanding by asking questions. The trainer should explain the task again, as required, until all soldiers understand the task.

B. Conference

Conference provides soldiers the opportunity to discuss the information presented. The trainer initiates and guides the discussion. Conferences are most effective when soldiers are familiar with the subject, when there is more than one correct technique or solution, and when time is not critical. Conferences normally do not require hands-on performance. An example of a conference is an AAR.

C. Lecture

Lecture presents information with little discussion other than a question and answer period at the end of the training. Lectures are used when time is limited, when soldiers know little about the subject, and when the lecture is preparing them for demonstration and practice.

Lectures are appropriate only if there is a large group to be trained. An example of a lecture is a pre-deployment briefing. Lectures are the least preferred method of training.

VI. Staff Training

Ref: FM 7-1 Battle Focused Training, p. 5-9 to 5-10.

Staff training develops and sustains planning, coordination, and other staff functions related to operational mission requirements. The staff derives its training objectives from the staff METL. The common training challenge for the staff is to synchronize and integrate BOS functions. Commanders must integrate staffs horizontally and vertically. Horizontal integration involves intra-CP cell coordination and inter-CP coordination at the same command echelon. Vertical integration involves inter-CP functional coordination among two or more command echelons.

Horizontal and Vertical Integration

Commanders accomplish horizontal and vertical integration by focusing staff training on C2 processes and procedures. These processes and procedures help staffs provide commanders with accurate, relevant, and timely information. Staffs use the MDMP and IPB to help commanders visualize and describe the current and future situations, and to establish and maintain an accurate COP.

Additionally, selected staff members must master various staff processes. Staff processes assist planning, coordinating, and monitoring operations. Staffs use these processes to help commanders direct operations during preparation and execution. Examples of staff processes are "Develop a R&S Plan," "Execute the Targeting Process," "Conduct A2C2 Activities," and "Conduct Civil-Military Operations (CMO)."

ABCS and FBCB2

The importance of ABCS and FBCB2 systems operator training to maintaining a staff's METL proficiency cannot be overstated. ABCS and FBCB2 systems provide digital automation support to help the staff visualize and describe the situation for the commander, and direct execution of the commander's decision through a COP. Staff training must sustain staff members and various ABCS and FBCB2 systems operator proficiency to optimize the staff's METL proficiency.

Staff training includes the following:

- Staff section, CP cell, and cell element-

- Training focuses on achieving individual, section, CP cell, and cell element task proficiency before progressing to staff group and full staff training

- Staff group training and drills focus on critical inter-CP cell staff control processes that contribute directly to full staff competency. Examples of inter-CP cell staff control-oriented processes are "Develop an R&S Plan," "Execute the Targeting Process," and "Conduct A2C2 Activities"

- Full staff training focuses on critical command-oriented staff processes that directly affect full staff proficiency. MDMP and IPB are examples of critical command-oriented staff processes

Multiechelon staff-

- Training focuses on full staff interaction with higher, subordinate, and adjacent unit staffs

- Involves inter-CP functional coordination among two or more command echelons

- Includes full staff, staff group, CP cell, cell element, and staff section training

The following table organizes CP cell/cell element/staff section, staff group, full staff, and multiechelon training exercises into crawl-walk-run skill proficiency training levels.

Skill Proficiency Training Levels

Crawl	Walk	Run
■ CP cell, cell element & staff section training ■ Individual training	■ Staff group(s) drills ■ Staff group training	■ Multiechelon staff training ■ Full staff training

Ref: FM 7-1, fig. 5-4, p. 5-10.

The following table provides some specific examples of staff training requirements into "crawl-walk-run" training events.

Sample Staff Events

Crawl	Walk	Run
■ Review staff TTPs ■ Develop cell and CP SOPs ■ Understand staff processes ■ Train TTPs ■ Conduct selective intra-CP cell coordination (e.g., coordinate among several main CP cells)	■ Train individual CP (TAC, main, rear or functional) ■ Conduct complete intra-CP cell coordination (e.g., among main CP cells) ■ Conduct staff process AARs (e.g., MDMP, CM&D, targeting, A2C2, etc)	■ Train an entire horizontal echelon staff (e.g., division level TAC, main and rear CPs) ■ Train an entire vertical echelon staff (e.g., corps through brigade main CPs) ■ Conduct unit/echelon and functional CP AARs

Ref: FM 7-1, fig. 5-5, p. 5-10.

Commanders train staffs through a mix of L-V-C training. At brigade level and higher, staffs conduct most of their training in the constructive environment, with limited use of virtual simulations. Effective staff training produces commanders and staffs capable of synchronizing operations across the full spectrum of operations.

VII. The Training Support System (TSS)

Ref: FM 7-1 Battle Focused Training, app. G.

Training support is an essential element of Army training. It enables realistic and challenging battle focused training in all domains-institutional, operational, and self-development-by helping commanders create the proper conditions for training.

The Training Support System (TSS) is a system of systems that provides products to assist the commander. The TSS includes training information infrastructures (TII); training aids, devices, simulators, and simulations (TADSS); training products; training services; and training facilities. Additionally, TSS provides a "reach-back" capability to the proponent schoolhouse that further expands training support to the commander.

Commanders strive to make battle focused training realistic and challenging by using the integrated TSS to facilitate an operationally relevant training environment anytime, anywhere. Effective training support is integrated into each phase of the Army Training Management Cycle to help commanders create the optimum conditions for training.

This appendix provides examples of the kinds of training support available to commanders to support their training mission at home station or when deployed. A training support center (TSC) is normally established, and collocated with deployed units, to ensure that continued training support and reach-back capability.

I. Planning

At the beginning of the training planning phase, commanders should establish contact with their home station or MACOM TSCs for coordination and support throughout the entire training cycle. Support Centers provide institutional knowledge of TSS, including linkage to Federal, DOD, Army-wide, industrial, and commercial support.

Commanders plan and develop a training strategy to train individual, collective, and leader tasks in live-virtual-constructive (L-V-C) environments. Virtual-constructive training support products are used to supplement, enhance, and complement preparation for live training exercises and to sustain proficiency. Additionally, training support products enhance progression of the unit training strategy through crawl-walk-run training.

Training Support Products and Services

Note: A complete listing of these products and services is included in DA PAM 350-9, available online at: http://www.usapa.army.mil/pdffiles/p350_9x.pdf

Official Departmental Publications:
- Administrative Publications
- Drills
- Field Manuals (FM)
- Army Training and Evaluation Program Mission Training Plans (ARTEP-MTPs)
- Soldier Training Publications (STP)
- Technical Manuals (TM)
- Training Circulars (TC)

Individual and Collective Training Support Materials:
- Battalion EXEVAL
- Career Model
- Combined Arms Training Strategy (CATS)
- Correspondence Courses
- Interactive Multimedia Instruction (IMI) Courseware
- Graphic Training Aids (GTA)
- Job Books
- Television Tapes (TVT)
- Training Support Packages

Training Aids, Devices, Simulators & Simulation (TADSS):
- A complete listing is included in DA PAM 350-9, available online.

Facilities:
- Ranges, Targets, Classrooms, Distributed Learning Facilities, Battle Simulation
- Facilities, Impact and Maneuver Areas

Services:
- Design and develop unit training and AAR briefing products
- Design and produce unit specific training aids and devices

As commanders examine their training strategy to determine who, what, when, and where to train, they determine what training support will be required. They consider the allocation of ranges for weapons qualification, gunnery, and other live fires; training areas for live engagement simulation exercises; simulators to support various levels of training exercises; simulations-both constructive and virtual-for staff and collective training; and training ammunition requirements for weapons training. Unit planning includes time and personnel required to execute accountability, maintenance and turn-in of specified training support products and facilities during the recovery from training.

II. Execution
Transition from planning to execution includes confirmation of scheduled facilities, products, and services. This is also an opportunity for commanders to identify and acquire material not previously identified in the planning phase and to check all unit and training support material, including testing for fidelity, reliability, and availability. Planning, pre-execution checks, and recovery from training for training support items is an integral part of the weekly training meeting.

III. Assessment
The TSS provides resources such as T&EOs, and feedback tools in V-C training support products, that enable commanders to plan, prepare, and execute effective training assessments. These tools support development of evaluation plans by providing documentation to gather feedback on the performance of individual and collective training.

IV. Individual Self-Development
Individual self-development, both structured and informal, is generally an extension of the proponent school, but can extend to local or extension colleges and universities. Proponent schools and the TSS develop self-development products, infrastructures, and tools that bridge and supplement institutional and operational experiences. Access to self-development products and registration for courses are provided through the Army Knowledge Online (AKO).

VIII. Situational Training Exercises (STXs) and Live-Fire Exercises (LFXs)

Ref: FM 7-0 Training the Force, p. 5-7 to 5-8. See also pp. 7-27 to 7-32 for further discussion of training exercises.

Situational Training Exercises (STXs)

Situational training exercises (STXs) are mission-related, limited exercises designed to train one collective task, or a group of related tasks and drills, through practice. STXs teach the doctrinally-preferred method for carrying out a task. STXs usually include drills, leader tasks, and individual soldier tasks. To ensure standardization, institutional schools and units develop STXs to teach the doctrinally-preferred way to perform specific missions and tasks. STXs may be modified based on the unit's METL, or expanded to meet special mission requirements.

STX training is especially helpful for training specific METL tasks. It is a useful technique primarily for training company team level and smaller units on a series of selected soldier, leader, and collective tasks using specific terrain. The concept provides an effective way to standardize TTPs and develop and rehearse tactical standing operating procedures (TACSOPs). STXs are a perfect opportunity to use crawl-walk-run training. Commanders narrow the focus and select specific collective tasks for the training. STX training may be resource-intensive, so commanders must maximize the benefit.

STX training under varying conditions gives the unit a distinct advantage when executing combat operations. STX training at night and during adverse weather provides a training opportunity to execute critical tasks and drills under naturally occurring light and weather conditions, and enhances training realism. Reverse cycle training should be planned to take advantage of every opportunity to replicate a 24-hour perational environment.

STX training is structured to expose leaders and soldiers to unexpected situations, favorable and unfavorable. Tasks must be executed confidently and competently during the fog of battle. Tough, realistic training challenges leaders and soldiers to overcome the hardships and uncertainties of combat. Challenging training inspires excellence by fostering initiative, enthusiasm, confidence, and the ability to operate in all elements of the operational spectrum. Even if a unit accomplishes the assigned task to standard, the unit may retrain the exercise with more difficult conditions.

Live-Fire Exercises (LFXs)

Live fire exercises (LFXs) closely replicate battlefield conditions and provide significant advantages. LFXs—

- Develop confidence and esprit-de-corps
- Provide soldiers with a realistic experience of the danger, confusion, and speed of combat operations
- Require demonstrated proficiency at lower echelons before LFXs are conducted at higher echelons

I. Preparation for Training

Ref: FM 7-0, Training for Full Spectrum Operations (Dec '08), pp. 4-33 to 4-35.

Formal near-term planning for training culminates when the unit publishes its training schedule and written event training plans (when necessary). Informal planning, detailed coordination, and preparation for executing the training continue until the training is completed. Preparation is the heart of training management. Commanders and other trainers use training meetings to assign responsibility for preparing all scheduled training.

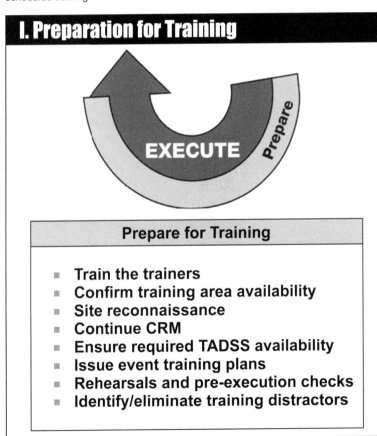

I. Preparation for Training

Prepare for Training

- **Train the trainers**
- **Confirm training area availability**
- **Site reconnaissance**
- **Continue CRM**
- **Ensure required TADSS availability**
- **Issue event training plans**
- **Rehearsals and pre-execution checks**
- **Identify/eliminate training distractors**

Ref: FM 7-1 (Sept '03), fig. 5-6, p. 5-11. (Bullets updated to '08 FM 7-0).

Preparation for Training

Ref: FM 7-0, Training for Full Spectrum Operations (Dec '08), pp. 4-33 to 4-35.

Preparation includes the following:

- Training the trainers
- Confirming training area availability
- Site reconnaissance
- Continuing CRM
- Ensuring required TADSS availability
- Issuing event training plans
- Performing rehearsals and pre-execution checks
- Continuing to identify and eliminate potential training distracters to maximize training attendance

Pre-Execution Checks

Identifying the responsibility for pre-execution checks is a critical portion of any training meeting. Pre-execution checks include the following:

- Identifying responsibility for training support tasks
- Monitoring preparation activities
- Assessing whether training can be executed to standard, given the training conditions

Subordinate leaders identify and select the collective, leader, and individual tasks necessary to support the identified training objectives. They do this based on as bottom-up feedback from internal training meetings. Commanders develop tentative plans, including requirements for preparatory training, multi-echelon training, concurrent training, and training resources. Often these plans take the form of verbal guidance issued during training meetings. When necessary, commanders prepare a written event training plan. All training plans include time and other resources necessary for retraining.

A. Selecting and Preparing Trainers

Trainers include leaders, evaluators, observer-controller/trainers, OPFOR personnel, and role players. These people are identified, trained to standard, and rehearsed before training events begin. Executing challenging, doctrinally correct, and professional training requires preparing leaders and trainers beforehand. This involves coaching them on how to train, giving them time to prepare, and rehearsing them. Commanders ensure that trainers and evaluators are tactically and technically competent on their training tasks. Commanders also make sure these people understand how the training relates to the unit METL and training objectives. Properly prepared trainers, evaluators, and leaders project confidence and enthusiasm to those being trained.

Training the trainers is a critical step in preparation for training. Leaders, evaluators, observer controller/trainers, and OPFOR personnel involved in any training event must know, understand, and be proficient on the standard for each task. All leaders are trainers, but all trainers are not necessarily leaders. A junior Soldier or subject matter expert may be the best person to train a particular collective or individual task. Subordinate leaders may be the trainer as well as the leader of an element conducting collective training.

B. Event Training Plans

A complex training event may require a formal event training plan. Commanders issue the event training plan as early as possible. They do this after completing a training site reconnaissance and identifying additional training support requirements with their subordinate leaders and trainers. This plan guides the organization in completing the training event. It identifies elements necessary for the unit to conduct the training to standard. It may be in the form of an operation order, or it may be oral guidance given in the weekly training meeting. Trainers coordinate to obtain the equipment, products, and ammunition needed to support training, based on the site reconnaissance and event training plan. Formal event training plans include the following:

- Confirmed training areas and locations
- Training ammunition allocations
- TADSS that have been coordinated for
- Confirmed transportation resources
- Soldier support items that have been coordinated
- Risk management analysis
- Designation of trainers
- Final coordination requirements

C. Inspections

Preparing for training requires inspections to ensure the needed resources are available. Inspections can be as simple as pre-training checks for a training event. Alternatively, they can be as complex as an organizational inspection program that scrutinizes the unit's entire training program. Inspections also aim to ensure equipment is ready and serviceable, trainers are prepared, resources are available, and safety is a priority. Inspections help leaders ensure the following:

- Their organizations have what they need to conduct quality training
- Their organizations conduct training to standard
- Training time is optimized
- Training is focused on the METL
- Training objectives are achievable
- Individual skills and knowledge are improved

D. Rehearsals

Rehearsal is a critical element of preparation. Often called a "ROC (rehearsal of concept) drill," it allows leaders and subordinates involved in a training event to develop a mental picture of responsibilities and events. It helps the organization synchronize training with times, places, and resources. A simple walkthrough or sand table exercise helps leaders visualize where individuals are supposed to be to perform a coordinated action at a certain time. Leaders see how training is supposed to unfold, what might go wrong, and how the training could change to adjust for intended and unintended events. Commanders and leaders also perform rehearsals to:

- Identify weak points in the event training plan
- Teach and coach effective training techniques
- Ensure training meets safety and environmental considerations
- Ensure leaders and trainers understand training objectives
- Determine how trainers intend to evaluate the performance of individuals or organizations
- Assess subordinate trainer competencies and provide feedback to them
- Give trainers confidence in the event training plan

Trainer Preparation Checklist

Ref: FM 7-1, Battle Focused Training (Sept '03), fig. 5-7, p. 5-14.

Leadership by example is especially important for trainers. Trainers must demonstrate task proficiency before teaching a task to others. Commanders and leaders must ensure that trainers are thoroughly prepared to conduct performance-oriented training. Trainer competence and confidence is contagious.

Prepare Yourself
- Know how to perform the task being trained (master the task).
- Rehearse training
- Back-brief the chain of command on your training plan and get their feedback

Know How to Train Others to Perform the Tasks
- Ensure that training is performance-oriented
- Conduct yourself in a confident manner
- Accurately answer your soldier's questions
- Train an assistant who can conduct the training to standard in your absence

Know How to set Up and Conduct an AAR

Prepare the Resources
- Identify and request TADSS
- Get equipment and materials before rehearsal
- Operate the equipment to become familiar with it, and check for completeness and spare parts

Ensure that Training Support Personnel (to include OPFOR)-
- Understand their support roles
- Know their roles as evaluators, OCs, and the OPFOR
- Are equipped and prepared to perform the tasks to standard
- Conduct reconnaissance and rehearsals

Prepare the Soldier
- Identify the soldiers to be trained
- Evaluate levels of training proficiency
- Train any prerequisite tasks or skills first
- Motivate the soldiers (tell them why the task is important, how it relates to METL)

Pre-execution Checks
- Are soldiers trained on prerequisite tasks prior to conduct of training?
- Have ranges and facilities been requested; has a reconnaissance been conducted?
- Are leaders certified to conduct range operations?
- Have convoy clearances been submitted and approved?
- Have TADSS been identified and requested?
- Have Class I, III, V supplies been requested and have pickup times and turn-in times been coordinated?
- Has transportation been requested?
- Are there risk assessments for each training event?
- Has the backbrief for the chain of command been coordinated?
- Is time scheduled for retraining?

II. Conduct Training

Ref: FM 7-1 Battle Focused Training, chap 5, pp. 5-62 to 5-63.

Conduct of training involves actions taken to execute the unit's training strategy outlined in the commander's QTG. Conduct of training begins with the execution of pre-combat checks and inspections. Conduct of training ends when designated training objectives for the particular training event or exercise are performed to the Army standard. Unit commanders and other trainers review results of the conduct of training during weekly training meetings and adjust training plans if necessary.

II. Conduct Training

EXECUTE

Prepare

Conduct

Conduct Training

- Conduct pre-execution checks
- Supervise, evaluate hazard controls
- Implement hazard controls
- Execute training
- Conduct AAR
- Retrain at first opportunity

Ref: FM 7-1, fig. 5-46, p. 5-63.

I. Conduct Pre-Combat Checks

Pre-combat checks are detailed final checks that units conduct immediately before and during the execution of training and operations. These checks are usually included in unit SOPs. They are normally conducted as part of troop leading procedures and can be as simple or as complex as the training or operation dictates. Pre-combat checks start in garrison and many are completed in the assembly area or in the training location; for example, applying camouflage, setting radio frequencies and distributing ammunition. Commanders must allocate sufficient time for subordinate leaders to execute pre-combat checks and inspections to standard.

Note: See facing page (p. 7-19) for sample list of Pre-Combat Checks.

II. Execute Training

Performance-oriented, standards-based training is the result of detailed planning and preparation. The proper execution of training to standard is a rewarding process. It places a significant burden on the trainer in terms of preparation and evaluation of performance. The payoff for properly executed training is a unit trained to standard on its wartime operational mission. Division and brigade commanders and their staffs, must be actively involved in the execution of battalion and company training. A unit executes training the same way it executes a combat mission. The chain of command is present, in charge, and responsible.

Using the principles of training, commanders ensure that properly executed training is well-structured, realistic, safe, and effective. Other important considerations include the following:

1. Focus on the Fundamentals
Units must be proficient on basic tasks before progressing to the more complex tasks. All basic tasks provide the foundation on which to build performance of individual soldier tasks, drills, and METL tasks to standard. C2, logistics operations, and NBC must be incorporated into all training.

2. Night and Adverse Weather Training
Night training and adverse weather training are keys to success in combat. All units in the U.S. Army, not just combat units, must be proficient in operating at night and during adverse weather conditions. Routine training under these conditions gives units a distinct advantage in combat operations.

3. Tough, Realistic Training
Training must be structured to expose soldiers and leaders to unexpected situations, both favorable and unfavorable. Tasks must be executed confidently and completely during the fog of battle. Tough, realistic training challenges leaders and soldiers to overcome the hardships and uncertainties of combat. Leaders must teach soldiers that combat cannot be reduced to a set of calculations or checklists. Challenging training inspires excellence by fostering initiative, enthusiasm, confidence, and the ability to apply learned tasks in the dynamic environment of combat.

4. Competition
Effective training can be competitive. Although soldiers, leaders, and units may sometimes compete with one another, they should always compete to achieve the Army standard. Once units can perform a task to the Army standard, leaders progressively increase the difficulty or conditions under which the task is executed. During competition, leaders should recognize soldiers or units exceeding established standards. Competition can be used to stimulate soldier interest and morale, select participants for higher level competitions, encourage higher levels of performance, and provide an event for a rigorous training period.

Pre-Combat Checks

Ref: FM 7-1 Battle Focused Training, fig. 5-47, p. 5-46.

Pre-combat checks are detailed final checks that units conduct immediately before and during the execution of training and operations. These checks are usually included in unit SOPs. They are normally conducted as part of troop leading procedures and can be as simple or as complex as the training or operation dictates. Pre-combat checks start in garrison and many are completed in the assembly area or in the training location; for example, applying camouflage, setting radio frequencies and distributing ammunition. Commanders must allocate sufficient time for subordinate leaders to execute pre-combat checks and inspections to standard.

- OPORD briefed. Leaders and soldiers know what is expected of them.
- Safety checks and briefings completed.
- All required TADSS are on hand and operational; for example, MILES equipment zeroed.
- Before-operations PMCS completed on vehicles, weapons, communications, and NBC equipment.
- Leaders and equipment inspected; for example, compasses, maps, strip maps, and binoculars.
- Soldiers and equipment inspected and camouflaged; for example, weapons, ID cards, driver's licenses.
- Soldier packing lists checked and enforced.
- Medical support present and prepared
- Communications checks completed.
- Ammunition (Class V) drawn, accounted for, prepared, and issued.
- Vehicle load plans checked and confirmed; cargo secured.
- Rations (Class I) drawn and issued.
- Quartering party briefed and dispatched.
- OPFOR personnel deployed and ready to execute their OPORD

III. Conduct After Action Reviews (AARs)

A significant part of learning occurs as a result of after action reviews (AARs), which ensure that the training audience understands when they have not performed to standard and how they must perform to do so. Accordingly, whenever possible, AARs are conducted immediately following performance during training sessions.

Note: See section After Action Reviews on pp. 8-11 to 8-20.

IV. Conduct Retraining

Retraining must be conducted at the first available opportunity. Commanders must program time and other resources for retraining as an integral part of their long-, short-, and near-term training planning cycle. Training is incomplete until the task is trained to standard. The critical question for commanders and trainers is, "When do you conduct retraining?" In short-

- Retraining is conducted as soon as possible after the AAR
- Commanders determine when retraining will be conducted based on current training plans and available resources
- Commanders program time and other resources for retraining

Retraining

When do you conduct retraining? Depends on the situation.

When you Retrain	Immediately	During Current Training		Future
Scope of Training	Individual	Squad/Crew	Plt/Co Team	Bn TF / Bde
Training Event	Weapon Qual	Clear Trench Line / Table VIII	Conduct Assault	Attack
Retraining Method	Refire until Qualified	MCOFT/ TWGSS/ PGS Refire	TEWT/ CCTT, STX Lanes	TEWT/ JANUS, Co STX

Bottom Line:

- Retraining must be conducted as soon as possible after the AAR
- Commanders determine when retraining will be conducted based on current training plans and availability of resources
- Commanders program time and other resources for retraining

Ref: FM 7-1, fig. 5-48, p. 5-66.

III. Recovery from Training

Ref: FM 7-1 Battle Focused Training, chap 5, pp. 5-67 to 5-68.

The recovery process is an extension of training and once completed, signifies the end of the training event. While recovery tasks vary depending on the type and intensity of training, most include maintenance training, turn-in of training support items, inspection of equipment, and the conduct of AARs that review the overall effectiveness of the training just completed.

III. Recovery from Training

Recovery from Training

- Conduct after operations maintenance checks and services
- Equipment accountability
- Turn-in support items
- Close out training sites
- Conduct AARs
- Individual soldier recovery
- Conduct final inspections
- Conduct risk management

Ref: FM 7-1, fig. 5-49, p. 5-67.

The following is a sample list of recovery activities:

- Perform post-operations preventative maintenance checks and services
- Ensure sensitive item accountability
- Ensure accountability of organizational and individual equipment
- Ensure that Class IV, V, TADSS, and other support items are maintained, accounted for, and turned in
- Close out training areas and ranges
- Conduct AARs of the training event and exercise just completed
- Allow time for the individual soldier to recover personal equipment and conduct personal hygiene
- Conduct final inspections

Conduct AARs During Recovery

Note: See pp. 8-11 to 8-20 for further discussion on After Action Reviews.

AARs conducted during recovery focus on collective, leader, and individual task performance, and on the planning, preparation, and conduct of the training just completed. Unit AARs focus on individual and collective task performance, and identify shortcomings and the training required to correct deficiencies. AARs with leaders focus on tactical judgment. These AARs contribute to leader learning and provide opportunities for leader development. AARs with trainers, evaluators, OCs, and OPFOR provide additional opportunities for leader development.

The essential questions are, "Did the training strategy improve the unit's METL proficiency, and if not, why not? What changes need to be incorporated in the company's training strategy?"

Did the unit's performance during this training exercise/event improve training proficiency on selected training tasks and objectives?

Did the unit's training strategy-

- Select the right type of events and exercises?
- Select the right mix of live and virtual simulators?
- Select the right "who," "what," "when," and "where"?

Did the unit's preparation for training-

- Select the right leader and unit training tasks?
- Select and sequence the right leader and unit training events and exercises?
- Adequately prepare trainers, evaluators, and OCs?
- Adequately prepare the designated OPFOR?
- Require changes to the unit's pre-execution checks?

The AARs conducted during recovery, along with the AARs that took place during the conduct of training, enhance future training. They provide the feedback that contributes to the development of training plans to correct identified deficiencies. Finally, these AARs contribute to the commander's overall evaluation of training effectiveness and unit assessment. However, AARs are not in themselves the end state of recovery. Recovery from training is complete when the unit is again prepared to conduct its assigned mission.

Training execution includes preparation for training, conduct of training, and recovery from training. Pre-execution checks are developed by the chain of command and provide the attention to detail needed to use resources efficiently. Completion of recovery from training is not the end of training. The assessment of training proficiency is critical to determining the effectiveness of the preparation and conduct of training just completed.

V. Training Exercise Development

Chap 7

Ref: FM 7-1 Battle Focused Training, app. D.

The training exercise selection process is used by commanders to achieve and sustain METL proficiency. To illustrate how the training exercise selection process helps-

• Train commanders and their subordinates at all echelons to implement mission command
• Develop and train staffs that can synchronize combined arms operations

To expand discussions on-

• Training adaptive leaders and units
• Use of live, virtual, and constructive training
• Crawl-walk-run training

Training Exercise Selection Process

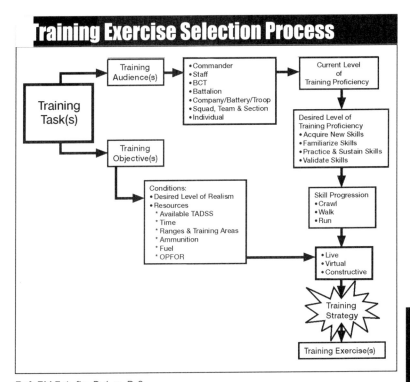

Ref: FM 7-1, fig. D-1, p. D-2.

Trng Execution & Exercises

Mission Command - Developing Competent, Confident, Adaptive Leaders and Soldiers

Ref: FM 7-1 Battle Focused Training, pp. D-3 to D-4.

Mission command requires competent, confident, adaptive leaders and soldiers. It requires commanders to teach their subordinate commanders, leaders, and units how to train for mission command. Training for mission command requires the commander to train on the four elements of mission command outlined in FM 6-0-

- Commander's intent
- Mission orders
- Subordinates' initiative
- Resource allocation

Commander's intent provides-

- A unifying idea that allows decentralized execution within an overarching concept
- Guidance and a point of common reference for subordinates to exercise initiative to accomplish overall goals
- The basis for decentralized decisionmaking and execution when subordinates understand the commander's intent two echelons up

Mission Command-Nested Concepts

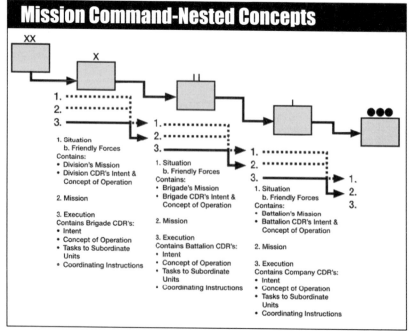

Ref: FM 7-1, fig. D-2, p. D-4.

A technique to train subordinates to understand the commander's intent two echelons up is to design training scenarios using nested concepts. Nested concepts provide the means to achieve unity of purpose where each succeeding echelon's concept is nested in the other.

Commanders who use nested concepts in training exercises provide subordinates an opportunity to-

• Practice decentralized decisionmaking and execution
• Exercise initiative within the commander's intent

The nested concept method gives commanders-

• The opportunity to engage and exploit the talents and initiative of subordinate commanders and soldiers at every level
• An effective technique to train their subordinates on the use of the four elements of mission command

Training for mission command requires commanders and leaders to emphasize use of mission orders along with nested concept training scenarios. Mission orders train subordinates to exercise initiative within the commander's intent. Commanders develop an environment of mutual trust and understanding that sponsors and fosters decentralized decisionmaking and execution. Additionally, commanders must-

• Underscore each subordinates responsibility for their assigned mission in the context of their commander's mission, intent and concept of operation
• Help subordinates understand the leadership effect of combat power. Leaders decide where and when to generate effects of maneuver, firepower, and protection

MAPEXs and TEWTs are leader-oriented training exercises in which commanders can use mission orders based on nested concept scenarios to train staffs and subordinate commanders in mission command. These exercises provide staffs and subordinate commanders with opportunities to-

• Develop and expand their battle command experience base
• Develop uniform understanding of key doctrinal concepts and terms, and use the doctrinal terms correctly
• Develop their ability to understand the commander's intent

The MAPEX uses troop leading procedures (TLPs) and the MDMP to-

• Give guidance (visualize)
• Prepare plans (describe)
• Issue orders (direct)

The TEWT provides an opportunity for commanders, staff officers, and other leaders to practice both the art and science of war. They-

• Practice the art of war by using discussions of tentative plans developed during MAPEXs to-
  - Encourage initiative and decentralized decisionmaking and execution
  - Develop uniform tactical thinking among commanders at every echelon (for example, BCT through company)
  - Improve mental agility of subordinate commanders
• Practice the science of war by training leader and staff tasks related to-
  - Direct fire planning, coordination, and preparation
  - Emplacing tactical and protective obstacles
  - Integrating indirect fires
  - "Walk-through" of selected CSS operations TTPs (for example, casualty evacuation [CAS EVAC])

1. Assess Training

Commanders consider several key questions when selecting training exercises. Commanders refer to their training assessment before they start the training exercise selection process to determine-

- What are the specific training tasks?
- What is the training audience for each specific training task?
- What is the overall training objective?

2. Identify Training Audience

Once commanders identify the training audience(s), they again refer to their training assessment to answer the following:

- What is the training audience's current level of proficiency?
- What is the required level of training proficiency for this training audience on this particular task? Is it to-
- Acquire new skills?
- Familiarize skills?
- Practice and sustain skills?
- Validate skills?

These questions help commanders determine whether to use a crawl, walk, or run training approach for any training exercise.

3. Determine Training Objectives

Commanders determine specific training objectives, then consider conditions necessary to achieve the level of proficiency for the training audience. Commanders ask the following questions when considering conditions-

- What is the desired level of realism?
- What resources are available to achieve the desired level of realism?

4. Select Training Exercise

Commanders select a particular training exercise or combination of exercises based on-

- Current level of proficiency compared with the required level of proficiency on specific tasks
- Resources available to replicate conditions necessary to achieve and sustain required levels of proficiency

The answers to these questions, considered along with the decision on crawl, walk, or run training skill proficiency level exercises, help the commander determine whether to use live, virtual, or constructive training simulators and simulations, or a combination of the three, for desired exercise quality.

V. Training Exercises

Ref: FM 25-101, app. C (STX and Live-Fire Exercise updated to FM 7-1).

Training Exercises

1 Map Exercise (MAPEX)

2 Tactical Exercise Without Troops (TEWT)

3 Fire Coordination Exercise (FCX)

4 Command Post Exercise (CPX)

5 Situational Training Exercise (STX)

6 Command Field Exercise (CFX)

7 Logistical Coordination Exercise (LCX)

8 Field Training Exercise (FTX)

9 Live Fire Exercise (LFX)

Ref: FM 25-101, app. C.

Commanders select a particular training exercise or combination of exercises based on specific training objectives and on available resources. When selecting exercises, commanders must consider several key questions:

- Who will be trained (soldiers, leaders, or units)?
- What are the training objectives?
- Which, if any, of the training exercises are most suitable to accomplish each objective?
- What are the available resources (time, training areas, equipment, money)?
- Which of the training exercises or combination will help meet the training objectives within the available training resources?

Realism vs. Level of Resourcing

Ref: FM 25-101, fig. C-1, p. C-2.

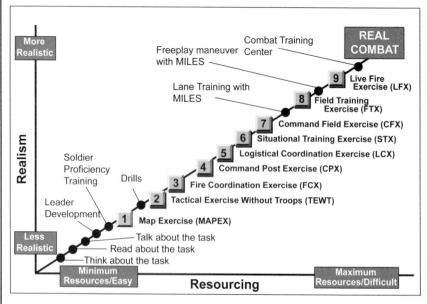

Suggested Exercise Participants

Ref: FM 25-101, pp. C-6 to C-9.

1. MAPEX

Battalion & Task Force Level
• Battalion cdr, CSM and XO
• Primary staff (S1, S2, S3, S4)
• Company cdrs & 1SGs
• Battalion motor officer
• Slice cdrs and leaders

Company & Team Level
• Company cdr, 1SG, and XO
• Platoon Leaders
• FIST chief
• Support leaders & co HQs personnel as appropriate
• Platoon sergeants

Platoon Level
• Platoon leader
• Platoon sergeant
• Squad ldrs & vehicle cdrs

2. TEWT

Battalion Level
• Battalion cdr, CSM and XO
• Primary and special staff
• Slice cdrs and leaders
• Company cdrs, XOs, plt ldrs

Company Level
• Company cdr, 1SG, and XO
• Platoon Leaders
• FIST chief
• Platoon sergeants

3. FCX

Battalion Level
• Battalion cdr
• S3, FSO, ALO
• Company cdrs and plt ldrs
• Squad and team leaders
• Slice leaders if applicable
• Weapon system personnel

Company Level
• Company cdr
• Platoon Leaders
• Squad and team leaders

Platoon Level
• Platoon leader
• Squad leader
• Team and section leaders
• Weapon system personnel

4. CPX

Battalion Level
• Battalion cdr, CSM and XO
• Battalion staff
• Company cdrs and plt ldrs
• Bn slice and spt leaders

Company Level
• Company cdr, 1SG, and XO
• Platoon ldrs and plt sgts
• FIST chief

5. LCX

Battalion Level
• Battalion XO
• S1 and S4 sections
• Bn motor officer and NCO
• Spt platoon leader
• Personnel services NCO
• Medical platoon leader

Company Level
• Company XO and 1SG
• Platoon ldrs, plt sgts
• Squad leaders
• Unit supply sgt & co medic
• Key soldiers

Exercise Selection Matrix
Ref: FM 25-101, fig. C-2, pp. C-4 to C-5.

Intelligence	1 MAPEX	2 TEWT	3 FCX	4 CPX	5 LCX	6 STX	7 CFX	8 FTX	9 LFX
Collect Information			X		X	X	X	X	
Process Information	X	X	X	X	X	X	X	X	
Prepare Intel Reports	X	X	X	X		X	X	X	
Maneuver									
Move	X	X	X	X		X	X	X	X
Engage Enemy									X
Control Terrain						X		X	X
Fire Support									
Process Ground Tgts	X	X	X	X		X	X	X	X
Engage Ground			X	X		X	X	X	X
Mobility, Countermobility & Survivability									
Provide Mobility						X		X	
Provide Countermobility	X	X	X	X		X	X	X	
Enhance Survivability		X	X	X		X	X	X	
Air Defense									
Process Air Targets		X	X	X		X	X	X	X
Attack Enemy Air Targets			X				X		
Deny Airspace	X	X	X	X		X	X	X	
Combat Service Support									
Arm	X	X	X	X	X	X	X	X	X
Fuel	X	X	X	X	X	X	X	X	X
Fix	X	X	X	X	X	X	X	X	X
Man the Force				X	X	X	X	X	
Distribution				X	X	X	X	X	X
Provide Sustainment Engineering	X	X		X	X	X	X	X	X
Provide Military Police Spt				X		X	X	X	X
Combat Service Support									
Acquire & Communicate Information and Maintain Status	X	X	X	X	X	X	X	X	X
Assess Situation	X	X	X	X	X	X	X	X	X
Determine Actions	X	X	X	X	X	X	X	X	X
Direct and Lead Subordinate Forces	X	X	X	X	X	X	X	X	X

1. Map Exercise (MAPEX)

The MAPEX portrays military maps and overlays. It requires situations on a minimum number of support personnel and may be conducted in garrison or in the field. When conducted in garrison, it is low-cost in terms of training dollars and facilities; it is an excellent training tool for a resource-constrained unit. Communications equipment may be used. A MAPEX helps the commander train his staff and leaders in planning, coordinating, and ex- ecuting operations tasks on map boards, chalkboards, training mock-ups, and sand tables. It is an excellent training tool before conducting other more costly exercises. A MAPEX trains the following:

- Functioning as an effective team
- Exchanging information
- Preparing estimates
- Giving appraisals
- Making recommendations and decisions
- Preparing plans
- Issuing orders
- Coordinating execution of orders

A MAPEX can be conducted internally at platoon, company, and battalion level or externally with a brigade or division MAPEX.

2. Tactical Exercise Without Troops (TEWT)

The TEWT is conducted on actual terrain with unit leaders and staffs, without soldiers. A TEWT allows the battalion TF or company commander to train his staff and subordinate leaders. It also allows him to analyze, plan, and present how he would conduct an operation on the actual terrain.

TEWTs are normally conducted internally. Because only the battle staff and selected support personnel are involved, the TEWT is an inexpensive way to familiarize leaders with the area of operations. A TEWT can be used:

- To analyze terrain
- To employ units according to terrain analysis
- To emplace weapons systems to best support the unit's mission
- To prepare and validate plans
- To plan CS and CSS operations

3. Fire Coordination Exercise (FCX)

The FCX is used to train the combined arms team chain of command and related fire control elements to rapidly synchronize fires on the battlefield.

The exercise can use reduced-scale targets and ranges to depict combat situations. The chain of command must respond in the form of maneuver and fire coordination techniques and procedures. Commanders use FCXs:

- To develop the chain of command into a team
- To synchronize fires within the combined arms team
- To train the chain of command prior to a live fire exercise
- To exercise the communications net
- To assist in integrating new weapons system
- To portray a rapidly changing situation for the chain of command to react to

FCXs are normally used to train platoon- through battalion-level. The entire task force chain of command can be trained.

4. Command Post Exercise (CPX)

The CPX may be conducted in garrison or in the field. It requires the establishment of the command post. When compared with the MAPEX or TEWT, it represents a greater commitment of soldiers' time and resources. A CPX an expanded MAPEX for staff and all commanders to lead and control tactical operations by using tactical communications systems. Of ten the CPX is driven by a simulation or is part a larger exercise. Normal battlefield distances between CPs may be reduced. A CPX trains commanders and staff—

- To build teamwork and cohesion
- To exchange information by proper reporting IAW tactical SOPs
- To prepare estimates, plans, and orders
- To establish and employ tactical communications
- To displace headquarters and command posts
- To integrate synchronized BOS

Battalions and companies may participate in a CPX as part of a larger force (brigade, division, and corps); they also may conduct internal CPXs.

5. Logistical Coordination Exercise (LCX)

LCXs allow leaders to become proficient at conducting unit sustainment operations such as supply, transportation, medical, personnel replacement, maintenance, and graves registration. LCXs provide a valuable, hands-on opportunity to deal with combat-related challenges of these activities. Most important, leaders can develop the SOPs so essential to their effective accomplishment. An LCX—

- Clarifies key elements of the battalion or TF logistics apparatus
- Exercises the flow of logistical information
- Incorporates a tactical war game that produces a wide variety of logistical requirements
- Allows plenty of opportunity for instruction and critique
- Exercises the communications network

As the primary leaders and soldiers train for the exercise, the interplay of CSS activities can be fully examined. Unit SOPs can be developed, modified, and verified. As proficiency in logistical operations is attained, LCX can be tied to other task force exercises to complete the integration of CSS with other combat operations.

6. Situational Training Exercise (STX)

Situational training exercises (STXs) are mission-related, limited exercises designed to train one collective task, or a group of related tasks and drills, through practice. STXs teach the doctrinally-preferred method for carrying out a task. STXs usually include drills, leader tasks, and individual soldier tasks. To ensure standardization, institutional schools and units develop STXs to teach the doctrinally-preferred way to perform specific missions and tasks. STXs may be modified based on the unit's METL, or expanded to meet special mission requirements.

STX training is especially helpful for training specific METL tasks. It is a useful technique primarily for training company team level and smaller units on a series of selected soldier, leader, and collective tasks using specific terrain. The concept provides an effective way to standardize TTPs and develop and rehearse tactical standing operating procedures (TACSOPs). STXs are a perfect opportunity to use crawl-walk-run training. Commanders narrow the focus and select specific collective tasks for the training. STX training may be resource-intensive, so commanders must maximize the benefit.

STX training under varying conditions gives the unit a distinct advantage when executing combat operations. STX training at night and during adverse weather provides a training opportunity to execute critical tasks and drills under naturally occurring light and weather conditions, and enhances training realism. Reverse cycle training should be planned to take advantage of every opportunity to replicate a 24-hour operational environment.

STX training is structured to expose leaders and soldiers to unexpected situations, favorable and unfavorable. Tasks must be executed confidently and competently during the fog of battle. Tough, realistic training challenges leaders and soldiers to overcome the hardships and uncertainties of combat. Challenging training inspires excellence by fostering initiative, enthusiasm, confidence, and the ability to operate in all elements of the operational spectrum. Even if a unit accomplishes the assigned task to standard, the unit may retrain the exercise with more difficult conditions.

7. Command Field Exercise (CFX)
The CFX lies on a scale between the CPX and FTX. Available resources determine where the CFX fits on the scale. The CFX can also be a backup for the FTX if maneuver damage, weather, or other factors prohibit the planned FTX. The CFX is an FTX with reduced unit and vehicle density, but with full C2, CS, and CSS elements. For example, the platoon leader in his vehicle represents the entire platoon.

CFXs are excellent vehicles for training leaders and staff with full command, control, communications, and logistical systems. They are less expensive and exercise intersystem linkages and real distances. They sharpen unit skills in such areas as-
- Intelligence
- Fire support
- Slice integration
- CSS
- Rear area operations
- Command, control, and communications

A CFX can train as much, or as little, of the task force as necessary, depending on the commander's assessment and training objectives.

8. Field Training Exercise (FTX)
FTXs are conducted under simulated combat conditions in the field. FTXs fully integrate the total force in a realistic combat environment. They involve combat arms, CS, and CSS units. FTXs encompass such training as battle drills, crew drills, and STXs to reinforce soldier and collective training integration. They are used to train the commander, staff, subordinate units, and slice elements—
- To move and maneuver units realistically
- To employ organic weapons systems effectively
- To build teamwork and cohesion
- To plan and coordinate supporting fires
- To plan and coordinate logistical activities to support tactical operations

9. Live Fire Exercise (LFX)
Live fire exercises (LFXs) closely replicate battlefield conditions and provide significant advantages. LFXs-
- Develop confidence and esprit-de-corps.
- Provide soldiers with a realistic experience of the danger, confusion, and speed of combat operations.
- Require demonstrated proficiency at lower echelons before LFXs are conducted at higher echelons.

I. Training Assessment

Ref: FM 7-0, Training for Full Spectrum Operations (Dec '08), pp. 4-37 to 4-40 and FM 7-1, Battle Focused Training (Sept '03), chap 6.

In the training context, assessment is the leader's judgment of the organization's ability to perform its mission-essential tasks and, ultimately, its ability to accomplish its doctrinal or directed mission. Training assessments address a wide variety of areas, including training support, force integration, logistics, and personnel availability. These assessments form the basis for determining the organization's training ratings for readiness reporting. Commanders consider the following when making assessments:

- Their own observations and those of subordinate leaders
- Feedback from AARs
- Results of unit evaluations, where performance is measured against standards to arrive at the assessment

Training Assessment

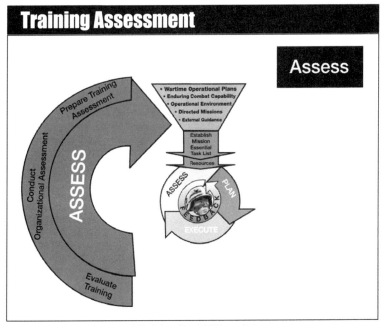

Ref: FM 7-1, Battle Focused Training (Sept '-03), p. 6-1.

Battalion and higher echelon commanders are concerned with overall unit readiness. Accordingly, they perform organizational assessments that aggregate numerous evaluations. These commanders establish an organizational assessment program that:

- Fixes responsibility within the staff and subordinate organizations for gathering and analyzing evaluation data and preparing recommendations

Sources of Evaluation Data for Organizational Assessments

Ref: FM 7-1, Battle Focused Training (Sept '03), fig. 6-1.

Battalion and higher-level commanders perform organizational assessments that aggregate a large number of evaluations. They include such diverse systems as training, force integration, logistics, and personnel.

Commanders establish a command assessment program that-

- Fixes responsibility within the staff and subordinate units for gathering and analyzing evaluation data and preparing recommendations
- Concentrates on the effectiveness of leader and organizational training
- Utilizes the CSM and other senior NCOs to gather feedback
- Allows the higher cdr to monitor outcomes and take action to reshape priorities, policies, or plans to overcome assessed weaknesses and sustain strengths

CTC take-home packages are an excellent source of feedback to include in an organizational assessment. These packages consist of videotapes and written documentation of AARs, a report of unit strengths and weaknesses as noted by OCs, and recommendations for future home station training.

- Personal observations of training
- Assessment and feedback from higher headquarters
- Staff visit reports
- Unit status reports
- Training briefings
- Training evaluations
- EXEVALs
- CTC take-home packages
- AARs from FTXs, gunnery periods, or other major training exercises
- AT reports
- CTT results (component of ITEP)
- UCOFT/MCOFT results
- AAR-generated reports from training activities, to include those from virtual training activities
- Emergency deployment readiness exercise (EDRE) reports
- Maintenance and logistical evaluations and technical inspection results
- Inspector General (IG) general and special inspections
- Commander's Organizational Inspection Program
- Force integration reports and feedback
- Army Audit Agency reports
- APFT scores
- Weapons qualification records
- Division (training support) assistance input

- Concentrates on the effectiveness of leader and unit training
- Uses command sergeants major and other senior NCOs to gather feedback on the individual, crew, team, and section training.
- Allows the senior commander to monitor outcomes and act to reshape priorities, policies, or plans to overcome weaknesses and sustain strengths.

I. Evaluation

In the training context, evaluation is the process used to measure the demonstrated ability of individuals and units to accomplish specified training objectives. Evaluations are one form of feedback. Commanders evaluate subordinate units two echelons below their unit. Training evaluations provide commanders with feedback on the demonstrated proficiency of individuals, staffs, and organizations against a standard. Training conducted without evaluation is a waste of time and resources. Evaluations can be informal, formal, internal, external, or any combination of them.

Training evaluations are a critical component of measuring readiness. Evaluation measures the demonstrated ability of individuals, leaders, staffs, and units to perform against the Army or joint standard.

Senior commanders and leaders focus on unit readiness by requiring evaluations of specific mission-essential and critical collective subtasks. They also use evaluation results to determine which observations, insights, and lessons constitute lessons learned. Lessons learned are distributed throughout their commands and used in planning future training.

Evaluation of individual and small-unit training normally includes every individual involved in the training. For large-scale training events, evaluators usually base their evaluation on the performance of a sample of individual and subordinate organizations.

An evaluation of training is not a test. Evaluations are not used to find reasons to punish leaders and subordinates. Leaders use evaluations as opportunities to coach and develop subordinates. Evaluations tell organizations and individuals whether they achieved the standard and help them determine the overall effectiveness of their training plans.

Results of evaluations can strongly affect the command climate of an organization. Senior commanders should underwrite honest mistakes and create a positive learning environment so the same mistakes do not reoccur.

The unit commander is responsible for assessing the readiness of the unit to execute its wartime mission. A critical component of this assessment is evaluation of training. The evaluation process is continuous, and must be planned for all training and considered as a way of life in the unit. Training evaluation is integral to standards-based training and is conducted by leaders at every level.

The analysis of the information is the key mechanism that commanders use in their assessment. Commanders can use evaluations to synchronize all unit functions. To evaluate training proficiency, commanders-

- Select the type of evaluation
- Develop an evaluation plan
- Conduct evaluation of training
- Conduct AARs
- Provide feedback up and down the chain of command

All training is evaluated to measure performance against the Army standard. The evaluation can be as fundamental as an informal, internal evaluation performed by the leader conducting the training, or the evaluation may be a very complex EXEVAL. In either case, evaluation is conducted specifically to enable the unit or individual undergoing the training to know whether the training standard has been achieved. Commanders establish a climate that encourages candid and accurate feedback for the purpose of developing leaders and trained units.

Evaluation of training is not a test; it is not used to find reasons to punish leaders and soldiers. Evaluation tells the unit or the soldier whether or not they achieved the Army standard, and therefore assists them in determining the overall effectiveness of their training plans or execution of training. Evaluation produces disciplined soldiers, leaders, and units. Training without evaluation is a waste of time and resources.

Each training event is evaluated during training execution. Planning for training must include resources (such as leader time, preparation, evaluators, and equipment) to facilitate evaluation. Leaders use evaluations as an opportunity to coach and mentor subordinates. A key element in developing leaders is immediate, positive feedback that coaches and leads subordinate leaders to achieve the Army standard. This is a tested and proven path to develop competent, confident, adaptive leaders.

Evaluation Ratings

Evaluation ratings are assigned by evaluators and should not be confused with leader assessment ratings. Evaluation ratings are ratings assigned directly to demonstrated task proficiency. Using T&EOs, evaluators observe the designated training tasks and grade the performance "GO" or "NO GO," as defined below-

- **"GO:"** The task or performance step of a task was performed to standard. A rating of GO is normally awarded if all steps in the task are passed.
- **"NO GO:"** The task or any performance step in the task was not performed to standard.

The completed T&EOs, with appropriate written comments, formal and informal AAR comments, coaching, and mentoring provide the participating leaders and soldiers with both immediate and documented feedback on demonstrated performance. Commanders later use the evaluator ratings as one source of input when making their training assessment ratings of T, P, or U for each METL task.

Evaluations are used to-

- Provide feedback on training proficiency, both strengths and weaknesses, to those participating in the training event
- Determine METL task proficiency
- Develop lessons learned for distribution throughout the command and the Army, when applicable
- Shape future training plans
- Coach and mentor subordinates
- Enhance leader development

A. Evaluators

Commanders ensure evaluators are trained as facilitators to perform AARs that elicit maximum participation from those being trained. External evaluators are trained in tasks they are evaluating and normally do not participate in the training being executed. In addition to being able to plan, prepare, and execute AARs, effective evaluators also:

B. Types of Evaluations

Ref: FM 7-0, Training for Full Spectrum Operations (Dec '08), pp. 4-38 to 4-39 and FM 7-1, Battle Focused Training (Sept '03), p. 7-6.

Evaluations may be informal, formalk internal, external, or any combination of these.

Informal	
Internal	**External**
■ Is a function of unit leadership whenever training is conducted (e.g., squad leader vehicle PMCS).	■ Is conducted by leaders during visits to training of subordinate units (e.g., CSM spot-checks Soldiers' range cards).
Formal	
Internal	**External**
■ An evaluation of squad and below proficiency (e.g., squad leaders evaluate squad individual and collective tasks).	■ An evaluation of battalion/ company/ platoon proficiency (e.g., battalion evaluations platoon ARTEP training events).

Ref: FM 7-1, Battle Focused Training (Sept '03), fig. 6-2, p. 6-6.

1. Informal Evaluations

Informal evaluations occur when leaders evaluate their unit's training against established standards. Leaders follow an informal evaluation with either an AAR or a critique, depending on the nature of the feedback to be provided. An example is a squad leader providing verbal feedback on a fire team leader's ability to control the team during a movement to contact. Another example is a leader visiting ongoing training and discussing his or her observations of individual and unit performance with subordinate leaders. In all cases, leaders evaluate training against the standard. This type of evaluation provides real-time feedback on the training environment and the proficiency resulting from training.

2. Formal Evaluations

Formal evaluations involve dedicated evaluators and are scheduled in training plans. Normally, formal evaluations are highlighted during short-range training briefings. As much as possible, headquarters two echelons higher perform formal external evaluations. Division commanders evaluate battalions, brigade commanders evaluate companies, and battalion commanders evaluate platoons. Feedback usually takes the form of an AAR followed by a written report. During and after formal evaluations, evaluators prepare their findings and recommendations. They provide these evaluations to the evaluated unit commander and higher commanders as required by the headquarters directing the evaluations.

3. Internal Evaluations

Internal evaluations are planned, resourced, and performed by the organization undergoing the evaluation. Unit-conducted situational training exercises are an example.

4. External Evalutations

External evaluations are planned, resourced, and performed by a higher headquarters or a headquarters outside the chain of command. The exercise director is normally two echelons above the evaluated organization. External sources should evaluate training whenever possible to objectively measure performance in terms of Army and joint standards.

C. Planning for Evaluations

Ref: FM 7-1, Battle Focused Training (Sept '03), p. 6-8.

The evaluation of collective training is critical to assessing a unit's capability to perform its METL tasks. For evaluation to be effective, it must be thoroughly planned and rigorously executed. Leaders must plan and prepare to ensure an accurate evaluation. For formal evaluations, commanders must ensure that the evaluators are trained and prepared to assume those duties. For informal evaluations, commanders must ensure that training plans prepare subordinate leaders to conduct the evaluation of their own units.

RC commanders may request assistance from their state adjutant general, regional readiness command, or affiliated unit to assist in planning, preparing, and evaluating training. However, the RC chain of command remains responsible for the evaluation.

The following information is required to facilitate long-range evaluation planning:

- Type of exercise (battalion FTX, company FTX, company STX, TEWT)
- Date(s) of exercise
- Type of evaluation (formal, informal, internal, external, or a combination)
- Support requirements (internal and external)
- Coordination for EXEVAL support

To enhance effective short-range planning, the commander and key leaders develop and provide the following information:

- Commander's intent and focus for the exercise
- Pre-execution checklist
- Level of evaluation; for example, down to platoon level
- Dates for training the evaluators
- Plan for conduct of evaluator training
- ARTEP-MTP or T&EOs

The commander and key leaders also provide a completed evaluation and control plan.

- Intent of the exercise and the evaluation
- Evaluation procedures
- Exercise scenario
- Training objectives
- Resource guidance
- Required coordination
- Discussion of evaluator's role in safety
- Rules of engagement
- Exercise operating procedures (ExOP)
- Reference-SMs, FMs, MTPs, and SOPs
- Evaluation checklists and T&EOs
- Guidance on conduct of AARs

Sample Evaluator Group Worksheet

Evaluation planners use an evaluator worksheet. This worksheet aids in developing the best evaluator organization.

Type of Exercise: FTX

Duration of the Exercise: 2 days

Frequency of Exercise: 2 platoons per day (4 platoons, 1 per company)

Level of Evaluation: Platoon and below

Tasks Selected for Evaluation:

Types of Evaluation:

Availability of Evaluator Personnel with Appropriate Skills:
- Platoon level-2 CPT staff officers
- Squad/crew level-2 platoon sergeants and/or staff NCOs
- Soldier Level-All of the above

Suggested Organization Based on the Above Information:
- Chief Evaluator(s)-Battalion commander/CSM
- Platoon Evaluators-1 officer/senior NCO per platoon
- Squad Evaluators-1 NCO evaluator per squad

Notes:
1. Each platoon has two evaluators at all times
2. Evaluations are conducted during the TF 1-77 FTX
2. AARs are conducted at the conclusion of each event
3. The chemical officer or NCO evaluates during cross-contaminated area task.

Ref: FM 7-1, Battle Focused Training (Sept '03), fig. 6-4, p. 6-8.

Refinement of the evaluation plan continues up to and during execution. This accommodates changes made to the events, the evaluation plan, and the resource allocations. OCs are not able to observe all training, so selected elements from the training unit are designated for evaluation. For a defend task, evaluators provide a formal evaluation of an entire platoon. This consists of overall formal evaluations for two squads with specific focus on one fire team within each squad. In this manner, a limited number of evaluators can develop a good snapshot of the platoon's overall proficiency.

- Are familiar with the evaluated organization's METL and training objectives
- Are tactically and technically proficient and rehearsed in the evaluated tasks
- Know the evaluation standards
- Know the evaluated organization's tactical and field standing operating procedures
- Consider such characteristics as the evaluated organization's missions, personnel turbulence, leader fill, and equipment status

Not only do individuals and units receiving the training learn from the evaluator; evaluators also learn while observing the evaluated organization.

External evaluators must be certified in the tasks they are evaluating and normally are not dual-hatted as a participant in the training being executed. Leaders, soldiers, and units learn from the evaluator. Evaluators learn by observing the unit. Unit leaders who serve as internal evaluators must also be certified in the tasks they evaluate. Some basic guidelines for the evaluator are listed below-

- Be trained (tactically and technically proficient) and rehearsed in the tasks to be evaluated
- Know the terrain. (Conduct reconnaissance of the training area.)
- Know the evaluation standards
- Follow the tactical and field SOPs for the organization being evaluated
- Apply relevant information about the evaluated unit, such as wartime missions, METL, personnel turbulence, leader fill, and equipment status
- Identify strengths as well as weaknesses
- Patiently observe all actions of a unit (Do not jump to conclusions.)
- Always use the chain of command (Do not take command of the unit.)
- Coach unit leaders
- Assist the commander and leaders in training safely. Be aware of specific safety considerations applicable to the training
- Be flexible; base evaluation on the unit's reaction to the tactical situation, not on personal knowledge of the preplanned scenario
- Do what the soldiers do. Experience the same conditions as the evaluated unit
- Know the OPFOR training objectives

D. Training Evaluators

Evaluators must be trained prior to conducting evaluations. Evaluator training is planned and executed during the preparation phase of training execution. Training ensures that the evaluators are technically and tactically competent and understand their responsibilities during evaluations.

- Pertinent Army doctrine
- Safety and environment considerations
- Conduct of required evaluator rehearsals
- Purpose and scope of the exercise
- Training objectives
- T&EOs
- Enemy situation (per OPORD)
- OPFOR organization

- Participating units' task organization and METL and how it supports the higher headquarters METL
- Participating unit's TSOPs
- Communications plan/network architecture
- Rules of engagement (ROE)
- Exercise operating procedures (ExOP)
- Intelligence plans
- Controller duties
- Reconnaissance
- Communications responsibilities and checks
- Required records and reports
- Casualty and damage assessment
- AAR

II. Feedback

Feedback is the transmission of verbal or written evaluative or corrective information about a process or task to individuals and organizations. It provides the basis for assessments. Sources of feedback include:

- Personal observations
- Reports from higher headquarters
- Staff assistance visits
- External evaluations, including CTC take-home packages
- Readiness reports
- Organized inspections
- DTMS reports

CTC take-home packages provide excellent information for the commander's assessment of readiness. These packages may include video and written AARs, a report of unit strengths and weaknesses, and recommendations for future home station training.

III. Certification

Certification is a measure of individual technical proficiency and is normally found in Army or MACOM regulations. Certification is not a normal part of day-to-day training. The decision to require certification is made at a higher headquarters and is the result of a deliberate process. Certification requirements for OCs and individuals to supervise live-fire ranges, driver licensing, etc., are examples of individual technical proficiencies that commanders may require to support training. Certification is more often applied to processes and procedures that support operations and training, such as destruction of classified documents or outdated medicines. Certification can also be validation of professional skills in such fields as law and medicine.

Commanders may require certification to confirm a unit's collective training proficiency to perform a specific type of mission or task. Certification of an infantry squad that has been tasked to conduct a specific stability or support task is an example of unit collective certification. Higher headquarters on a "by exception" basis normally directs this confirmation requirement.

IV. Lessons and Lessons Learned

As the Army continues to grow and learn, it is necessary to maintain doctrinal currency and relevancy. Maintaining currency and relevancy means collecting, assessing, sharing, and integrating into training and education the observations, insights, lessons, and TTPs learned during training exercises and operational deployments.

Commanders and other leaders, while assessing training exercises and operational deployments, or at the conclusion of any AAR, may note issues that should be shared with the rest of the Army. The outputs from an AAR-what worked and what did not work-are lessons learned. In many cases, these lessons may be significant beyond just the unit involved in the training.

Conducting AARs and integrating TTP and lessons learned from those AARs back into ongoing training and operations are an inherent command responsibility. Important or significant observations, insights, lessons, and TTP should be shared with the rest of the Army by sending them to the Center for Army Lessons Learned (CALL) at Fort Leavenworth, Kansas. CALL shares this information with the Army through a variety of electronic and paper-based products.

Although CALL has the lead to gather and disseminate lessons learned, CALL cannot cover every BOS or operational deployment without help from commanders and units. Branch proponents work with in-theater commanders to gather lessons in general, and lessons about BOS in particular.

V. Retraining

Leaders understand that not all tasks will be performed to standard on the first attempt. Thus, they allocate time and other resources for retraining in their training plans. Retraining allows participants to implement corrective action. Retraining should be completed at the earliest opportunity, if not immediately, to translate observations and evaluations into tasks trained to standard. Training is incomplete until the organization achieves the Army standard. Commanders do not allow an organization to end training believing that a substandard performance was acceptable. In some cases, a "restart" or "redo" of an event may be necessary before moving to the next training event.

II. The After Action Review (AAR)

Ref: FM 7-0, Training for Full Spectrum Operations (Dec '08), pp. 4-39 to 4-40 and FM 7-1, Battle Focused Training (Sept '03), app. C.

The after action review is a method of providing feedback to organizations by involving participants in the training diagnostic process in order to increase and reinforce learning. Leaders use formal or informal AARs to provide feedback on training. The AAR provides a forum for structured review and information sharing. AARs allow participating individuals, leaders, staffs, and units to discover for themselves what happened during the training, why it happened, and how to execute tasks or operations better. The AAR is a professional discussion requiring active participation by those being trained. AARs:

- Are two-way discussions, rather than one-way critiques, of the performance of an individual or organization
- Increase the likelihood of learning and foster the development of a learning organization by actively involving participants
- Use "leading questions" to encourage key participants to self-discover important observations, insights, and lessons from the training event
- Emphasize corrective action rather than dwelling on what went wrong
- Focus directly on attainment of training objectives derived from the METL
- Emphasize meeting Army or joint standards rather than pronouncing judgment of success or failure

AARs are often "tiered" to develop leaders at multiple echelons. For example, feedback from squad or section AARs should be brought into platoon AARs. Feedback from platoon AARs should feed discussion in company AARs. After completing an AAR with all participants, senior trainers may continue the professional discussion with selected leaders. Some AARs are formal gatherings of unit key leaders. Others are simply one-on-one discussions between a commander and an observer-controller/trainer over a vehicle hood.

Unit leaders must be trained to complete informal, internal evaluations as well. They must be able to plan, prepare, and execute AARs effectively whenever and wherever needed. Taking too much time between an event and the AAR can cause a loss of learning. This means leaders remain:

- Familiar with their unit's METL and how it supports their higher headquarters' METL
- Tactically and technically proficient in the evaluated tasks

AARs should be conducted during training as well as at the end of training events or during recovery. Leader feedback to subordinates during training allows subordinates to take corrective action immediately. Frequently providing feedback gives organizations opportunities to correct deficiencies before a training event ends. If leaders only conduct end-of-exercise AARs, valuable lessons may be lost.

AARs with leaders focus on tactical judgment. These AARs contribute to leader learning and provide opportunities for leader development. Including evaluator, observer-controller/trainer, and OPFOR performance in AARs provides additional leader development opportunities. These AARs contribute to the commander's overall evaluation of training effectiveness and assessment of unit proficiency.

Types Of After Action Reviews

There are two types of AARs: formal and informal. A formal AAR is resource-intensive and involves the planning, coordination, and preparation of the AAR site; supporting training aids; and support personnel. Informal AARs require less preparation and planning.

Types of After-Action Reviews

Formal Reviews	Informal Reviews
▪ Have external observers and controllers (OCs)	▪ Conducted by internal chain of command
▪ Take more time	▪ Take less time
▪ Use more complex training aids	▪ Use simple training aids
▪ Are scheduled beforehand	▪ Are conducted when needed
▪ Are conducted where best supported	▪ Are conducted at the training site

Ref: FM 25-20, fig. 1-3, p. 1-4 (not included in FM 7-0).

See also p. 8-5 for further discussion of evaluations.

A. Formal

Leaders plan formal AARs at the same time that they finalize the near-term training plan (6 to 8 weeks before execution). Formal AARs require more planning and preparation than informal AARs. They require site reconnaissance and selection, coordination for training aids (terrain models, map blow-ups, etc.), and selection, setup, and maintenance of the AAR site.

During formal AARs, the AAR facilitator (unit leader or OC) provides an exercise overview, and focuses the discussion of events on the training objectives. At the end, the facilitator reviews key points and issues, and summarizes strengths and weaknesses discussed during the AAR.

B. Informal

Leaders and OCs use informal AARs as on-the-spot coaching tools while reviewing soldier and unit performances during training. The informal AAR is extremely important, as all soldiers are involved. For example, after destroying an enemy observation post (OP) during a movement to contact, a squad leader conducts an informal AAR to make corrections and reinforce strengths. Using nothing more than pinecones to represent squad members, the squad leader and squad members discuss the contact from start to finish. The squad quickly-

- Evaluates their performance against the Army standard
- Identifies their strengths and weaknesses
- Decides how to improve their performance when training continues

Informal AARs provide immediate feedback to soldiers, leaders, and units during training. Ideas and solutions the leader gathers during informal AARs can be immediately put to use as the unit continues its training.

The After Action Review (AAR)

Ref: FM 7-0 Training the Force, pp. 6-4 to 6-5.

The AAR, whether formal or informal, provides feedback for all training. It is a structured review process that allows participating soldiers, leaders, and units to discover for themselves what happened during the training, why it happened, and how it can be done better. The AAR is a professional discussion that requires the active participation of those being trained. The AAR is not a critique and has the following advantages over a critique:

- Focuses directly on key METL derived training objectives
- Emphasizes meeting Army standards rather than pronouncing judgment of success or failure
- Uses "leading questions" to encourage participants to self-discover important lessons from the training event
- Allows a large number of individuals and leaders to participate so more of the training can be recalled and more lessons learned can be shared

The AAR consists of four parts-

1. Review what was supposed to happen (training plans)
The evaluator, along with the participants, reviews what was supposed to happen based on the commander's intent for the training event, unit-training plan, training objectives, and applicable T&EOs.

2. Establish what happened
The evaluator and the participants determine what actually happened during performance of the training task. A factual and indisputable account is vital to the effectiveness of the discussion that follows. For force-on-force training, OPFOR members assist in describing the flow of the training event and discuss training outcomes from their points of view.

3. Determine what was right or wrong with what happened
The participants establish the strong and weak points of their performance. The evaluator plays a critical role in guiding the discussions so conclusions reached by participants are doctrinally sound, consistent with Army standards, and relevant to the wartime mission.

4. Determine how the task should be done differently the next time
The evaluator assists the chain of command undergoing the training to lead the group in determining exactly how participants will perform differently the next time the task is performed.

Leaders understand that not all tasks will be performed to standard and in their initial planning, allocate time and other resources for retraining. Retraining allows the participants to apply the lessons learned during the AAR and implement corrective action. Retraining should be conducted at the earliest opportunity to translate observation and evaluation into training to standard. Commanders must ensure that units understand that training is incomplete until the Army standard is achieved.

The AAR is often "tiered" as a multiechelon leader development technique. Following an AAR with all participants, senior trainers may use the AAR for an extended professional discussion with selected leaders. These discussions usually include a more specific AAR of leader contributions to the observed training results.

Step 1. Planning the After Action Review

Ref: FM 7-1 Battle Focused Training, pp. C-2 to C-4.

Commanders are responsible for planning, preparing, executing, and evaluating training. All training is evaluated.

To maximize the effectiveness of AARs, formal or informal, leaders must plan and prepare. AAR planning is part of unit near-term planning (6 to 8 weeks out). During planning, commanders assign OC responsibilities and ensure the allocation of time and resources to conduct AARs.

The AAR plan provides the foundation for successful AARs. The amount and level of detail needed during the planning and preparation process depends on the type of AAR to be conducted and available resources. Commanders develop an AAR plan for each training event. It contains-

- Who will observe the training and who will conduct the AAR
- What trainers should evaluate
- Who attends
- When and where the AAR will occur
- What training aids will be used

OCs use the AAR plan to identify critical places and events they must observe to give the unit a valid evaluation. Examples include unit maintenance collection points, passage points, and unit aid stations. The AAR plan also includes who will observe and control a particular event. The OC is the individual tasked to observe training, provide control for the training, and lead the AAR.

I. Planning the AAR

1. Selecting and training observor/controllers (OCs)
2. Reviewing the training and evaluation plan
3. Scheduling stopping points
4. Determining attendance
5. Choosing training aids
6. Reviewing the AAR plan

1. Selecting and Training Observer/Controllers

When planning an AAR, commanders should select OCs who-

- Can demonstrate proficiency in the tasks to be trained
- Are knowledgeable of the duties they are to observe
- Are knowledgeable of current doctrine and TTPs

When using external OCs, commanders strive to have OCs who are at least equal in rank to the leader of the unit they will evaluate. If commanders must choose between experience and understanding of current TTPs or rank, they should go with experience. A staff sergeant with experience as a tank platoon sergeant will be a better OC than a sergeant first class that has no platoon sergeant experience.

Commanders are responsible for training OCs to include training on how to conduct an AAR. Each OC leads AARs for the element the OC observes, and provides input to the OC for the next higher echelon. Ideally, inexperienced OCs should observe properly conducted AARs beforehand.

2. Reviewing the Training and Evaluation Plan

The commander must specify what the training is intended to accomplish, and be specific on what is to be evaluated. T&EOs provide tasks, conditions, and standards for the unit's training as well as the standard by which leaders measure unit and soldier performance.

T&EOs are extracted from the ARTEP-MTP or developed from the ARTEP-MTP and appropriate STPs. A copy of the T&EO is given to the senior OC. The senior OC distributes the T&EO to the OC team members who review and use it to focus their observations. Using the evaluation plan, OCs can concentrate on critical places and times to evaluate unit performance.

3. Scheduling Stopping Points

Commanders schedule time to conduct AARs as an integral part of training events. Commanders plan for an AAR at the end of each critical phase or major training event. For example, a leader plans a stopping point after issuing an OPORD, when the unit arrives at a new position, after consolidation on an objective, etc.

Commanders should allow approximately 30 to 45 minutes for platoon-level AARs, 1 hour for company-level AARs, and about 2 hours for battalion-level and above. Soldiers will receive better feedback on their performance and remember the lessons longer as result of a quality AAR.

4. Determining Attendance

The AAR plan specifies who attends each AAR. At each echelon, an AAR has a primary set of participants. At squad and platoon levels, all members of the squad and platoon should attend and participate. At company or higher levels, it may not be practical to have everyone attend because of continuing operations or training. In this case, unit and OPFOR commanders, unit leaders, and other key players may be the only participants. OCs may recommend additional participants based on specific observations.

5. Choosing Training Aids

Training aids add to an AAR's effectiveness. Training aids should directly support discussion of the training and promote learning. Local training support center (TSC) catalogs list training aids available to each unit. Dry-erase boards, video equipment, terrain models, and enlarged maps are all worthwhile under the right conditions. For example, if reconnaissance reveals there were no sites that provided a view of the exercise area, the AAR facilitator may want to use a terrain table

Terrain visibility, group size, suitability to task, and availability of electrical power are all things to consider when selecting training aids. The key is planning and coordination. The bottom line: use a training aid only if it makes the AAR better.

6. Reviewing The AAR Plan

The AAR plan is only a guide. Commanders and OCs should review it regularly to make sure it is still on track and meets the training needs of the units. The plan may be adjusted as necessary, but changes take preparation and planning time away from subordinate OCs or leaders. The purpose of the AAR plan is to allow OCs and AAR leaders as much time as possible to prepare for the AAR.

Assessment & AARs

Step 2. Preparing the After Action Review

Ref: FM 7-1 Battle Focused Training, pp. C-4 to C-6.

Preparation is the key to the effective execution of any plan. Preparation for an AAR begins before the training and continues until the actual event.

II. Preparing for the AAR

1. **Reviewing training objectives, orders and doctrine**
2. **Identify key events**
3. **Observing the training and taking notes**
4. **Selecting AAR sites**
5. **Collecting observations from other observer/controllers**
6. **Organizing the AAR**

1. Reviewing Training Objectives, Orders, And Doctrine

OCs must review the training objectives before training, and again immediately before the AAR. Training objectives are the basis for observations and the focus of the AAR. OCs review current doctrine, technical information, and applicable unit SOPs to ensure that they have the tools to observe unit and individual performance properly. OCs read and understand all OPORDs and fragmentary orders (FRAGOs) the unit will issue before and during training in order to understand what is supposed to happen. The detailed knowledge OCs display as a result of these reviews gives added credibility to their evaluations.

2. Identifying Key Events

OCs identify which events are critical and make sure they are positioned in the right place at the right time to observe the unit's actions. Examples of critical events include-

- Issue of OPORDs and FRAGOs
- Troop-leading procedures (TLPs)
- Contact with opposing forces
- Resupply and reconstitution operations
- Passage of lines

3. Observing the Training and Taking Notes

OCs must keep an accurate record of what they see and hear, and record events, actions, and observations by time sequence to prevent loss of valuable information and feedback. OCs include the date-time group (DTG) of each observation so it can be easily integrated with observations of other OCs. This provides a comprehensive and detailed overview of what happened.

One of the most difficult OC tasks is to determine when and where to observe training. The OC does not always need to stay close to the unit leader. The best location is where one can observe the performance of critical tasks and the overall flow of unit actions. The OC cannot compromise the unit's location or intent by being obvious. The OC should be professional, courteous, and low-key at all times.

4. Selecting AAR Sites

AARs should occur at or near the training exercise site. Leaders should identify and inspect AAR sites and prepare a site diagram showing the placement of training aids and other equipment. Designated AAR sites also allow pre-positioning of training aids and rapid assembly of key personnel, thereby minimizing wasted time.

The AAR site should allow soldiers to see the terrain where the exercise took place. If this is not possible, the trainer finds a location that allows them to see the terrain where the most critical or significant actions occurred. The OC should have a terrain model or enlarged map or sketch and a copy of the unit's graphics to help everyone relate key events to the actual terrain.

The OC should make soldiers attending the AAR as comfortable as possible by removing helmets, providing shelter from the elements, having refreshments available (coffee, water), thereby creating an environment where participants can focus on the AAR without distractions.

5. Collecting Observations from Observer/Controllers

The senior OC needs a complete picture of what happened during the training to conduct an effective AAR. OCs for subordinate, supporting, and adjacent units provide the senior OC with a comprehensive review of the unit they observed and the impact those units have on the higher unit's mission.

The enemy's perspective is critical in identifying why a unit was or was not successful. During formal AARs, the OPFOR leader briefs the OPFOR plan and intent to set the stage for a discussion of what happened and why.

6. Organizing The AAR

The OC gathers all the information, organizing notes in chronological sequence in order to understand the flow of events. The OC selects and sequences key events in terms of their relevance to training objectives, and identifies key discussion and/or teaching points.

The purpose of discussion is for participants to discover strengths and weaknesses, propose solutions, and adopt a course of action to correct problems. OCs organize the AAR using one of the following three techniques:

- **Chronological order of events.** This technique is logical, structured, and easy to understand. By covering actions in the order they took place, soldiers and leaders are better able to recall what happened.
- **Battlefield operating systems (BOS)**. This technique structures the AAR using the BOS. Focusing on each BOS and discussing it across all phases of the training exercise, participants can identify systemic strengths and weaknesses.
- **Key events/themes/issues**. Particularly effective when time is limited, key events focus discussion on critical training events that directly support training objectives the chain of command identified before the exercise began.

The Six Warfighting Functions (FM 3-0)

1. **Movement and Maneuver**
2. **Intelligence**
3. **Fires**
4. **Sustainment**
5. **Command and Control**
6. **Protection**

Note: The "six warfighting functions" (TBP in the 2008 edition of FM 3-0 Operations) replace "battlefield operating systems."

Step 3. Conducting the After Action Review

Ref: FM 7-1 Battle Focused Training, pp. C-7 to C-8.

The training exercise has reached a stopping point, AAR preparation is complete, and key players are at the designated AAR site. If necessary, the OC reviews the purpose and sequence of the AAR to ensure that everyone present understands why an AAR is conducted. It is now time to conduct the AAR.

III. Conducting the AAR

1. Introduction and rules
2. Review of objectives & intent
3. Commander's mission & intent
4. OPFOR commander's mission & intent
5. Summary of events (what happened)
6. Closing comments (summary)

1. Introduction And Rules

The introduction should include the following thoughts:

- An AAR is a dynamic, candid, professional discussion of training that focuses on unit performance against the Army standard. Everyone must participate if they have an insight, observation, or question that will help the unit identify and correct deficiencies or maintain strengths.

- An AAR is not a critique. No-one, regardless of rank, position, or strength of personality, has all the information or answers. AARs maximize training benefits by allowing soldiers to learn from each other.

- An AAR does not grade success or failure. There are always weaknesses to improve and strengths to sustain.

Example AAR Observation Worksheet

Training/exercise title:

Event:

Date/time:

Location of observation:

Observation (player/trainer action):

Discussion (tied to task / standard if possible):

Conclusions:

Recommendations (indicate how unit have executed the task(s) better or describe training the unit needs to improve):

Ref: FM 25-20, fig. 3-1, p. 3-3 (not included in FM 7-1).

Soldier participation is directly related to the atmosphere created during the introduction. The AAR leader should make a concerted effort to draw in soldiers who seem reluctant to participate. The following techniques can help the OC create an atmosphere conducive to maximum participation. The OC should-

- Reinforce the idea that it is permissible to disagree
- Focus on learning and encourage people to give honest opinions
- Use open-ended and leading questions to guide the discussion of soldier, leader, and unit performance
- Enter the discussion only when necessary

2. Review Of Objectives And Intent

The OC reviews unit training objectives the AAR will cover. The OC then restates the tasks being reviewed, including the conditions and standards for the tasks.

3. Commander's Mission and Intent (What Was Supposed To Happen)

Using maps, operational graphics, terrain boards, etc., the commander/leader restates the mission and intent. The OC may guide the discussion to ensure that everyone present understands the plan and the commander's intent. Another technique is to have subordinate leaders restate the mission and discuss the commander's intent.

4. OPFOR Commander's Mission and Intent

In a formal AAR, the OPFOR commander explains the plan to defeat friendly forces. Using the same training aids as the friendly force commander, participants can understand the relationship of both plans.

5. Summary of Events (What Happened)

The OC guides the review using a logical sequence of events to describe and discuss what happened. The OC does not ask "yes" or "no" questions, but encourages participation and guides the discussion by using open-ended and leading questions. An open-ended question allows the person answering to reply based on what was significant to the soldier. Open-ended questions are much less likely to put soldiers on the defensive. Open-ended questions are more effective in finding out what happened. For example, it is better to ask, "SGT Johnson, what happened when your Bradley crested the hill?" than, "SGT Johnson, why didn't you engage the enemy tanks to your front?"

As the discussion expands and more soldiers add their perspectives, what really happened becomes clear. The OC does not tell the soldiers or leaders what was good or bad. The OC must ensure that specific issues are revealed, both positive and negative in nature. Skillful guidance of the discussion ensures that the AAR does not gloss over mistakes or unit weaknesses.

6. Closing Comments (Summary)

During the summary, the OC reviews and summarizes key points identified during the discussion. The OC should end the AAR on a positive note, linking conclusions to future training. The OC then leaves the immediate area to allow unit leaders and soldiers time to discuss the training in private.

Step 4. Follow-Up: Using Results of the AAR

Ref: FM 7-1 Battle Focused Training, pp. C-8 to C-9.

AARs are the dynamic link between task performance and execution to standard. They provide commanders a critical assessment tool to plan soldier, leader, and unit training. Through the professional and candid discussion of events, soldiers can compare their performance against the standard and identify specific ways to improve proficiency.

IV. Follow-Up

1. **Identify tasks requiring retraining**
2. **Fix the problem**
   - **Retrain immediately (same training event)**
   - **Revise Standing Operating Procedure (SOP)**
   - **Integrate into future training plans**
3. **Use to assist in making commander's assessment**

Leaders should not delay retraining except when absolutely necessary. If the leader delays retraining, the soldiers and unit must understand that they did not perform the task to standard and that retraining will occur later.

One of the most important benefits of the AAR comes from applying results in developing future training. Leaders can use the information to assess performance and to plan future training to correct deficiencies and sustain demonstrated task proficiency.

Time or the complexity of the mission may prevent retraining on some tasks during the same exercise. When this happens, leaders must reschedule the mission or training in accordance with FM 7-0 and FM 7-1. As part of this process, leaders must ensure that deficient supporting tasks found during the AAR are also scheduled and retrained.

Revised Standing Operating Procedures

AARs may reveal problems with unit SOPs. If so, unit leaders must revise the SOP and ensure that units implement the changes during future training.

Summary

The AAR process makes the U.S. Army different from all others. The AAR is a key component in giving our nation the best trained Army in the world.

The Leader's SMARTbook (3rd Rev. Ed.)
Index

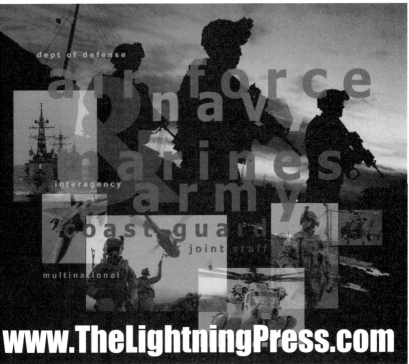